Eye on Israel

Eye on Israel

How America Came to
View Israel as an Ally

Michelle Mart

State University of New York Press

Published by
State University of New York Press, Albany

© 2006 State University of New York

For information, address State University of New York Press,
194 Washington Avenue, Suite 305, Albany, NY 12210-2384

Production by Judith Block
Marketing by Michael Campochiaro

Library of Congress Cataloging-in-Publication Data

Mart, Michelle, 1964–
    Eye on Israel : how America came to view Israel as an ally / Michelle
Mart.
         p. cm.
    Includes bibliographical references and index.
    ISBN 0-7914-6687-6 (hardcover : alk. paper)—ISBN 0-7914-6688-4
(pbk. : alk. paper)
    1. Jews—Public opinion.   2. Israel—Public opinion.   3. Public
opinion—United States.   4. Jews in literature.   5. Jews in motion
pictures.   6. United States—Foreign relations—Israel.   7. Israel—
Foreign relations—United States.   I. Title.

DS143.M32 2006
305.892'4—dc22   2005012108
ISBN-13 978-0-7914-6687-2 (hardcover : alk. paper)
ISBN-13 978-0-7914-6688-9 (pbk. : alk. paper)

10 9 8 7 6 5 4 3 2 1

For David, Hannah, and Tobias

Contents

Preface

In December 1962, President John F. Kennedy told Israeli Foreign Minister Golda Meir that the United States had a "special relationship with Israel." The president had just reiterated to the foreign minister that the United States would not sacrifice its relationship with the Arabs for exclusive regional ties with Israel. But he softened the blow to Israeli political ambitions by evoking the lofty vision of a "special" tie between the two peoples, "comparable only to that which it has with Britain." Although Kennedy hoped to achieve the short-term political goal of mollifying the foreign minister, his words did not emerge from a vacuum. They carried a host of associations for Americans and Israelis—policymaker and ordinary citizen alike—and symbolized pervasive cultural and political attitudes toward Israel and Jews in general.

Historians cavil about a "special relationship" and its nature.[1] Despite these disagreements, it is clear that by 1962 many Americans treated Israel as an ally with unique ties to the United States. Given the history of antisemitism in the early part of the century, as well as the debates in the United States about the founding of Israel after World War II, this consensus by the early 1960s represents a remarkable realignment of American attitudes. The story of that transformation of American opinion and policy is the subject of this book, which will trace multiple changing cultural narratives about Jews and Israelis, both subtle and obvious, as they appeared in popular fiction, the press, and the writings of cultural critics and policymakers. Through these narratives, shaped by the ideology and political realities of the Cold War, Americans saw their own reflection: Israelis became surrogate Americans. Hence, tracing the vision of Israel in the American imagination can also provide a window on how Americans constructed their own identity after World War II.

Before the Second World War, Jews were viewed almost universally in the United States as "outsiders," different from other Americans. Popular images ascribed to them included clannishness, pushiness, overconcern with money, physical weakness, unattractiveness, and urbanity. One crucial aspect of the shift in postwar attitudes is that cultural narratives changed to include Jews who possessed ideologies, values, and histories in common with old-stock Americans; as a result, these "outsiders" became "insiders." For example, Israeli pioneers, forging a country out of the desert, were frequently noted, celebrated, and compared with American pioneers of years past. In contrast, postwar writers and journalists paid little attention to urban Israelis except when they too seemed engaged in a heroic enterprise to bring development to a backward land. Importantly, many of these postwar cultural narratives were modeled on the images celebrated by Zionists earlier in the century. Thus, the vision American Jews (and other Zionists) had for a Zionist homeland became integrated into the broader American image of the postwar Israel.[2] The focus of discussion in the following pages is not so much the origin of the images as much as on why they became widely embraced in the postwar United States and how that affected attitudes toward the Jewish state.

The transformation of Jews and Israelis from outsiders to insiders had implications beyond the latest Hollywood movie or *Life* magazine profile. The shift in cultural narrative both reflected and helped shape the climate of political opinion in which U.S. leaders made policy toward Israel.[3] U.S. global power politics, of course, put a huge premium on anti-Communist alliances in the late 1940s and 1950s, while images of Israel and Israelis emerged to celebrate, in part, Western partners in a hostile Cold War world. Cold War ideology—as manifest in cultural values and language as well as in political relationships—contributed in a variety of ways to this series of narratives and myths about the American-Israeli relationship. The celebration of the pioneer in Israeli life, for instance, alluded not only to the American past; it also invoked the present through Cold War values which contrasted the progressive, modern West with the "backward" East.

American cultural narratives of Israel and Israelis changed over time in interaction with foreign policy events and other political circumstances. Hence, the American images of Israel and Jews in 1960 differed significantly from those of 1948. Yet, the emergence of Jews and Israelis as insiders was far from preordained, so a study of this early period of American-Israeli relations helps explain why Jews shed their outsider label. In its first decade of existence, the Jewish state underwent huge political and economic changes, while American foreign policy and culture felt the repercussions from a series of hot and cold wars. American policymakers sought to realize abroad the power and influence of what seemed an unprecedented "American Century." At the same time, domestic culture justified this great influence by such ideologies as democracy, progressivism, Judeo-Christian beliefs, the importance of the frontier, and so-called traditional nuclear families. To the extent that Israelis were depicted as sharing these ideologies, they appeared similar to Americans. Policymakers, subject to the same cultural messages as other Americans, were also influenced by changing views of Jews. Culture was clearly an important factor in constructing the American-Israeli relationship. And the effects were felt at home as well: changing perceptions of Jews and Israel in the American mind helped pave the way for a broad, new acceptance of Jews in American life.

The focus of this study is the image of Israel in American culture. It is not intended to be a comprehensive history of American-Israeli relations. The policy sections that are woven into the narrative are designed to show how cultural images became embedded in the rhetoric of foreign relations. This book traces the dramatic transformation of Jews and Israel in the American cultural and political imagination at midcentury, from curious minorities to kindred spirits and reliable allies in the Cold War. Visible in movies, novels, magazines, and newspapers, the new understanding of Israel and Jewish identity that emerged in this period continues to influence American politics, culture, and foreign policy to this day.

Acknowledgments

This project has been many years in the making, and I have been fortunate to have had the help and wisdom of teachers, friends, and colleagues. I am grateful for their insights and corrections, though any faults which remain in this book are mine alone.

At different points I have received criticisms and comments from many colleagues. For their generosity of time and ideas, I thank in particular Carol Anderson, Michael Berkowitz, Frank Costigliola, Bob Dean, Hasia Diner, Peter Hahn, Michael Hogan, Steven Katz, Douglas Little, Emily Rosenberg, Jonathan Sarna, Geoff Smith, Susan Tannanbaum, and Stephen Whitfield. In addition, I have received thoughtful feedback from anonymous reviewers for *Diplomatic History*, *Modern Judaism*, and *Religion and American Culture*. Andrew Hrycyna, a brilliant and exacting editor, is one friend and colleague who stands out for the inordinate amount of time that he spent going over the manuscript, making thoughtful suggestions to improve its structure and strengthen its argument.

Archivists, librarians, and staff from several institutions have made the research for this book much less arduous. In particular, I benefited from the helpful professionals at the Harry S. Truman Library, the Dwight D. Eisenhower Library, the National Archives, the Franklin D. Roosevelt Library, the David Ben-Gurion Archives at S'de Boker, Israel, the Library of Congress, the Museum of Television and Radio in New York, and New York University Library. I am indebted to the librarians and staff at Penn State, Berks who assisted me in tracking down numerous sources and citations.

I am also fortunate to have wonderful colleagues at Penn State and financial support for my research. Since my arrival here, the university has been very generous in grants for research and course releases for which I am most grateful. My colleagues have been engaging and supportive; they make it a pleasure to be a member of this faculty.

The editors and staff at State University of New York Press have been helpful and easy to work with. I am grateful to Michael Rinella, Judith Block, and Michael Campochiaro for their work and support. I also appreciate Alex Trotter's work on the index.

Work on this book began when I was in graduate school, although it changed forms many times. I was fortunate to have two thoughtful and outspoken advisors, Brad Perkins at the University of Michigan and Marilyn Young at New York University. Both offered challenges and encouragement. Marilyn Young worked with me on every aspect of the dissertation, offering invaluable criticism and patient support. The University of Michigan and New York University, especially, were generous in supporting my graduate studies and, thus, the genesis of this project.

Walter LaFeber, who was my undergraduate adviser at Cornell, spurred both my interest in American foreign policy and my decision to become an historian. Since I first sat in Walt LaFeber's survey course of American foreign relations, I have been inspired by his example as a teacher and his extraordinary record of scholarship. He has offered thoughtful criticism and advice since I left Cornell, for which I am most grateful.

Long before I knew that I would become an historian, a group of exceptional teachers set me on the path of research and scholarship at Hunter College High School in New York City. In particular, the late E.I. Marienhoff, showed me how to construct strong, rigorous arguments and inspired the confidence to withstand disagreement.

While I have received remarkable support from teachers and professional colleagues, I have been blessed to feel warmth and confidence from many good friends and a loving family. To each of them, I offer my heartfelt thanks. My mother, Sheila Mart, and my late father, Eric Mart, have always been my champions, confident that I could do whatever I set my mind to. My sister, Madeleine Mart, has always been loving and supportive.

My children, Hannah and Tobias, have been my joy and inspiration over the past eight years. I look at them and want to do my best work, but am always reminded of what is ultimately most important in life. My husband David Walker has lived with this book for many years. But he has been with me every step of the way, offering insightful criticism and extraordinary editing. This book has come to fruition due to David's faith, support, and love. I am most blessed.

1

Images of the "New Jew" in Postwar Culture

Building on the Legacies of Antisemitism and the Holocaust

In 1947, the best-selling novel and Academy Award-winning film *Gentleman's Agreement* captured the earnestness with which some Americans attacked antisemitism and its accompanying evils. Laura Hobson's book and the film based upon it made it clear that antisemitism—like all prejudice—was un-American, since it persecuted people for imagined differences. Such assumptions were emblematic of the widespread celebration of universal brotherhood that permeated popular and political culture in the years after World War II, and began to transform images of American Jews in these years. Previously, American Jews were almost always depicted in popular culture as outsiders and were usually objects of discrimination. Yet, after World War II and the upheaval of the Holocaust, public antisemitism became increasingly unacceptable as it came into conflict with the moral ideals Americans embraced in the war against Nazi Germany and Fascism. Moreover, the "new Jew" of the American imagination acquired a special kind of symbolic moral status. Thus, in popular fiction, the press, government propaganda, and the comments of social critics and politicians, a new American image of Jews began emerging in the postwar years: Jews as cultural and political insiders.

Not surprisingly, American views of Israel—the world's only Jewish state—were grounded in the images of Jews that permeated popular culture, both before but especially after World War II. Thus, a study of the postwar image of Israel in American culture must begin with a look at the images of "new Jews" and their cultural antecedents.

ANTISEMITISM IN THE UNITED STATES

As part of a pluralistic nation, Americans had always grappled with the definition of their own nationality. The terms of that struggle had changed over time, including early in the twentieth century when an unprecedented wave of southern and eastern Europeans came to American shores. To many, new European immigrants and other minorities represented immutable "races" which were inferior to the "traditional" American group—White, Anglo-Saxon, Protestant. One concrete result of this racialist thinking was the reversal of unrestricted immigration in the 1920s. Jews, along with European Catholics, were objects of the new restrictions and considered to be a separate race by many government policymakers, scientists, journalists, and average Americans. Jews also faced educational quotas that cut their presence in colleges and universities, employment discrimination, bars to social clubs and resorts, and residential screenings. "Ingrained prejudices of respectable people," argues Leonard Dinnerstein, were "confirmed as proper in the 1920s."[1]

Even many Americans who did not subscribe to antisemitic ideas still believed that there was no room for diverse minorities in the United States. Some press stories blamed Jews for the antisemitism that they faced since they didn't blend in with the rest of the population. Moreover, in the 1930s, some in the press—particularly in Christian vehicles such as *The Christian Century*, *The Christian Science Monitor*, and *The Lutheran Companion*—charged that Jewish behavior such as "clannishness" and radical activities invited persecution in Europe. The emphasis on assimilation permeated popular fiction as well. According to more than one study of Jewish images on film, de-semitization and de-Judaization were rampant in 1930s films as recognizably Jewish characters disappeared from the screen, while White, Anglo-Saxon Protestant characters predominated in Hollywood.[2] Hollywood's de-semitized images of the 1930s were consistent with changing ideas about race and national identity in the popular culture. As social scientists repudiated nineteenth and early-twentieth-century biologically deterministic views of race, racialist thinking declined among other Americans as well.[3] By the eve of World War II, anthropologists and sociologists focused on the "culture concept" as the locus of identity. Social scientists believed that prejudice could be defeated and tolerance encouraged through education.

Shortly before the war, officials in the U.S. Office of Education tried to put this prescription into action with a series of radio broadcasts called, *Americans All . . . Immigrants All*. This series was the first of its type which stressed that the country was comprised of diverse people who all agreed on certain ideals. Yet, the thrust of this message as well as broader academic and popular beliefs of the time was assimilationist: although Americans should be tolerant of diversity, differences among specific groups would fade over time. A revealing example of how these ideas were integrated into wartime propaganda was the comic book *They Got the Blame: The Story of Scapegoats in History* put out by the YMCA, with the assistance of *Scholastic Magazine* and the government's Office of War Information.[4] Scapegoating was irrational, the comic argues, "a flame of insanity" which could be defeated through mere exposure and education. The comic ends with a ringing restatement of war aims: "the united nations are determining to build a world free of prejudice and intolerance."

The message of this YMCA comic was echoed throughout the public culture during the war, from popular entertainment to sociological studies. Wartime films inevitably highlighted the un-American side of prejudice, most dramatically through the multiethnic platoon in which soldiers overcame differences and relied on each other for their lives. Similarly, Swedish sociologist Gunnar Myrdal in his study of the position of African Americans in the nation, *An American Dilemma*, argued that the war was being fought to overcome prejudice: "In fighting fascism and Nazism, Americans had to stand before the whole world in favor of racial tolerance."[5]

In the postwar years, many political leaders, as well as writers, filmmakers, and other contributors to the public culture, believed that it was even more important to live up to the ideals which they had embraced during the war, and to defeat the still powerful forces of prejudice in American society. Civic groups and others believed that public education would end prejudice. For example, in 1948, the National Council of Christians and Jews organized American Brotherhood Week "to strengthen [the] Nation through the unity that grows out of brotherhood." Educators, publishers, and Hollywood and radio executives (with President Harry S. Truman as honorary chairman) participated in the project.[6]

Ironically, antisemitism peaked in the United States during World War II. Hence, wartime views of Nazi persecutions were not always charitable toward Jews. Many Americans did not believe that the victims of the Nazis were completely innocent. In his analysis of public opinion surveys from 1938–1939, sociologist Charles Stember finds that anywhere from 27–61 percent of respondents believed that the German Jews were at least partly responsible for their own persecution. Reasons cited for the hostile attitudes toward the Jews included common antisemitic stereotypes.[7]

Thus, dedication to the Allied cause and opposition to Hitler's policies toward Jews were not necessarily one and the same. The strength of anti-semitism before and during World War II is reflected in the refusal of the federal government to allow the majority of Jews fleeing the Nazis to seek refuge in the United States. Refugee policy was executed by the State Department, where it was clear to many observers that powerful officials were antisemitic.[8]

Nevertheless, after the war, it became increasingly unacceptable to voice antisemitic views in the *public* culture. As the editors of *Look* magazine observed, "Hitler made anti-Semitism disreputable."[9] Stember documented a clear decline in antisemitism after its World War II high. Even though prejudice was still harbored in private, "The mere repression of bigotry," he argued, "constitutes a social gain." The decline of prejudice was expressed in different ways. For example, the number of respondents to a survey who labeled Jews as a race dropped significantly, while the number who labeled Jews as a religious group rose by half as much. Not surprisingly, the status of Jews also increased as they rose in class. As the following discussion will illustrate, when prominent voices in the political and popular culture denounced prejudices based on race, the very meaning of race as a category and the borders between different groups changed in radical ways. With regard to the image of Jews, this change was clear: previously referred to in common stereotypes as "not white," in the late 1940s and 1950s, Jews "became" white in the public culture.[10]

THE DECLINE OF ANTISEMITISM IN POPULAR FICTION

Novels and films after the war which focused on antisemitism were a popular, cathartic way to reaffirm moral values and expunge discomfort over past insensitivity to prejudice. Yet, a fictional discussion of anti-semitism in the postwar period was no easy task. In the three centuries since Jews had lived on the American continent, their status vis-à-vis their neighbors was not always clear. In addition, Jewish artists, themselves, were ambivalent about whether they should assimilate completely into the mainstream. Despite the adherence among some Jews to what Marshall Sklare called "the nineteenth century social contract" that one's Jewishness was only to be shown in private life, the wide appeal of universal ideals in postwar America, the horror of the Holocaust, and the growing political, social, and economic security of American Jews combined to overwhelm the caution that minorities should not call attention to themselves.

Crossfire is an example of a film that tackles antisemitism head-on. This hard-boiled 1947 *film noir* hammers out the message that all prejudice is evil and murderous.[11] The film opens on a brutal fight, as the sounds of breaking furniture are heard over the darting shadows. Hours later, a tough Detective Finley (Robert Young) looks over the crime scene and the body of the victim, Samuels, whose name is mentioned a couple of times, making his Jewish identity clear to the audience. We learn that Samuels spent the evening in a bar where he met three soldiers, one of whom, Montgomery (Robert Ryan), soon appears on the threshold. We later find out that the antisemitic Montgomery murdered Samuels because he was Jewish. But the senselessness of the crime means that the detective will overlook the most obvious solution. As the investigation unfolds, so does a parallel story of how groundless stereotypes become destructive prejudices.

There are a number of clues that signal to the audience that the abrasive Montgomery (Monty) is evil and his antisemitic beliefs are, therefore, indefensible. He is harshly critical of those around him; for example, he makes fun of a shy southern soldier with a thick accent. Monty rails against the falling standards of the U.S. Army which was full of "stinking civilians." His anger seems un-American. The civilian character of the army is a point of pride in American ideology, especially so soon after the victory of World War II. The self-important Monty is the only truly nasty character and the only one who makes antisemitic statements. Thus, by syllogistic logic, the film argues that only nasty, and in this case violent people make antisemitic statements.[12]

In contrast to the other characters, Monty uses common stereotypes to describe Jews. He explains that he followed Samuels out of the bar that evening, because "if a Jew-boy was setting up the drinks somewhere we might as well get in on it." According to Monty, Jews are both too wealthy and too stingy with their money. Monty's hatred of Jews is also fueled by the prejudice that Jews aren't good fighters and don't do their fair share of service in the army. He tells Finley, "I've seen a lot of guys like [Samuels] who played it safe during the war. . . . Some of them are named Samuels, some got funnier names." Monty's references to Samuels as "Jew-boy" reminds us of the common, overlapping language of prejudice that often questioned the masculinity of particular groups. (Throughout American history, for example, African Americans had been referred to by Whites as "boys.")

Crossfire and other works of fiction which addressed antisemitism used stereotypes which were apparently widespread in the public culture.

Charles Stember found in surveys from 1938, 1940, and 1946 that a majority of respondents felt that Jews had a variety of objectionable traits: (1) greed, unscrupulousness, an inordinate concern with money; (2) pushiness, aggressiveness, selfishness; (3) clannishness, covering for each other; (4) bad manners, a lack of cleanliness, an unrefined nature. Monty's opinions, thus, matched those of many of his countrymen in the late 1940s. The familiarity that many Americans had with the antisemitism depicted in *Crossfire* as well as with the steps to eradicate it was also reflected in the fact that the film was a "modest commercial success" and a bigger critical success, nominated for the Academy Award for best film.[13]

Far from drunken brawls that lead to murder, the extremely popular *Gentleman's Agreement*, both a novel and a film in 1947, demonstrates the social evils of antisemitism.[14] Even one review which called the plot "flagrantly thimble-rigged" argued that it was "required reading for every thoughtful citizen in this parlous century."[15] The didactic novel by Laura Hobson focuses on a writer who poses as a Jew for six weeks to do research for an exposé on antisemitism. Phil Green learns that antisemitism can be found everywhere, even among good-hearted liberals who don't know that they are prejudiced, as well as among self-hating Jews who are anxious to fit into the Gentile world. Hobson drew on her own experience to explain the pervasiveness of social antisemitism. She later recounted being at a dinner party before the war when the subject of Hitler's persecution of the Jews was discussed. One guest concluded, "The chosen people ask for it, wherever they are."[16]

Hobson's novel is a hollow construction designed to illustrate how age-old stereotypes are articulated. Phil's sister, for example, uses an expression which plays on the supposed stinginess of Jews, "That cheap Pat Curran keeps trying to Jew us down." One doctor makes a subtle comment implying that Jewish doctors pad their fees. A colleague of Phil's assumes that Jews don't fight and so asks Phil if he was a correspondent during the war. Phil's in-the-closet Jewish secretary, who has changed her name to get her job, doesn't want to see the company hire Jews who may be "too ethnic." "Don't you hate being the fall guy for the kikey ones?" she asks Phil.[17] And, Phil discovers that there are any number of social restrictions in real estate, clubs, and resorts. The novel's title refers to the unspoken agreement among some property owners that they will not rent or sell to Jews.

Even if social antisemitism is not as dangerous as that which led to the Holocaust, Phil argues that it is infuriating, because it automatically assumes that you are not equal to other people. He explains the importance of opposing all prejudice when his girlfriend Kathy calls restricted resort owners "nasty little snobs." "Call them snobs and you can dismiss them," Phil responds. "See them as persistent traitors to everything this country stands for . . . , and you have to fight them. Not for 'the poor, poor Jews,' but for the whole damn thing this country is—"[18] Thus, Phil equates universal morals and identity with the definition of being American. Phil's mother, the moral center for Phil and for the film audience, expands this equation even more by calling for a triumph of universalism, using the one world political vocabulary of the day. "Maybe it won't be the American century, after all," she tells her son, "or the Russian century or even the Atomic century. Wouldn't it be wonderful, Phil, if it turned out to be everybody's century, when people all over the world, free people, found a way to live together." With the Holocaust in recent memory and the wartime ideals of a unified world still fresh, both the film and the book articulate broadly felt cultural values in the immediate postwar era: particular identities must be repudiated, because of their dangerous potential.

The novel makes clear that prejudice is un-American, because it is a short distance from genteel restrictions to crude name calling or worse. Phil's son, Tommy, comes home crying from school one day after he is called "a dirty kike."[19] Phil's Jewish friend, Dave, finds his career and economic future threatened when he can't locate a place for his family to live in the restricted housing market of New York City suburbs. Crossfire's Finley, like Phil, explains that antisemitism must be fought on all fronts, because distinctions in degrees of prejudice are not that significant: "This business of hating Jews comes in a lot of different sizes. . . and because we stand for all these kinds, Monty's kind grows out of all the rest." Prejudice is a cultural and psychological behavior that can be unlearned. Phil is convinced that he understands the experience of all who have been the object of discrimination through his own sympathetic ruse: "I know about *everyone* who was *ever* turned down . . . ." Thus, antisemitism is the same as all other prejudice and can be defeated through cultural education.

The earnest tone of *Crossfire* and *Gentleman's Agreement* belies the difficulty of discussing antisemitism in Hollywood from the 1930s through the 1950s. Before the United States entered World War II, Hollywood producers and filmmakers worried about antisemitism, especially when isolationists led by Senators Gerald Nye and Bennett Clark, and aviator Charles A. Lindbergh, charged in 1941 that Jews and Hollywood were leading the country into war. Hollywood fears of antisemitism increased after the war when new charges of subversion were based on alleged Communist influence in films. The House Un-American Activities Committee (HUAC) hearings in Hollywood which began in October 1947, just weeks before *Gentleman's Agreement* opened, made studio heads more jittery; people in and out of the industry regarded the investigations as antisemitic, because many of those accused were Jews. Most importantly, those prominent in the congressional investigations—such as Martin Dies and Charles Rankin—were openly antisemitic and supported by leaders of Fascist and racist groups.[20]

The depiction of Jews in the postwar period is complicated further by the insecurities of the Jewish studio heads about their own ethnic identity. Jewish moguls were anxious to assimilate into the American mainstream, but ever fearful of antisemitism which they thought "lurked everywhere."[21] As a response, in part, to the schismatic pulls felt by these Jews, Hollywood de-emphasized ethnicity. Hence, films of the 1940s focused on the similarites between Jews and non-Jews, emphasizing assimilation and the melting pot ideal. In other words, Hollywood repressed ethnic differences and omitted most depictions of particular religious and cultural characteristics. Increasingly in the 1950s, Jewish heroes took on the attributes of other Americans, while ethnic characteristics were reserved for those few, older, less sophisticated characters who were *defined by* their Jewishness. For example, Jose Ferrer's portrayal of Lt. Barney Greenwald in *The Caine Mutiny* (1954)—unlike the character in Herman Wouk's novel on which he is based—doesn't mention his Jewish identity or its impact on the mutiny court martial. In contrast, Gertrude Berg's Molly Goldberg of *Molly* (1950) plays the stereotypical *Yiddishe Mama*.[22]

Characters in some films, such as *Gentleman's Agreement*, are de-semitized by their appearance. Gregory Peck's Phil is tall, dark, handsome, and earnest. John Garfield (Dave) was one of Hollywood's few leading men whose Jewish identity was known, and, along with Peck, he, too, was a matinee idol. The film places much emphasis on the similarities between Jews and non-Jews, as illustrated by the appearance of the actors. Elaine Wales, Phil's Jewish secretary, is a blond, stereotypically non-Jewish type who lies about her ethnicity and no one suspects that she is Jewish. Even in the book, the idea that Jews are physically indistinguishable from other Americans is a recurrent theme. As Phil contemplates his scheme to be Jewish, he notes how similar he and Dave are—in coloring, size, and features. The idea that Jews were not physically distinct was a common theme in other fiction of the period that challenged antisemitism. For example, in the 1949 film *Take Me Out to the Ball-game*, a Jewish baseball player is very similar to his two Irish buddies except that he happens to be taller than his teammates (an additional detail that plays against the common image of Jews).

Antisemites in these works of fiction are anything from insensitive name-callers to violent murderers. The novels and films also demonstrate that prejudice is wrong by ennobling the Jewish characters. This valorization was another side to the prejudices about Jews. Stember found that stereotypes about Jews in the late 1930s and early 1940s included "admirable" qualities as well as negative ones. In three surveys from 1938 and one from 1940, 51–67 percent of respondents found positive qualities in Jews. The characteristics included: ability in business, persistence, ambition, intellectual talent, religious and familial loyalty, thriftiness, and integrity.[23] Meanwhile, the character of Samuels in *Crossfire* embodies certain positive qualities. He is sensitive and kind to a young soldier who is unsure of where he fits in once the war is over.[24] Samuels is depicted as a patriotic figure who was discharged from the army after being wounded. His record echoed the efforts of journalists and Jewish groups to correct the misperception that Jews had not done their fair share in the war.[25]

The whole premise of *Gentleman's Agreement* assumes that being a Jew is nothing more than experiencing antisemitism. Phil just decides that he'll be Jewish for a few weeks. He reasons that his friend Dave is just like him: they look alike, they grew up together, they're both modern American men. Phil does not seek out any other Jews, research Jewish history or culture, or visit a synagogue. He merely throws himself up against discrimination. After Phil's son Tommy is insulted by the other children for being Jewish, Dave tells Phil, "Well you can quit being Jewish now. That's all there is to it." A well-known physicist, Dr. Lieberman, confirms Phil's belief that Jewish identity is synonymous with being a victim. He tells Phil "it is a matter of pride to go on calling ourselves Jews. Only when there are no antisemites, calling ourselves a Jew won't matter." When antisemitism and other prejudices are eliminated, ethnicities will cease to exist.

Such sentiments reinforce the pervasive universalist ethos reflected in public education projects such as American Brotherhood Week and *They Got the Blame*. The organizers of these projects and the creators of *Gentleman's Agreement*, indeed, argue that differences among people are merely imagined. This theme was commonly sounded by journalists as well in the late 1940s. For example, the photojournalists from one agency collaborated on a project entitled "People are People the World Over." For an entire year, *Ladies Home Journal* published photos showing similarities in the way people from all countries cooked, shopped, washed, and raised their children. Similarly, a 1947 series in *The New Republic* by journalist Bruce Bliven did its best to educate Americans that antisemitism—although disturbingly pervasive—was based upon *imagined* differences between Jews and other Americans.[26]

The press and popular fiction depicted the virulence of antisemitism and the innocence of the Jews who suffered from it. Importantly, they also presented solutions to the problem. The first way to combat antisemitism was to deal with the issues rationally. Contemporary social and political critics also stressed the irrationality of antisemitism. Jean-Paul Sartre, for example, argued that antisemitism was a "passion" and must, therefore, be opposed with dispassion.[27] The solution proposed in *Gentleman's Agreement* and *Crossfire* is to demonstrate the meaninglessness of ethnic identity and thereby explain to the audience that antisemitism is wrong, because it is unfair and un-American. This view echoed numerous examples found in contemporary press and nonfiction books.[28] Phil explains to his young son Tommy that being a Jew is no different than being a Protestant or a Catholic. When he finishes his articles, he explains to Tommy that the "game" they've been playing is called "identification."[29]

Crossfire uses a similar rhetorical structure. By the end of the film, the detective, Finley, explains everything to the childlike southern soldier Leroy in order to enlist his help in capturing Monty. Finley tries to show Leroy that prejudice against all groups is unfair: "Doesn't Monty make fun of your accent and call you a hillbilly and say you're dumb?" He tells him how his own immigrant grandfather was beaten to death by a mob because he was a Catholic. "Hating is always senseless," Finley argues. "One day it kills Jews, the next day Irish Catholics, the next day Protestants and Quakers." *Gentleman's Agreement* also stresses the un-American aspect of antisemitism. For example, Phil argues in his article that the founding fathers knew that "equality and freedom were the only choice for wholeness and soundness in a nation." Furthermore, the works of fiction demonstrate that Jews are good Americans; Dave and Samuels fight patriotically in the war.

The demonstration of Jewish patriotism through military service points to another theme of this fiction. Sometimes a rational approach is not enough. Sometimes, according to these authors, men have to stand and fight for what is right. Moreover, the war was also a personal test of manliness for the soldiers. Dave, Samuels, and others are meant to disprove the stereotype that Jews are not real men or fighters. Dave is also ready to fight when some soldiers use slurs against him in a restaurant. Thus, they meet the gendered criteria which define heroes in popular American fiction. The third major prescription to combat antisemitism found in these works is to celebrate universal morals and the common humanity of all people. *Gentleman's Agreement* and *Crossfire* do this by downplaying the importance of ethnicity, and equating American freedom and democracy with universal morality.

Two other popular works of fiction which highlighted antisemitism among soldiers were the best-selling 1948 novels *The Naked and the Dead* and *The Young Lions*.[30] Irwin Shaw's novel *The Young Lions* tells the story of three soldiers during World War II, one German and two Americans, one of whom is Jewish. The most likable of all the characters is the Jew, Noah Ackerman. The reader's sympathies are with Noah when his commanding officers and bunkmates begin taunting him with antisemitic comments. The captain charges that Noah failed to clean his bunk area properly, so he confines the whole barracks to base on Saturday night. Sergeant Rickett, along with the other soldiers blame the "Jewboy" for the punishment. Rickett admonishes him that the barracks has to be "white-man clean."[31] This exchange reminds readers of the common assumption of earlier racialist thinking: Jews were often referred to as non-White. It would not be until the decline of antisemitism in the 1950s that Jews would be seen as completely "white," distinguished from other minority groups, such as African Americans, Chinese, or Arabs.

The men in the barracks come up with a litany of stereotypes about Jews: "I don't mind your killing Christ, but I'll never forgive you for not washing that window"; "[Jews] run all the banks and all the whorehouses in Berlin and Paris"; "I actually heard of a Jew who volunteered [for the army]." Noah suffers the taunts with dignified silence and soon finds himself ambushed and beaten by his bunkmates. Noah demands satisfaction and stoically endures beatings from the biggest men in the company. Outside the pages of a novel, many real soldiers experienced such abuse during World War II. Historian Arno Mayer recalled his experiences in the army that were not unlike those of Noah Ackerman's: "I experienced a kind of anti-Semitism I wasn't prepared for. It reached a point where I had a couple of teeth knocked out."[32]

The story of antisemitism which Noah must endure is paralleled with the transformation of another character of Shaw's, the young Christian Diestl, from a proud Austrian to an unfeeling Nazi. Even before he has joined the Nazis, he explains the necessities of antisemitism to a young American tourist: "I know it is ridiculous to attack any race. . . . But if the only way you can get a decent and ordered Europe is by wiping out the Jews then we must do it."[33] Sometime later, Christian has become a Nazi soldier, rounding up Jews to be sent off to death camps. By the end of the war when Christian finds himself passing through a concentration camp, he is decidedly indifferent to his surroundings.

The Naked and the Dead is also an epic of World War II which demonstrates the evils of prejudice and beneath its cynical exterior shows the path to redemption from this sin. Antisemitism in Norman Mailer's novel arises from the displacement of anger the men of this platoon feel toward themselves and others. For example, Gallagher, a working-class Irish Catholic from Boston who resents losing at poker and feels guilty that he is throwing away money when he has a pregnant wife at home, turns angrily to a Jewish orderly playing in the game, "That Jew had been having a lot of goddamn luck," he thinks, "and suddenly, his bitterness changed into rage." The other soldiers' prejudices are also expressions of their anger; Sergeant Croft's childhood, for example, was dominated by a father who humiliated his son. Thus, the two Jews in Mailer's platoon are subjected to any number of slurs from the majority of the soldiers. Gallagher taunts the first, Goldstein, about wanting a soapbox when he expresses an opinion about the military campaign. At other times, the Jews are addressed as "Izzy" and "dumb Jew bastard."[34]

The antisemitism among the lower-class characters in these films and novels is crude and outspoken, but the works make clear that this is not a class issue. Rather, it is a danger that affects society as a whole. Mailer's Lieutenant Hearn recalls how he grew up as the scion of a wealthy midwestern family hearing veiled antisemitic remarks at home. And, Noah, in *The Young Lions*, suffers antisemitism at the hands of officers as well as other enlisted men.

Antisemitism is not the only prejudice that is seen as dangerous. Befitting the period's universal ideals, all prejudices are connected and all are depicted as wrong. The officers criticize a number of groups. Croft remarks to the Mexican Martinez (whom he has named "Japbait" for his scouting abilities) that an Italian soldier in the platoon is "a funny wop." Martinez is uncomfortable with the remark as he feels, himself, not that far removed from the Italian in the eyes of the Anglos. Martinez' good record as a soldier is due in part to his determination to be the hero in battle that he could never be at home, because he isn't "white, Protestant, firm, and aloof." In a moment of angry panic, Gallagher conflates his prejudices shouting at a Japanese prisoner "You look like a fuggin Yid with all that hand waving."[35]

Shaw's and Mailer's novels showed how people could overcome their seemingly intractable differences to discover their commonalties, such as their masculine identity and ability to fight together. Noah becomes buddies with his friend Johnny, planning to move to his town and work for his father after the war. Noah clings to an idealized vision of Americana and asserts that he will never tire of the simple life. Historian John Higham—using the language of postwar universalism—puts Noah's motivation in the context of contemporary social concerns: "Totalitarianism convinced Americans that racial and religious divisions constituted the last, . . . the most vicious cleavages in a beleaguered society that was otherwise knit together by a sturdy web of ideals."[36]

MOVING BEYOND UNIVERSALISM

The war, in general, pushed Americans toward a universalism that made antisemitism intolerable. The rejection of antisemitism in the public culture is reflected in crusading fictional works (such as *Crossfire*) which reaffirmed the moral purpose of the United States. Such fiction asserted that antisemitism was unacceptable, because Jews were just like other Americans. Yet, the neat lessons of absolute universalism had their limits in a post-Holocaust world. The particular reality of the Holocaust leads the popular culture and the image of the Jew in new directions. While the war is in the background of works about domestic antisemitism (one character in *Gentleman's Agreement* refers to the "ovens of World War II"), the fiction about war-torn Europe and the Pacific tackles the complexities of acknowledging differences among various groups of people, while endorsing universal values. Thus, the novels of Shaw, Mailer, and other works depict the differences among people to endorse, nevertheless, a universal ideal. They show Jews who are distinguished by their appearance, characteristics, or fate as victims who rise above their status to provide a universal example or moral.

American ideas about Jews were manifest in both antisemitic stereotypes as well as valorizing celebrations of Jewish character. Such ideas were widespread in the media and political culture as well as in fiction. Popular images that resonated most strongly with an understanding of the Holocaust were those of Jews as weak, pitiful victims, helpless in the face of an overpowering enemy. Images of Jewish victimhood remained widespread even two years after the Holocaust. For example, in November 1947, *Life* reported on the U.S. tour of two eight-year-old orphans of Hitler's concentration camps, which was arranged by an organization of

American Jewish women trying to raise money to support European orphans. Such ideas of Jewish victimhood remained vivid for years to come, as former President Harry S. Truman demonstrated in a 1955 speech to the Combined Jewish Appeal of Greater Boston when he concluded: "The Jews have already been the most persecuted of peoples . . . in the history of the world."[37]

The most prominent images of Jewish difference in popular culture were the real or imagined physical distinctions that set them apart from other Americans and Europeans. For example, Samuels, the murder victim in the 1947 film *Crossfire*, is physically distinguished from the Gentile characters looking as if he is of east European origin: he has dark wavy hair and bushy eyebrows, and is short and heavyset. Noah, from *The Young Lions*, is similarly distinguished from his Gentile fellows. He has a small stature, is physically weak, and, by the end of the war, noticeably frail. Norman Mailer also creates a World War II Jewish soldier who embodies many of the physical stereotypes about Jews. Roth was "a small man with an oddly hunched back and long arms . . . he had a long dejected nose and pouches under his eyes."[38] Roth is barely able to clear the jungle brush. For the other soldiers, Roth's physical weakness becomes a badge of Jewish identity.

In their portraits of Jews physically distinct from their neighbors, these Jewish authors have not only internalized the idea that Jews are weak, but also the idea that Jews are unattractive. In his 1950 novel *The Wall* about the Warsaw Ghetto, John Hersey creates Rachel who is "cursed" with a "Semitic face." There are numerous references to Rachel's appearance which all the characters in *The Wall* seem to agree is ugly. The implication is that she is ugly *because* she is "Jewish-looking." Noach Levinson, the archivist among these dwellers in the ghetto, also embodies common stereotypes about Jews. He has the looks of a Jewish *schlemiel* to suit his bookish occupation: "there was actually something repellent about his looks. . . . He had the face of an intellectual, narrow and drawn forward, and upon his unruly nose sat a pair of steel-rimmed glasses whose lenses were so thick that Levinson's eyes seemed . . . far larger than most human eyes."[39]

The aesthetic which prizes "non-Jewish" looks continues to dominate popular fiction into the 1950s. Joseph Viertel in his 1955 novel *The Last Temptation* creates two characters who try desperately to escape from Nazi Europe. To a limited extent, they are able to assimilate and, thus, escape because they don't "look" Jewish. Deborah calls Vic "her tall warrior" and she has "pretty, delicate features." In contrast to this pair, Deborah's childhood friend Gussie is described as Jewish-looking: "She looked it—plump and dark, and her thick glasses behind which she constantly blinked made it worse." Furthermore, Gussie's "prominent, bulbous nose, her black kinky hair, and plump figure" were highlighted. Deborah's and Vic's physical appearance is one of the temptations which fool them into thinking that they can shed their Jewish identity. Both Hersey's and Viertel's novels show the folly of trying to assimilate and to deny one's own identity. Yet, the standard of beauty remains a non-Jewish one. The de-semitizing aesthetic comes to dominate the images of Jewish heroes who appear increasingly "Aryan" through the decade. Jews who act less like victims are, increasingly, depicted as less "Jewish-looking," while those characters with stereotypically Jewish features are depicted as weak. Thus, the physical descriptions of Jewish frailty and homeliness are metaphors for the Jewish condition of victimhood.[40]

The lesson of World War II and, ultimately, of the Holocaust, argue these Jewish authors, is to transcend limitations and to become heroes instead of victims. Shaw's frail Noah becomes an exemplary soldier. He patriotically enlists when war breaks out. In the army, he stands up to the antisemitic taunts of his fellow recruits, finally fighting his tormentors in supervised matches, explaining, "I want every Jew to be treated as though he weighed two hundred pounds." When he and his platoon find themselves in the fields of France, it is Noah who becomes the natural leader. He is the bravest, quickest, and most practical in the field. A couple of the other men are literally helpless without him. He has not only served his country, but become ennobled in the process. When his friend from boot camp meets up with him in Europe, he recognizes this change in Noah: "Although he was terribly frail now and coughed considerably, he seemed to have found . . . a thoughtful, quiet maturity. . . . Noah talked gently, without bitterness, with none of his old intense, scarcely controlled violence."[41]

Norman Mailer goes farther to create a heroic Jewish soldier who has overcome the limitations of his identity both physically and psychologically. Joey Goldstein, in *The Naked and the Dead*, is physically strong, blond, blue-eyed, thoroughly de-semitized, and a sharp contrast to the other Jewish soldier, Roth. Indicating how Jewish—and Israeli—heroes increasingly will be depicted in the 1950s, Goldstein—with looks of an all-American boy—is the one who will survive the war. Mailer makes the "non-Jewish" looking Goldstein comfortable with his American and Jewish identities, while Roth becomes consumed by his own feelings of difference and inferiority. Clearly, the physical depiction of these two characters reflected the aesthetics—embraced by most Jewish authors and filmmakers—which valued "non-Semitic" and "non-ethnic" types.

Other fictional characters, like Mailer's Roth, internalize the negative stereotypes about Jews and are, initially, unable to overcome their status as victims. Deborah Mamorek in *The Last Temptation* recalls being ashamed when she was the only Jewish child in her class taught by an antisemitic teacher. The pain created by this self-hatred, and how it made Jews feel and act like victims, is a common theme in the fiction of the late 1940s and 1950s. Joseph Viertel's characters Vic and Deborah survive the Holocaust and make it to Palestine, but they pay a steep price in their sense of self worth. Even in Jerusalem, Vic, although he denies it, is ashamed of his Jewish identity: "I'd say I was self-conscious. As if I'd been born with one eye or one leg. A man with an infirmity through no fault of his own but glad to be friends with healthy people."[42] The status of Jews as victims was enshrined not just because of stereotypes and because Jews absorbed the antisemitic judgments of those around them. Jews were the archetypal victims following World War II because of the unredeemable evil of the Nazis during the war.

Many postwar fiction writers detailed the evil of Nazi crimes against the Jews. Hersey's popular novel about the Warsaw ghetto, *The Wall*, describes the humiliations which Jews faced at the hands of the Nazis, putting, as William Shirer wrote in his review, the Holocaust in terms "we of the predominantly Christian West can feel and can comprehend."[43] The complete innocence of the Jewish characters in the postwar fiction makes the humiliation more acute. In the aftermath of the war and the undeniable revelations about the Holocaust, any ambivalence about responsibility for the persecution disappeared. *The Wall*, *The Last Temptation*, and *Anne Frank: The Diary of a Young Girl*, for example, all center on young women or girls who experience Nazi persecution and display courage in the face of it. Even after more than two years in hiding, Anne Frank is still able to see the good in people, "I don't think . . . of all the misery, but the beauty that still remains. . . . He who has courage and faith will never perish in misery!"[44] Remaining on the bestseller list for half a year, Anne's diary appealed to a sense of hopeful redemption after the inhumanity of the war. One critic wrote that she "brings back a poignant delight in the infinite human spirit."[45] Rachel Apt, in *The Wall*, also has an honest and nurturing spirit which draws other people to her and earns her the nickname of "Little Mother." Deborah Mamorek is yet another innocent girl who grows strong from the persecution which she suffers.

It is worth pausing to note why Anne Frank's diary is included in this discussion of images of the Holocaust. Although this book is not a novel, it shares some of the characteristics of a fictional work: it uniquely personalizes the Holocaust and it was turned into a play and a film. Also, it was in some ways treated like a novel. One review called the diary part of the "literature of Jewish martyrdom of this age," and another made an explicit comparison with Hersey's novel: "It is in reality the kind of document that John Hersey invented for *The Wall.* . . . The common life effect which Mr. Hersey sought to suggest . . . here follows with utter spontaneity."[46]

The descriptions of Nazi treatment of Jews in the postwar literature came on the heels of wartime press stories that had doubted the evidence of a Holocaust in the making or the unique position of Jews in it.[47] By the time fighting had engulfed Europe and the brutality of Nazi policies was undeniable, news reports about Nazi persecutions still lessened the chance that Americans would feel it was a priority to halt the genocide. First, as the persecution of the Jews became familiar, it was relegated to ever smaller spaces on the inside of papers. Second, as Deborah Lipstadt notes, "the press subsumed Nazi antisemitic policy under the rubric of general wartime suffering." And, finally, Lipstadt argues, the stories of gas chambers and ovens were so shocking that many were reluctant to accept their veracity. When *New York Times* reporter Bill Lawrence wrote an account of his visit to the death camp Maidanek in August 1944, the editors of the paper printed an unprecedented editorial asserting the reliability of Lawrence. Yet, while some reporters might have understood the brutality of the camps after 1944, even by April 1945, when publishers and editors were brought to four liberated camps by Allied commander Dwight D. Eisenhower, they did not recognize that "the fate of the Jews had been unique in both ideology and scope."[48]

The willful ignorance on the part of many Americans about the wartime events in Europe continued in some respects after the slaughter stopped. Many misunderstood the particularly Jewish aspects of the Holocaust, the scope of Hitler's operation, or that antisemitism was endemic to Nazi rule. As *The Nation* observed in early 1948, "the average American does not yet realize how important anti-Semitism was for Adolf Hitler as a weapon in his struggle for world domination."[49] A number of cultural critics have argued that immediately following the war the tragedy was completely universalized in public consciousness and only understood as a campaign of World War II. Tony Kushner observes, "For many years . . . , neither British nor American society was able to come to terms with the specifically antisemitic aspect of the Nazis' extermination programme."[50]

Thus, Kushner and others have argued that the universalizing message of the Holocaust was tied to liberal ideology which opposed "any form of Jewish separatism, even when the reality of the Nazi extermination programme became clear." Given the universal rhetoric dominant in the political and popular culture throughout the 1940s, the reluctance to discuss Hitler's crimes as persecution of the Jews instead of as a violation of universal morality was predictable. Moreover, political leaders and writers feared that any focus on the special fate of the Jews would only fuel the still widespread antisemitism. This fear was borne out by numerous expressions of antisemitism and polls such as a wartime one of American G.I.s, many of whom reported that "Hitler was *partly right* in his treatment of the Jews." This fear, in turn, strongly affected the universalist tone of Jewish-American literature in the late 1940s and early 1950s. Dorothy Seidman Bilik observes: "Fear of American anti-Semitism and horror at a more virulent German strain contributed to a bland Jewish American fiction that extolled sameness, brotherhood, and caution."[51]

The failure to highlight the Jewish fate in the Holocaust also reflected a misunderstanding of the details of the Final Solution. To be sure the horror of the Nazi deeds was not lost on the Allied public—on both sides of the Atlantic. For example, when the British first saw newsreels of the camps in April 1945, "Observers at the cinema and in the photographic exhibitions reported the audiences' and visitors' stunned silence." Nevertheless, the implications of the evidence were sometimes ignored. For instance, in the media and government reports on the liberation of Bergen-Belsen, there were few references to Jews, although Jews comprised two-thirds of the prisoners.[52]

Even if many Americans were reluctant to recognize the particularly Jewish side of the Holocaust, the Jewish victims seemed to be defined by their relationship to the Nazis. Tony Kushner concludes, "the victims emerged as a devastated people without a past or a future." The elevation of victimhood as a symbol of universal martyrdom after the war was, I would argue, of great importance in accelerating the acceptance of Jews as insiders in American culture. Dorothy Seidman Bilik notes that this connection had a powerful effect on the image of the Jew: "During this most tragic decade in Jewish experience, the Jew was universalized and mythologized as a symbol of twentieth century man, a homeless victim in an indifferent universe."[53]

The widespread reaction to the unfathomable nature of the Holocaust and the tendency to universalize its lessons in public culture seems to belie the idea that the particular characteristics of Jews and their status as victims called for the establishment of Israel as retribution for the Nazis's actions. Yet, to understand the importance of the Holocaust for the establishment of the Jewish state, one needs to be reminded that the universalizing and particularizing images of the Jews were not mutually exclusive. Instead, they competed with each other in the public consciousness to widen the support for Israel by appealing to sometimes different constituencies. And, most importantly, while the lessons of the Holocaust may have been broadened and the victims of the crime universalized, Jews were nevertheless predominantly identified as victims in these years. Thus, by this logic, all victims of the Nazis were not Jews, but all Jews were victims. If all Jews are symbols of persecution, they have a particular role in the service of a universal lesson.

Two examples of popular fiction that briefly depicted the aftermath of the Holocaust are the 1947 novel *The Young Lions* and the 1948 film *The Search*.[54] At the end of Shaw's novel, Noah, his friend Michael, and the rest of their company liberate a concentration camp. The men are overcome by the horror of the scene before them:

> The smell, by itself, would have been enough to make them silent, but there was also the sight of the dead bodies sprawled at the gate and behind the wire . . .
>   . . . although the objective appearance of their skull-like faces and their staring, cavernous eyes did not alter very much, either in weeping or smiling. It was as though these creatures were too far sunk in a tragedy which had moved off the plane of human reaction onto an animal level of despair.[55]

The horror of the camp is particularized as a Jewish experience to the extent that Michael is always looking to his stoic friend Noah to try to read his reactions. But Jews are not the only inhabitants of the camp. They are one group among the Poles, Russians, Albanians, and German Communists, and they still seem to be a minority which can be persecuted even here. One Albanian leader of the prisoners tells the American Captain Green that the other prisoners "will not stand for" a Jewish memorial service which a rabbi has requested to hold in the camp.[56] Green furiously gives his guarantee for the safety of the worshippers saying that he will station machine gun placements around the courtyard during the service. Although the Holocaust is treated as a human tragedy which affected everyone, Jews—as a group—are still defined by their status as victims and are in need of protection after the war.

Just as implied in *The Young Lions*, *The Search* also indicates that Americans will have a special role in healing the wounds of World War II. *The Search* is a 1948 film about the tragedy of refugee and orphan children in postwar Europe.[57] Americans are the victorious soldiers as well as the people who will care for the victims after the shooting has stopped. The United Nations Refugee Relief Agency is an international organization, but it is staffed by many Americans, most prominently a motherly Mrs. Murray. The film, shot on location in the American-occupied zone of Germany, has a serious, semidocumentary tone befitting the subject of refugee children, "one of the saddest, most arresting dramas of our time," wrote critic Bosley Crowther in his review of the film.[58] The opening scene shows relief workers taking displaced children off a train; the camera pans over the sad-looking, frail children as the narrator tells us, "the war is over, but there is still want and misery." When the children are registered at the United Nations Refugee Relief Agency, we meet a French Catholic child, a Polish one, a Jewish child who had to sort the clothes of the gas chamber victims, and a little blond boy who cannot speak a word. In a flashback, we learn that the mute boy, Karel, is from a cultured Czech family; he becomes the focus of the film as he learns to speak once again, and is finally reunited with his mother. The special case of the Jews is, at times, highlighted. One Jewish boy who is scared to reveal his identity pretends to be a Christian until Karel's mother and a kindly priest assure him that he will no longer be persecuted for being Jewish. Nevertheless, a clear choice was made to feature the Czech not the Jewish boy as symbolic of young war victims.

Although *The Search* focuses on the importance of rescuing innocent victims such as these children from the devastation of the war, rescue, by itself, is not enough. In this film, as well as in other fiction and nonfiction accounts of the war and its aftermath, there is a search for meaning in the tragedy. In the case of the Jews, the most visible group of victims, writers, and filmmakers find that meaning in the continuing persecution itself. Thus, it is the fate of Jews to suffer, but in that suffering they are elevated morally and are a beacon for the world. In *The Naked and the Dead*, the Jewish soldier who successfully survives the war, Goldstein, embraces his difference, because he sees it as inescapable. His grandfather told him when he was a boy that Jews "must always journey from disaster to disaster, and it makes us stronger and weaker than other men." Goldstein takes this statement of Jewish survival and difference to heart, and gains strength from it. He is driven forward even when his body is about to collapse by a sense of mission: "Israel [the Jewish people] is the heart of all nations. . . . The conscience and the raw exposed nerve; all emotion passed through it."[59] No other character in the novel has Goldstein's drive to survive even when the futility of the effort seems overwhelming. The sense of moral choseness found in Goldstein became a defining characteristic of Jews and Israelis in subsequent fiction.

The Naked and the Dead was written just three years after the end of World War II and the allusions to Jewish endurance in the face of the Holocaust are unmistakable. Already aware of the specifics of the Holocaust, Goldstein is overcome by the tragedy of the Jews's fate: "There was nothing in him now but a vague anger, a deep resentment, and the origins of vast hopelessness." Nevertheless, Goldstein does endure, in part, because he believes that he and other Jews must survive to redeem humankind. Of course, millions of Jews did not survive the war, but their deaths can nevertheless uplift others. In *The Young Lions*, after seeing the horror of the camp and hearing his captain stand up for the right of Jews to hold a memorial service, Noah exalts that "The human beings are going to be running the world!"[60] As Noah asserts this redemption, he is shot by a defeated and dejected Nazi who is wandering alone through the woods. Following Noah's example, Michael finally finds his own courage and shoots the Nazi. The particular mission of the Jews, then, has universal value.

Those who attempt to deny their Jewish identity—whether by assimilation into the larger society or collaboration with the enemy—do not find redemption. Joseph Viertel's Vic, who calls Jewish culture a fiction and refuses to circumcise his son, is an example. John Hersey, in *The Wall*, also emphasizes the importance of taking pride in Jewish identity. One character who does not learn this lesson attempts to smuggle himself out of the ghetto and pass as a Gentile. He is admonished by his rabbi that he cannot shed his Jewish identity so easily: "You are a product of [Judaism's] traditions . . . of humility, . . . of the Torah, of family bonds, . . . above all, of being persecuted. . . . The heritage is in your heart."[61] The rabbi's entreaty conflates Judaism and the history of persecution against the Jews. Yet, he argues, Jews are set apart by more than their status as victims, and their unique qualities are valuable to all people. A similar view is found in contemporary nonfiction rhetoric. For example, in a review of a history of the Jews, critic R. M. MacIver writes: "the ethnoreligious system of Judaism expresses the particular *genius* of a people." MacIver and others stressed the universal value of this ethnoreligious system.[62]

As in *The Naked and the Dead*, Hersey's Jews are the heart of humankind and the guardians of universal morality. One of the ghetto fighters writes that "we are indeed involved in the struggle of Humanity against anti-Humanity."[63] Such sentiments were expressed in nonfiction as well. Anne Frank wrote of her conviction that Jews serve a moral purpose in the world, and will never be completely a part of any other national group.

Others agreed with Frank. In her introduction to the diary, Eleanor Roosevelt wrote that Anne's words made her aware of the "ultimate shining nobility of [the human] spirit."[64] In *The Wall*, one character tells his fellow ghetto residents that honesty and justice are "implanted in the wandering blood of the Jews." He concludes with a call to celebrate universal humanity, while acknowledging the unique contributions which each group brings to it.[65] Importantly, as will be discussed in subsequent chapters, the language of absolute struggle between "Humanity" and "anti-Humanity" paralleled the shrill view found in Cold War rhetoric of a world divided between good and evil. In this dialectic, there was no mistaking on which side the Jews stood.

CONCLUSION

After the horrors of World War II, most Americans in the late 1940s were persuaded of the moral and practical importance of universalism, the extension of moral concern across and regardless of national or ethnic boundaries. Throughout popular culture and the press, universal values, at home and abroad, represented that which was noble, decent, and civilized. This postwar embrace of universalism led many Americans to reject prejudices, especially antisemitism, in the public culture. Yet, as this chapter has shown, Jews were not merely embraced in the popular culture, because they were just like other Americans. Jews were also depicted as having particular qualities that were valued. The Jew who had been unquestionably an outsider was now becoming an insider, because of his difference, not in spite of it. The new Jews of the popular imagination were similar to other Americans, but they also had special moral lessons to teach their fellows, lessons learned through years of prejudice and the Holocaust.

Thus, the new Jews of early postwar popular culture represented the beginning transformation of Jews from outsiders to insiders; and these images are essential for understanding American attitudes toward the formation of Israel. As the next chapter will discuss, Americans justified their support or opposition to the formation of Israel within the framework of tension between universal and particular identities. The new cultural image of Jews which brought together the two poles of the universal and particular, helped to justify the creation of Israel within the popular and political culture.

2

The United States and the Founding of Israel

A Particularist State with a Universal Mission

In November 1947, Henry Wallace, former vice president and soon-to-be presidential candidate, wrote an article about the plight of Jewish displaced persons who still remained in refugee camps more than two years after the war had ended. Wallace's article appeared in *The New Republic* just weeks before the United Nations General Assembly vote that would endorse the partition plan for Palestine and the creation of both Jewish and Arab states. It reminded readers that the proposed Zionist state was needed to bring some closure to the tragedy of the Holocaust. Wallace vividly described the legacy of misery in a camp run by the International Refugee Organization in Cinecitta, a few miles outside of Rome. While the refugees "str[o]ve to leave the continent on which their dear ones were massacred," Wallace observed, at the present immigration quotas, it would be seven to eight years before most would get into the United States or other countries that they had chosen. Meanwhile, the former vice president argued that there was an answer to this misery which he found nearby in a villa rented by the American Joint Distribution Committee to house about one hundred and fifty refugees. In contrast to the camp run by the International Refugee Organization, in this villa, "There is self government. There is spirit. There is purposeful existence." The residents were training themselves for life in Palestinian settlements, and also receiving some technical training from the American Jewish agency ORT (Organization for Rehabilitation through Training). Just like those in Palestine, this "embryo Kibbutz . . . stands in sharp contrast to the despair at Cinecitta," argued Wallace.[1]

Henry Wallace was not alone when he concluded that the Zionist goal of expanding Jewish settlements and establishing a political entity in Palestine was the obvious remedy to the devastation of the Holocaust. Indeed, the humanitarian impulse to help refugees after the war was a common justification for the establishment of Israel, even among those—such as Harry S. Truman—who had not previously supported any part of the Zionist dream. What distinguished the argument of Wallace and other Zionists from that which emphasized the humanitarian imperative was that the former highlighted the particular persecution as well as characteristics of the Jews. Theirs was not a universal humanitarian cause, but one specifically designed to right the wrongs of the Holocaust. Importantly, this elevation of the particular needs of the Jews over universal humanitarian standards privileged the claims of the Jews to Palestine over the claims of the Arabs to the same land. Not all were convinced by this argument. Arab leaders, not surprisingly, argued that there was little connection between the Holocaust and the creation of Israel. Some American leaders as well as writers were also scornful of the elevation of particular Jewish claims over universal, humanitarian principles.

The clash between universalistic and particularistic interpretations of the Jewish fate continued on in the 1940s and 1950s, but both could be—and were—used to support the creation of the Jewish state. Although the emphasis on Jewish particularity seems to have contradicted the universal ideal, these two contemporaneous and competing formulations reinforced and broadened support for a new Jewish state in the Middle East. Thus, two seemingly contradictory narratives about the meaning of the Holocaust ended up recommending the same course of action: establishment of a Jewish state.

CREATING A JEWISH STATE IN POPULAR FICTION

The debate about the founding of Israel played itself out on various fronts. The conflict of justifications at the policy level also manifested itself in popular culture, which, as always, provided a backdrop, reflecting and helping shape the struggle of ideas and attitudes being acted out in politics. Much popular fiction of the late 1940s and early 1950s depicted the creation of a Jewish state in the Middle East as the natural reparation for the tragedy of the Holocaust. In the fiction, survival is often rooted in the Jewish community, not in individuals. For example, in John Hersey's 1950 novel *The Wall*, which tells the story of Jews in the Warsaw Ghetto, characters who reject the community are treated with contempt. When the Jewish community as a whole is divided by political differences, such as those between the Socialists and the Zionists, all the Jews lose, Hersey argues, and their divisions make them powerless against the Nazis. The characters Rachel Apt and Dolek Berson teach this lesson to the rest of the community and, in so doing, become symbolic parents to the Jewish future. Rachel worries that she must "wean" her fighters away from her so that they can go on without her. The family metaphor is completed by the birth of a baby, "Israel," born in a bunker amid final preparations for the battle against the Nazis. Not long after Israel is welcomed into the world, he is killed for the sake of the others, because his crying endangers all hiding in the bunker. The tragedy of Israel's death is one of many that the Jews endure before the war is over, but his mother remains optimistic about survival and having another baby.

The Jews of both the novels *The Wall* and Joseph Viertel's *The Last Temptation* (1955) as well as those in the films *The Sword in the Desert* (1949) and *The Juggler* (1953) find their greatest hope for Jewish survival in the new Jewish state. These two films were unusual in the 1940s and 1950s. Reflecting the widespread fear of arousing antisemitism, Hollywood filmmakers were just as reluctant to make films about modern Israel as they were to focus too much attention on the Jewish aspects of the Holocaust.[2] Nevertheless, in all four works, Palestine (and, later, Israel) is the indisputable *home* for Jews. In *The Last Temptation*, the group of smuggled Jews are treated as long lost relatives by the locals who shower the refugees with warm clothes and "exotic" fruits (the refugees have reached paradise!). Deborah is ever prodding the self-hating Vic to believe that Jews actually deserve their own country. To Vic's proposal that they leave Jerusalem during the heaviest fighting, Deb argues *"This is our very last place in the entire world."*[3]

Joseph Viertel implies that Deborah, like many other European refugees from the Holocaust, had for many years loosely associated her Jewish identity with Zionism. Her older brother, for example, left for Palestine during the 1930s to help build the new state. The assertion of a long-standing identification of European Jews with Zionism confers emotional and secular legitimacy on the creation of the modern Jewish state in Palestine apart from ancient biblical promises. Rachel, in *The Wall*, started working for the Zionists when she was about fifteen or sixteen. She is soon a committed Zionist and decides to smuggle her little brother out of the ghetto to reach Palestine alone. Just as the European refugees in *The Last Temptation* are welcomed with open arms by the Palestinian Jews, the Zionists in *The Sword in the Desert* and *The Juggler* are eager to take in the survivors of the Holocaust.[4] *The Sword in the Desert*, set in 1947, opens on the nighttime scene of a boat full of Jewish refugees approaching the Palestine coast. One old man tearfully says how it took "two thousand years" to get there. *The Juggler* also begins with a boat full of refugees arriving in Israel shortly after independence. One, Hans Muller (Kirk Douglas), an embittered survivor who lost his whole family in the Holocaust, is told by refugee camp officials, "Now, you're home." The camp doctor also tries to reach out to the emotionally scarred Hans: "Every person is precious to us. . . . That's why we have an Israel, for no other reason."

The Zionist claim to the land is not legitimate merely because the Jews call it home and they have biblical ties to Israel. These films and novels argue that the Jews deserve Israel because of the persecution that they suffered in Europe. Rachel knows that their physical survival can only be achieved in Palestine. Deborah brings her family to Palestine when she realizes that they can't be Jews anywhere else. *The Juggler* and *The Sword in the Desert* are shaped by the refugees' story. One of the underground leaders in the latter film tries to explain to the mercenary American captain who ferries refugees out of Europe why it's important that these refugees reach Palestine. Most, he argues—as the camera comes to rest on a terrified little girl clutching her doll—have "heard the screams of their loved ones" as they were dragged into the ovens. The depiction of Jews as perpetual victims legitimates their claim to Israeli independence, and reminds Americans that Jews are always threatened. In *The Last Temptation* and elsewhere, the Independence War is described in what would later become familiar David and Goliath terms: Vic judges that the *Haganah* doesn't "even have a chance in a million."[5] Viertel's description of the war is similar to Hersey's description of the Warsaw Ghetto revolt. Both highlight the ever-present threat that the Jews will lose. And, in *The Sword in the Desert*, one young Zionist tells her lover, "Israel hasn't got one chance in a thousand."

The David and Goliath metaphor, implicit in these fictional portrayals, became used explicitly in media, political, and, soon thereafter, historical rhetoric about Israel. For example, Israeli President Chaim Weizmann used language which was already widespread in American culture, strengthening an image of Israel as a young, outmatched, fellow democracy. Weizmann evoked the image of a David and Goliath contest in the Middle East in a telegram to Truman in late 1948 describing the beginning of the Independence War earlier in the year: "Our people almost unarmed withstood the onslaught and successfully defended their independence." This metaphor lent itself to overdramatization. In a 1951 letter, Weizmann described the matter of peace with its neighbors as a "question of life and death" for Israel.[6] Similar language and emphasis on Israelis as victims was widespread in the American press. For example, a May 1948 editorial from *The Philadelphia Inquirer* strongly condemned British support for the Arabs. Israeli Haganah forces were described as "hardy and well-trained but desperately small." Similarly, the fighters trying to take Jerusalem in the summer of 1948 were a "weary, hungry, decimated band of Jews." Other articles argued that Israelis would "need . . . a shield of David to keep their nation alive"; luckily, they were led by David Ben-Gurion, "a modern-day David."[7]

But even more than the appeal of Israel as a threatened David, Jewish persecution justified the establishment of Israel for writers in the postwar period, because the state seemed to be the only way to heal the wounds of the Holocaust. *The Juggler's* Hans arrives in Israel emotionally withdrawn and suffering from delusions, leading him to assault a police officer whom he imagines to be a Nazi. The residents of the *kibbutz* where he stays finally coax Hans out of his shell, getting him to admit that he needs help. Deborah, in *The Last Temptation*, also, finds solace in Israel after the terror of Europe. She confesses that she has a fantasy that her feet will turn into roots, so that she will be forever rooted in the land.

In *The Sword in the Desert*, Palestine also represents the best way to heal the wounds of Jewish refugees. The Jewish children in the UNRRA camp have a special salvation after the war: Palestine. The UNRRA camp officials share in this belief, throwing a going away party for a group of Jewish children as they leave for Palestine. The party room is decorated with a large *Mogen David*, portraits of Theodore Herzl (the founder of political Zionism) and David Ben-Gurion, and large Hebrew letters. The children, all dressed in what look like matching *kibbutznik* shorts, shirts, scarves, and knapsacks, march out smiling and singing. The children are overjoyed to be going to the mandate territory and it seems that the United Nations is more than willing to send them there. Real life refugee policy in Palestine was much more complicated. The British blocked much Jewish immigration, especially after their 1939 White Paper. Moreover, Zionists often expressed hostility to British imperialism and described it as dishonest and unjust.[8]

The establishment of Israel is, of course, complicated by the presence of the British and the Arabs. *The Last Temptation* and *The Sword in the Desert* discredit the mandate role of the British and delegitimize the Arab claim to the land. One British officer in *Desert* explains the politics of the region and why everyone should be concerned with the Middle East: "if we pull out before there is an agreement, the entire Middle East may go up in flames and with it the world. . . . This isn't a Jewish or an Arab or a British problem; this is a problem for all mankind." This sentiment supports what historians Peter Hahn and William Stivers, among others, have labeled the most important contemporary foreign policy goal for Americans in the region: the maintenance of stability.[9]

Not surprisingly in an American culture which had long had a love/hate relationship with British social and political values, there were contradictory views of the ally's role in Palestine. The British in Viertel's story are neither as philosophical nor as honorable as those in *The Sword in the Desert*. Many of them are antisemitic. One officer says that "Hebrews" never learned to get along with others and contrasts them to Arabs who are respectful and "never pushing."[10] The British soldiers in the novel treat the Arabs with politeness and the Jews with derision. Although this film and novel give different impressions of the British, in both, the British are the main dramatic antagonists to the Jews. The secondary antagonists to the Jews are the Arabs. Arabs—prominent in *Temptation*, but nearly absent in *Desert*—are depicted as inferior to the Jews, and alien to all that is Western and modern.

THE LIMITS OF THE HOLOCAUST

Although there could be no doubt in American postwar culture of the sympathy that many felt for the victims of the Holocaust, for some, this was not enough to justify the creation of a Jewish state. One source of American reluctance was the nature of the proposed nation, an exclusively Jewish state. Laura Hobson's *Gentleman's Agreement* raised this question through the character of Dr. Lieberman. Lieberman, a physicist, makes a distinction between Palestine as a refuge and Zionism as a movement for a state. He is clearly against the latter and likens its proponents to confirmed Communists in that they have closed minds. Furthermore, Lieberman explains that he is against religious nationalism, and the rejoining of church and state that Zionism represents. Lieberman's view expresses the fear heard in contemporary political debates that Zionism would create an undemocratic, racial, and theocratic state. Although the novel champions universalism, it is against religious and ethnic particularism, and leaves Lieberman's view as the only word on Zionism, the question of a particularistic state is introduced more as an ongoing controversy rather than as a settled issue.

One of the most strident, persistent voices in the public, political debate over the establishment of a particularly Jewish state was that of former diplomat Alfred Lilienthal who had been active in the anti-Zionist American Council for Judaism. Although the American Council for Judaism, the foremost Jewish anti-Zionist organization in the United States continued lobbying and education efforts into the 1950s, it remained alienated from most American Jews and unable to affect the direction of policy. Lilienthal's arguments, while they failed to win widespread support, are instructive, because they reveal some of the political contradictions entailed in supporting the creation of a Jewish state in the center of the Middle East.

Lilienthal's central argument against the formation of a Jewish state was that in the debate over a universal or particular Jewish identity, the universal (and, for him, spiritually based) identity had clearly won out. Jewish history, he wrote, has been a "continuous struggle between these conflicting ideologies—nation versus faith—chosen people versus universality—segregation versus integration." As an American Jew, Lilienthal argued that his religion did not distinguish him from other Americans politically. Moreover, he was indignant that being a Jew meant he should automatically support Israel: "American Jews should no longer be forced, by smears and fears [from within the Jewish community], to have a foreign policy separate from that of Methodists or Episcopalians." He charged that this insidious demand of "dual loyalty," coming from the Israeli government as much as from American Jews, was unfair and unprecedented among all other ethnic groups. In the wake of World War II, Lilienthal makes the universalistic argument that Jewish racialism is "poppycock" and akin to Nazi ideas.[11]

Lilienthal was particularly bitter about the press coverage of the Palestine debate and the new Jewish state. He argued that throughout the country the press was "knuckling down" to Zionist pressure. He pointed to interviews with newspaper editors conducted by the National Opinion Research Center in October 1947, one month before the partition vote in the United Nations. Fifty percent of those interviewed opposed partition, 30 percent favored it, and 10 percent called for a federalized state in Palestine. Despite these numbers, Lilienthal implied that some illegitimate forces must be at work since the opinions were not reflected in the "clear pro-Zionist slant" of the news stories. Lilienthal also criticized press coverage of the Arabs in the Middle East. He asserted that Arab refugees were not usually discussed, and if they were discussed were "depicted as tools of the Grand Mufti of Jerusalem, as pro-Nazi Falangists, or as desert marauders." He found the same biases in reviews of books on the issue, arguing that books which were not clearly pro-Zionist (few in number compared to those supportive of Israel) were given poor reviews. Similarly, those who chose to speak out against biased views of the Middle East were labeled pro-Arab or antisemitic, with mainstream voices often "lumped together with" antisemitic extremists.

Lilienthal's determination to view the press coverage of Israel as the result of a pro-Zionist conspiracy oversimplified and misunderstood the complex factors that contributed to an evolving American image of the Jewish state. First, since Lilienthal was so concerned with this issue, he erroneously assumed that newspaper editors should be equally consumed with it, thus charging that a dearth of editorials was due to Zionist pressure. One could point to the same data and make the opposite argument: a lack of editorials signaled an anti-Zionist bias on the part of the papers. Second, and far more significantly, because Lilienthal was an American Jew who felt no identification with a Jewish state, he failed to consider that other Jewish and non-Jewish Americans might be genuinely attracted to such a state and see something of themselves in it. Instead, he believed that there must be an illegitimate hegemony at work forcing Americans to support a Jewish state against all rational judgment. In addition, Lilienthal overstated the early support for Israel. From 1947 at least through 1955, the political and cultural attitudes toward Israel were increasingly friendly, but remained complex and not always easy to read.

The attitude of a Jewish anti-Zionist such as Alfred Lilienthal demonstrated the limitations of the Holocaust to create political support for a Jewish state. Lilienthal deplored the crimes committed in the Holocaust, but saw them as unconnected to Jewish nationalism. Instead, he clung fast to liberal values of nation states based upon universal values, allowing for pluralistic identity. Lilienthal and others who agreed with him thus raised the question of why many American *liberals* came to favor the creation of Israel and embraced the state once it was a reality. Some liberals, such as *The Nation* editor Freda Kirchwey, were early supporters, while many, such as Eleanor Roosevelt, came later to Zionism.

Eleanor Roosevelt only called for the creation of a Jewish state after the end of 1947. Her attitudes toward Zionism and Israel are interesting, because throughout her career she had championed universal causes such as world peace and human rights. Yet she came to support the creation of an exclusively Jewish state in a disputed area of the Middle East, thus following a common political trajectory of many American liberals in the early years of the Cold War.

The revelations about the Holocaust and the plight of its survivors strongly affected Eleanor Roosevelt. At first glance, this would appear to be the source of Roosevelt's support for the creation of a Jewish state. During the war, her own lingering antisemitism disappeared as she worked hard to assist persecuted European Jews. She became deeply frustrated and awakened to the destructiveness of antisemitism when—despite her best efforts to lobby State Department and other Washington officials—she was unable to pry open American doors to Jewish refugees. Following the war, Roosevelt's compassion for the refugees grew, and she was particularly moved by visits to European refugee camps, writing of the plight of Jewish displaced persons in her "My Day" syndicated column. She identified with this issue, as she did with many political issues, through the stories of individuals. She was, for example, affected by an old woman in one of the camps who knelt in the road before Roosevelt, grabbed her knees, and repeated "Israel" over and over. Roosevelt remarked, "I knew for the first time what that small land meant to so many, many people." She continued to write about the issue in 1946 expressing exasperation with Britain's refusal to let Jews into Palestine. In August 1947, the former first lady and member of the American delegation to the United Nations urged the president to pressure Britain into letting a ship full of refugees into Palestine.[12]

Clearly, Eleanor Roosevelt drew very different lessons from the Holocaust than did Alfred Lilienthal. At the same time, Roosevelt's views also reflect the limits of the Holocaust to create political support for Zionism. Her commitment to Jewish immigration to Palestine did not mean that she—at first—supported the establishment of a Jewish *state* there. At the end of 1946, Roosevelt favored the political solution of a UN trusteeship over the area. Other American liberals were also unconvinced that freer Jewish immigration to Palestine necessitated the creation of a Jewish state. For Truman, the argument that he should support Zionist demands because Jews were victims of the Holocaust was wearing thin even by the fall of 1946. Zionist and White House advisor to Truman David Niles observed in a letter to David Ben-Gurion that this feeling was common among many Americans, not just Truman: "The feeling of guilt for the Holocaust is no longer so great . . . and the longer the solution to the D.P. [displaced person] problem [is] put off, the more interest [will] lag."[13]

Niles' predictions may have proved true of some Americans, but not all. By 1947, when the future of Palestine had been turned over to the UN by the British mandate authorities, Eleanor Roosevelt was starting to change her ideas about the mandate territory. She was in favor of a Jewish homeland in Palestine, but was still not sure about partitioning the land into separate Arab and Jewish states. As it turns out, the decisive reason that Roosevelt supported a Jewish state was not the Holocaust, but the integrity of the United Nations and its internationalist principles. The turning point in her thinking came in November 1947 when the majority report from the UN committee appointed to study the issue was approved by the General Assembly. By this vote, the UN endorsed partition of Palestine into Jewish and Arab states. Roosevelt's support for the UN was so great that she considered partition a test of the new organization.

Over the next six months, Roosevelt argued in correspondence with President Truman and Secretary of State George Marshall that the United States had to work to implement partition or risk damaging the international organization. Her pressure on the president and the secretary was steady, and she even threatened to resign her position from the American delegation to the UN when she suspected that the United States was backing away from partition. Her priorities remained consistent, writing to Marshall, "My greatest concern is for the UN even though I also have concern for upholding what I think is a moral obligation [to support a Jewish homeland]." This overarching concern for the UN was even reflected in her reaction to American recognition of the Jewish state in May 1948. Although Roosevelt had argued strenuously that the United States should recognize the new state as soon as it was announced, she protested to both Truman and Marshall that the White House had not warned the American delegation to the UN ahead of time and had, therefore, weakened the organization and the trust among its members.[14] Many others also found the swift American decision for recognition a great surprise. Marshall reported to Truman that he had had difficulty preventing resignations both from the UN delegation and the State Department over this issue.[15] The press was also taken by surprise. *Newsweek*, for example, described the "Recognition Bombshell" at the UN, and argued that the actions of the United States "dealt a severe blow to the United Nations prestige"; the *Washington Star* concurred that swift U.S. recognition "hit UN delegates like a smash to the face."[16]

Despite her criticism of how the United States extended recognition, Eleanor Roosevelt quickly criticized the Arabs for their invasion of Israel in 1948 since it was "irresponsible" and showed "little respect for the rest of the world."[17] Moreover, once Israel was an established fact, Roosevelt became an ardent admirer of the Jewish state and her people. Her previous objections to Zionism were left behind and, indeed, have been forgotten by many historians who have written about the founding of Israel and American-Israeli relations.

THE EVOLUTION OF TRUMAN'S ATTITUDES

Like Eleanor Roosevelt, Harry S. Truman chose to support the creation of a Jewish state only shortly before its formation. He, too, was moved by the image of pitiful Holocaust refugees who needed reparation for the crimes of the Nazis—although he came to his sympathy for Jews later in life. Like many postwar liberals, including Roosevelt, Truman had voiced antisemitic views in his younger days, and had used racial and ethnic epithets. In contemporary disputes over refugees and Palestine, Truman continued to use broad labels for Jews.[18] Nevertheless, by World War II, Truman's attitudes reflected the popular emphasis on universal values as the foundation of American identity. As he wrote in his diary on 7 June 1945:

> . . . by amalgamation, we've made a very good country. . . .
>   I've no more use for Polish-Americans, Irish-Americans, Swedish-Americans or any other sort of hyphenate than I have for Communist-Americans. They all have some other loyalty than the one they should have. Maybe the old melting pot will take care of it.[19]

Truman's rejection of antisemitism by the late 1940s undoubtedly reflected the changing standards of what was acceptable in postwar public culture. Truman's views about prejudice and Jews were also influenced by his personal relationships. His friendship with Eddie Jacobson and Max Lowenthal, and his working relationship with White House assistant David Niles and adviser Samuel Rosenman, probably made him more sensitive to antisemitism.[20]

By 1948, Truman was also a universalist who couched his support for Israel in humanitarian terms. Thus, the president extended recognition and friendly support to Israel, and justified his policy in both universal and particular terms. The president echoed the common assumptions of popular culture and the media, believing that Jews deserved a home by virtue of their humanity and the imperative to treat them without prejudice. Such an assumption by Truman and liberal Americans was not surprising at a time when antisemitism was becoming unacceptable in the public culture and universal values were championed. Supporters and opponents of Zionism both invoked the universalist ideals and language to support their position.

At the same time, Truman and other supporters of Israel argued that Jews were the particular victims of the Nazis and of years of anti-semitism. Universalism and particularism found common ground, and it is important to understand why. Policy toward the issue of World War II refugees was relatively straightforward and enjoyed widespread consensus, at least in the abstract. Many Americans, beginning with Truman, had a deep compassion for the most prominent victims of German brutality. As Americans had advanced across the continent of Europe and seen for themselves the grim realities of Nazi regimes, compassion for the victims and condemnation of the perpetrators grew. Moreover, after the war, when the United States shared responsibility for occupying Europe, the urgency of resettling refugees was motivated not only by morality, but also by practicality. The issue grabbed big headlines and had the potential to bring condemnation upon American occupation forces abroad.

Yet, the issue of finding justice for Jewish war refugees came to intersect with the much-less-straightforward question of a Jewish national entity in the Middle East. From 1945–1948, Truman and many other policymakers in his administration, looked upon the issue of the Zionist movement in the Middle East as a humanitarian problem. They believed that a sizable number of Jewish displaced persons should be brought to Palestine to begin a new life. In the summer of 1945, Harry Truman was worried about war-devastated Europe and the thousands of displaced persons on the continent. He sent Dean of the University of Pennsylvania Law School Earl Harrison to investigate the refugee situation. Harrison recommended that one hundred thousand Jewish refugees be allowed into the British mandate territory of Palestine. Since their 1939 White Paper, the British had effectively cut off immigration to the territory and ended land sales to Jewish residents. Jews numbered four hundred fifty thousand, roughly 30 percent of the Palestine population.[21]

Truman's endorsement of the Harrison Report won him praise from longtime Zionist activists as well as Jewish and non-Jewish Americans who saw the creation of the Jewish state as the embodiment of universal ideals. Seventy-eight percent of Americans polled in 1946 agreed that one hundred thousand Jews should be let into Palestine.[22] Nevertheless, Truman continued to face political pressure and complaints on the refugees' behalf, including the charge that conditions in the refugee camps at the end of 1945 had not improved in the six months since the fighting was over.

During the war, many American politicians had supported the Zionist goal of creating a Jewish state in Palestine.[23] A year before the war ended, both political party platforms had included pro-Zionist planks, and both houses of Congress had pending resolutions endorsing a Jewish commonwealth in the Middle East (the Taft-Wagner bill in the Senate and the Wright-Compton bill in the House). Furthermore, thirty-three state legislatures had passed pro-Zionist resolutions and forty governors and half of Congress had signed pro-Zionist petitions to the president.[24] Yet, the popularity of the issue only served to highlight an ironic complication of its "universal" implications. In addition to the objections of the British and the rising violence from both Arabs and Jews, with the flush of postwar universalist aspirations in both popular and policy discourse, Americans were increasingly uncomfortable with the idea of a state founded on particularist criteria. Accordingly, the Taft-Wagner bill was reintroduced in the Senate in October 1945 with the phrase "Jewish commonwealth" removed and a proviso added that all men, regardless of race or creed, would get equal rights in the new state.

The redrafted bill provided one answer to the American rejection of a state based on narrow religious or ethnic lines. Yet, the simple rewording did not change the fact that the proposed Zionist state would be undeniably Jewish in character. What did change was the image of that state and the place of Jews and other ethnic groups in American culture. In the political narrative used by American policymakers as well as in contemporary popular culture, the proposed Jewish state came to embody universalism based on political ideals, so religious and ethnic differences—in Israel and in the United States—were less important and, therefore, nonthreatening. Thus, the universalist ideals of the postwar period could be flexible and public discussion of the Zionist issue selective, highlighting the humanitarian imperative of caring for Jewish displaced persons. For example, the highly publicized *Exodus* incident in mid-1947 cemented already strong American popular support for the Jewish position and became a symbolic focus of Zionist rhetoric. The ship *Exodus*, originally came from the United States and had an American captain and crew; it held more than four thousand refugees determined to reach British-controlled Palestine. The attempt to smuggle in the human cargo was unsuccessful: the British rammed the boat, killing two Americans and one refugee, and wounding more than thirty others. The refugees were sent back to Cyprus and, eventually, to Germany on prison ships. The publicity surrounding the incident dramatized the tragic plight of the Holocaust survivors confronted with the implacable British military, and the support of individual Americans for the immigrants.[25]

Many Americans, including Truman, were moved by such stories. In his memoirs, Truman recalled that his primary motivation in recognizing the new state was humanitarian. He wrote that the fate of the displaced persons was "of deep personal concern to me." Truman's ideal policy would have allowed the settlement of the refugees *without* the creation of a Jewish state. He emphasized that the British and Arabs had to work out a peaceful solution, because "he had no desire to send half a million American soldiers to keep the peace in Palestine." He saw the issue as one of short-term necessity to let the refugees in, but preferred to leave a long-term political solution up to the UN.[26] From all accounts, there is no reason to question the sincerity of Truman's humanitarian concern. At the same time, the contemporary and later descriptions of that concern have often drowned out the other factors in American policy and have contributed to the narrative that exaggerated Truman's role in the creation of Israel. This narrative and the moral urgency of Truman's position became, in turn, synonymous with American policy toward Israel. Thus, Truman's individual role and convictions came to symbolize U.S. policy, and his humanitarian vision soon defined the American popular image of Israel and the proprietary role of the United States in its formation.

IMAGES OF THE FOUNDING OF ISRAEL

The narrative that emphasized the United States' role, especially that of Truman in the formation of Israel, is illustrated by what came to be one of the most potent images of Israel: the country as a newly born baby. (This narrative was echoed in the press and popular fiction—as seen in John Hersey's *The Wall*.) In this typology, Truman played an essential role. Three days after the formation of the state, Assistant Secretary of State Robert Lovett wrote that while "the President's political advisors, having failed to . . . make the President a father of the new state, have determined at least to make him the midwife." That same day, Rabbi Samuel Thurman of the United Hebrew Congregation of St. Louis, Missouri, where he had made Truman's acquaintance years before, wrote to the president: "America is now at Israel's cradle—virtually, as its mother. As such, it has a high responsibility—I trust, of no little maternal affection and concern." The chief rabbi of Israel concurred with Thurman, telling the American president that "God put you in your mother's womb so that you could be the instrument to bring the rebirth of Israel."[27] Whether Truman is described as a male instrument and father or a female midwife and mother, he is always a parental figure to the new state.

Truman, himself, did nothing to discourage the idea that he played a key role in the formation of Israel. Along with his memoirs which stress his singular humanitarian vision, Truman ventured bolder metaphors. In 1953, at a reception for the Jewish Theological Seminary, when Eddie Jacobson referred to Truman as "the man who helped create the State of Israel," Truman interrupted his friend saying, "What do you mean 'helped create'? I am Cyrus, I am Cyrus" [the Persian who was credited with the Jews' return to Jerusalem].[28] Years earlier, Truman had written to Emanuel Neumann, president of the Zionist Organization of America, that "one of the proudest moments of my life occurred at 6:12 PM on Friday May fourteenth . . ." [when the United States recognized Israel].[29] Interestingly, almost all of the government, press, and historic accounts of Israel's formation include a "time of birth"—a vital statistic in the arrival of a baby.

After he left office, Truman continued to receive praise from American Jews and Israelis for his role in 1948, speaking at dinners of the United Jewish Appeal, Greater Miami Combined Jewish Appeal, National Israel Bonds Dinner, and the Convention of the Zionist Organization. The praise was sometimes effusive, as seen in the Light of the World Award presented to him by an Israeli academy at a 1957 Zionist convention.[30] Even in 1969, Golda Meir, extended birthday greetings, adding, "we're in your everlasting debt."[31] Thus, Truman, Israel, and American Jews all seemed to collaborate in writing the retrospective narrative about Truman's great role—and by extension, that of the United States—in the creation of Israel, according to a humanitarian, universal imperative, not a narrow political one.

From another perspective, the role of Truman and the United States in the formation of Israel was not great. Following his vocal support for allowing Jewish refugees into Palestine in 1945 and 1946, Truman gladly stood on the sidelines while the United Nations Special Commission on Palestine (UNSCOP) hammered out a political solution. Truman supported UNSCOPs plan for partition of Palestine into a Jewish and an Arab state which was endorsed by the General Assembly in November 1947. (Partition was favored by the Zionists and opposed by the Arabs.) As violence in the mandate rose, Truman's support for partition grew lukewarm—especially in light of strong opposition to the UN plan from the U.S. State Department. The president concurred that perhaps a temporary trusteeship would be necessary, although he postponed any decisions for a policy change. Thus, Truman was politically embarrassed by the seeming reversal of his own administration in March 1948 when the U.S. Ambassador to the United Nations spoke in favor of a trusteeship proposal without a *direct* authorization from the White House.[32] By

May, Truman's own support for partition was again firm, and he extended recognition to the state as soon as it was declared.

The narrative about the president's pivotal role was encouraged by members of Truman's administration and was firmly in place soon after Israel was founded. For example, in February 1951, Administrative Assistant Philleo Nash responded to queries regarding Truman's role in the creation of Israel with the pronouncement that "the President of the United States and the President of Israel could almost be said to have equal claims to being the father of the new country." Nash's selective account of events cited Truman's early support for the creation of a Jewish state and his recognition of affinity between the State of Israel which was based on "democratic freedom" and the United States. He wrote that Truman provided economic aid "to stabilize the new born state" and welcomed Israel into the "family of nations." He argued that there was a special bond between "one of the oldest republics in the world" and "the newest." Finally, Nash's heroic picture of Truman's efforts on behalf of Israel rested on "a warm personal friendship" between the first president of Israel, Chaim Weizmann, and Truman.[33] The relationship between the presidents here and in countless other accounts has come to personalize the relations between the two countries to that between two friends. Truman did have a sense of responsibility to Weizmann, the grand old man of Zionism. For example, when the President was angriest at the constant lobbying of the Zionist organizations in March 1948, he was still open to the entreaties of Weizmann.

Truman's sentimental view of Weizmann was, in part, due to the intervention of his friend and former business partner Eddie Jacobson of Kansas City, Missouri.[34] Special Counsel Clark Clifford and Special Assistant for Minority Affairs David Niles were also important influences on Truman's decision to recognize Israel.[35] Their advice, in turn, was based on humanitarian arguments as well as domestic politics. Clifford was most instrumental in the short-term logistics of endorsing partition in the United Nations and negotiating a truce with the State Department which allowed the president to be the first leader to recognize the state, while Niles' role was most important as a liaison to and advocate for the Zionists.[36] Clifford based his argument to recognize Israel on the humanitarian and biblical justifications which he believed motivated the president. He recalled that Truman was upset by the refugees of World War II and the evil of the Holocaust, saying that "Every thoughtful human being must feel some responsibility for the survivors" and the recognition of the Jewish state was "everything this country *should* represent."[37] Furthermore, he argued that the British Balfour Declaration had already promised the state to the Jews and that the Bible promised the Jews the land of Palestine.

Despite Clifford's defensive denials, ("political considerations were not a factor for me or President Truman") it was clear that his motivations were also political.[38] This political concern became paramount in the eight months between the time the United States extended de facto and de jure recognition. In these months, Clifford and Truman's other advisors exerted strong pressure on the president to grant de jure recognition and economic assistance to Israel. (Truman granted both after the country's first election in January 1949.)[39] Clifford was convinced that there was, in the words of one historian, "overwhelming" popular support for a Jewish homeland.[40] According to public opinion polls, American support for the Zionists was both broad and stronger than the "almost nonexistent support for the Arabs."[41]

Clifford seemed determined to satisfy both partisans for Israel and the majority of Americans before the fall election. For example, he assured the president of the American Jewish Congress that the administration would quickly work towards de jure recognition.[42] And, Clifford agreed with his colleague Chester Bowles who urged bolder U.S. action supporting Israel. Bowles and other Democratic leaders assumed that the political fate of the party and its support for Israel were intertwined. Bowles failed to grasp the irony of his recommendation when he warned Clifford that if Truman did not make a strong statement about de jure recognition soon, "the opposition will charge him with playing politics with our foreign policy."[43] Clifford and Bowles were most concerned about the sentiments of Jewish voters who—although only 3 percent of the national population—constituted 4 percent of votes cast and were a powerful force in the Democratic Party.[44] Moreover, Jewish voters were significant in the key swing states of New York, Ohio, Illinois, and California.

While it seemed clear that domestic political factors influenced White House policy toward Israel, Zionist supporters and policymakers steadfastly denied such a crass quid pro quo by arguing that universal ideals necessitated support for Israel. By invoking universalism, they saw their actions as noble, not self-interested. Moreover, their actions could be seen as reflective of shared liberal domestic goals of eliminating anti-semitism and treating Jews like other Americans. Leaders of Zionist organizations remained active in their contacts with the White House and Congress, basing their appeals on what was already a widely accepted idea that the issue was nonpolitical. For example, Rabbi Baruch Korff, of the Political Action Committee for Palestine, wrote to Senator Howard

McGrath in February 1948: "the world looks to the President and Congress to make their decision in line with the traditional American policy of support for oppressed peoples."[45]

Pro-Israeli policymakers such as David Niles and Clark Clifford based their advice, in part, on evidence of national support for Zionism as well as on the steady stream of letters which arrived at the White House from organizations and individuals in support of a Jewish state. A number of cities and towns across the country, along with local unions, passed resolutions and gathered petitions calling for the establishment of a Jewish state.[46] The White House received hundreds of thousands of postcards, telegrams, and letters supporting the Jewish state from 1946–1948. The correspondence came from numerous organizations, including the American Jewish Congress, the American Christian Palestine Committee, the Lawyers Committee for Justice in Palestine, and the American Federation of Labor. Also, individual Jewish leaders and members of Congress pressed the Zionist case to the administration.

The deluge continued after May 1948, when the subject of the correspondence switched to de jure recognition, lifting the arms embargo, and opposing the internationalization of Jerusalem. The letters from prominent individuals were personally answered by David Niles. The administration kept careful tallies of this correspondence, both the numbers received and the originating organizations of those letters or telegrams sent by individuals.[47] The White House cited this correspondence as evidence of overwhelming support for the creation of Israel. For example, on 15 May 1948, the President's Press Secretary Charles Ross told reporters that the White House had received roughly five hundred telegrams about recognition—all but three in favor of Truman's decision.[48] Ironically, then, the correspondence that could have been dismissed by critics as evidence of crude political calculation by policymakers, could be cited as a sign that support for the Jewish state had grassroots, democratic origins and, thus, in the sometimes confusing world of American political culture, was "above" politics.

Along with the correspondence and the lobbying efforts of the Zionist organizations, Truman's political advisors also saw overwhelming support for the creation of Israel in the press, particularly after the UN had passed the partition resolution in November 1947. It's worth noting that this press support still did not reflect a strong *Zionist* sentiment. One historian observed that the press support was based on subscription to the universal ideal as expressed in the UN sanction of partition more than on "any great love for the Zionist cause."[49]

Although a politically and culturally triumphant narrative of universalism both opposed prejudices at home and favored the establishment of a Jewish state, a look at opposing political views finds that a universalist framework was also invoked by some *critics* of Zionism to justify their views and actions. Groups such as the American Council for Judaism, American Friends of the Middle East, and some Protestant organizations and publications such as the *Christian Century* argued that Americans should not support Israel, because of its religious and ethnic exclusiveness, its "difference" from the rest of the Middle East, its expansionist, aggressive aims, and the displacement of Palestinian refugees caused by its creation. Jewish anti-Zionists, in particular, focused on the danger of trying to create an exclusive racial, theocratic state out of an age-old religious tradition that crossed all borders. Among government policymakers, the most vocal critics of the formation of Israel were found in the State Department where a number of officials met and worked with the American Council for Judaism. The State Department officials also objected to United States' support for a Jewish state, because they argued that the policy would irrevocably harm American relations with the oil producing Arab countries and, perhaps, invite the Soviets into the region. Furthermore, state officials argued that the Jewish state would have dangerously close ties with the Soviet Union, because Soviet agents had been infiltrated among Jewish refugees from that country and eastern Europe.[50]

State Department opposition was based on the experience and advice of those, especially on the Near Eastern and African Affairs (NEA) desk, who viewed Palestine as part of the Arab Middle East. In the rest of the government, media, and especially among Zionist lobbyists, the State Department soon gained the reputation of being an "Arabist," Anglophilic stronghold. The department received thousands of letters criticizing its pro-Arab positions. One reason that the department's opposition failed to win support was because it went against powerful and popular humanitarian imperatives. Moreover, it had no ideological or rhetorical resonance to counter the passionate pro-Israeli images.[51]

State Department advisors emphatically asserted that the United States' interests lay with the Arabs because of oil which was vital to the European recovery.[52] The State Department also championed the interests of the industry, because there was a close, informal relationship between oil executives and diplomatic personnel. For example, the Arabian American Oil Company (ARAMCO) regularly gave the State Department confidential reports on its assessment of events in the Arab countries based on firsthand observations.[53] Indeed, many of the oil executives came out of the State Department or other government positions. The oil lobby, although less notable, was not less active than was the Zionist lobby. One historian explains the apparent inconsistency by arguing that the Zionist lobby was "public by nature," while the oil lobby was "discreet by nature."[54]

Both the oil executives and State Department officials exaggerated the dangers that the Arabs would cut off the West's oil supply, while Clifford argued that the Arabs were dependent on oil sales. Clifford's point is illustrated by the actions of Saudi King Ibn Saud who put off Arab calls to cancel ARAMCO's concession, arguing that the royalties enabled Saudi Arabia to "better to assist her neighboring Arab states in resisting Jewish pretensions." Apparently, State Department officials also exaggerated the danger to their own relations with the Arab governments. One official, years later, explained that "we career men" knew each other personally and stayed close despite U.S. recognition of Israel.[55]

Truman, who already viewed the Palestine situation from the perspective of finding homes for war refugees, was predisposed against the State Department argument and the elite world of diplomacy. Years later, he spoke angrily of what he considered State Department patronization of him on the issue of Palestine: "The difficulty with many career officials in the government is that they regard themselves as the men who really make policy." A few days after he assumed office, he recalled, "I'd already had a communication from some of the 'striped pants' boys warning me . . . to watch my step, that I didn't *really* understand what was going on over there and that I ought to leave it to the *experts*." When Secretary of Defense James Forrestal reminded Truman that they would need oil in the event of a war, Truman responded that he "would handle the situation in the light of justice, not oil."[56] Yet, as we have seen, the split between humanitarian principles and crude politics was not as clear cut as some asserted. Truman (and others) played it both ways: he was sincerely motivated by humanitarianism, yet he reaped the political benefits of bucking diplomats to support a "moral" and politically popular cause.

The split between an elite State Department concerned with multinational oil business and an earnest president upholding humanitarian principles strengthened the narrative that Israel had an indisputable moral purpose and that opposition to that purpose was politicking for monied interests. For example, the State Department's temporary reversal of American support for partition in March 1948 led to charges from the press and public that the department was "dishonoring" the country with a "gentleman's agreement" based on oil politics. *The New York Times* called the switch on partition an "act of moral cowardice."[57] This dichotomy also furthered the idea that since support for the refugees was popular, Israel's champions, as well as the country itself, was by nature *populist*. Increasingly, in politics and fiction, Israel's populist and democratic elements were highlighted, and the country seemed to be a symbol of the universal political and moral ideals for which the United States stood.

The dichotomy between oil politics and humanitarian principles had another effect on the public debate over the formation of Israel. Such a contrast tied support for the new Jewish state firmly to the concurrent efforts to eradicate prejudice, at home and abroad. The description of the State Department's policy as a "gentleman's agreement" to protect oil interests echoed the name popularized by Laura Hobson of mean-spirited attempts to discriminate against American Jews. Thus, in contrast to the State Department's position, supporting a national home for victims of discrimination seemed to uphold morality and universal principles of one world, free of prejudice.

Overall, the arguments made in support of Israel found broader appeal, and greater political and cultural resonance in the late 1940s than did those against the Jewish state. The fight against antisemitism, a "universal" cause, helped to justify the struggle to establish a Jewish state which was, at first glance, a narrow, particular cause. Yet, supporters of Israel, and many Americans, redefined the Zionist enterprise as a reflection of post-World War II humanitarianism and universalism. They argued that rationally understood morality should guide social and political behavior, both at home and abroad. The decline of American antisemitism and the creation of Israel were, thus, both part of a narrative of a universalist ideal triumphant in the aftermath of war.

PARTICULARISM AND THE IMAGE OF ARABS

Ironically, though not surprisingly, the universalist ideal used to justify both the eradication of domestic prejudice and support for the creation of Israel had very little to do with Jews particularly. This was, after all, an attempt to use rationally understood morality to guide social and political behavior. But, popular and political support for Israel was *also* justified in very particularistic terms, reinforcing the growing perception of the early Cold War that there were indeed "two worlds" diametrically opposed to each other. Postwar Communism resembled the enemy of wartime Fascism, a totalitarian system that had made Jews its most unfortunate victims. So, Truman and others seemed to subscribe to contradictory interpretations of Jewish suffering. They argued that the particular suffering and identity of Jews justified the creation of Israel.

Once Israel was an established fact, Truman asserted that the creation of the Jewish state was reparation for Nazi persecution. In his own memory, Truman reinforced the narrative that the Holocaust *demanded* the creation of Israel:

> That terrible story of human hate and cruelty is, however, counter-balanced in the pages of history by the story of human love and charity in the story of the worldwide effort to save the survivors of that persecution and to bring them into safe haven, into *the* homeland of their own. . . .[58]

Prominent Jews in a number of nonpolitical fields also called for a Jewish state for the victims of the Nazis. Benny Goodman, for example, sent a telegram to the White House in the spring of 1947 supporting increased Jewish immigration to Palestine: "The degradation of any people is not to be tolerated. We must endeavor to permit helpless Jews to walk with dignity into Palestine."[59]

Through the persuasion of many liberals, Truman came to believe there was a connection between the fate of Holocaust survivors and the creation of a Jewish state. The Nation Associates, in the pages of the weekly *Nation* and through correspondence to the White House and Congress, lobbied hard for a Jewish state. The advisory board of the Nation Associates included a number of prominent liberals, such as Thurman Arnold, Erskine Caldwell, Helen Gahagan Douglas, Lillian Hellman, John P. Lewis, Walter Lowdermilk, Reinhold Niebuhr, Eugene O'Neill, Walter White, and Stephen Wise. *Nation* editor Freda Kirchwey frequently wrote to Truman in support of Israel and its interests. The editorial policy of the magazine also reflected these views, detailing all of the political developments and wrangling in the Middle East. *Nation* activists also brought their case to Congress and to the Democratic Party organization.[60]

The idea that Jews deserved their own state, because of the crimes of the Nazis, affected how Americans viewed critics of Israel, especially the Arabs. While the status of Jews as both victims and survivors of totalitarianism was examined in the postwar period, the wartime role of their new antagonists was held up to scrutiny in the public culture and found wanting. If support for Israel was in part defended out of a particularist understanding of the Holocaust, that story brought with it, almost inexorably, a temptation to cast Israel's contemporary opponents in the guise of Nazi perpetrators. Moreover, in the popular and political culture, Arabs became associated with the evils of totalitarianism in general and Jews with the antitotalitarian fight of the new Cold War.

The Arabs were the subject of criticism in the press and often depicted as inferior to the Jews.[61] More specifically, in the narrative that described Israel as a redemption for the Holocaust, the Arabs faired poorly because of wartime links to the Nazis. This was especially true, because in the years immediately following the war, the public culture was saturated with books and articles about the war and its aftermath, about the moral lesson of the conflict, and the evil of the Axis. The leader who personified the pro-Axis tilt among some Arabs was Hajj Amin Al-Husseini, the Mufti of Jerusalem. Hajj Amin was a strong opponent of both the British and the Zionists, and an active Arab nationalist. Exiled from his native Palestine by the British, he spent part of the war in Baghdad helping to organize a pro-Axis coup in mid-1941. He was supported by both Arab governments and Axis members. When the coup failed, he left for Berlin where he spent the rest of the war, collaborating with the Nazis. Hajj Amin even signed an agreement with Benito Mussolini in late 1941 that Jews in Palestine would be exterminated by the Germans once the Nazis were successful in overrunning the Middle East. Following the war, after a brief detention in France, Hajj Amin escaped to Cairo where he remained a leader for Palestinian Arabs.

Palestinian Arab loyalty to the Mufti in the 1930s and 1940s had more to do with a strong desire for self-determination than with support for Fascism or any other ideology he might have espoused. One Palestinian writer, Said Aburish, recalls that his family and their neighbors followed the Mufti—known by ordinary Palestinians as the "father of the revolution"—because he and members of the Arab Higher Committee were planning a Palestine independent of Britain.[62]

Whatever the motivation behind the Palestinians' support for the Mufti, his association with the Nazis was a particularly potent way to discredit the man and, therefore, the cause of the Palestinians in American popular culture. In Hollywood films of the 1940s, for example, Arabs were often depicted as Nazi spies.[63] Moreover, pro-German sympathies of other Arab leaders—such as King Farouk of Egypt—were used to tarnish the image of Arabs in general. Zionist partisans argued, directly and indirectly, that those who stood in the way of justice for the Jewish refugees had been allied with the Nazis.[64] Arab behavior toward Israel was also compared with European antisemitic practices.[65] Another common way to tarnish the Arabs with the Nazi brush was to remind

Americans of the danger of "appeasement" in the Middle East. With the rhetoric of World War II fresh in the public culture, the term "appeasement" became a code word for pro-Nazi (and, later, pro-Communist) policies. Moreover, the term was often used to put Americans on the Israeli side, as in the following example: "a friendly Jewish state—(and it *would be* friendly)—would be a far more reliable outpost . . . than the Arabs would ever be, no matter how far appeased."[66]

Editor of *The Nation* Freda Kirchwey was one Zionist who frequently used this type of language to emphasize the connection between the Arabs and the Nazis. Her lobbying included frequent letters to the White House and the United Nations detailing the wartime activities of the Mufti. Soon after the 1948 war began, The Nation Associates prepared a pamphlet of documents describing King Farouk's and Hajj Amin's dealings with Berlin. *The Nation* was not alone in its denigration of Hajj Amin as a leader. *Time*, for example, referred to him as merely the Egyptians' "stooge." In addition, articles in *The Nation* argued strongly that the Mufti should not be involved in international negotiations over Palestine since he was a "war criminal."[67]

Individual pro-Zionist letters to politicians also relied upon similar images of an unholy alliance between the Nazis, Arabs, and British. For example, one New York rabbi wrote to Democratic Committee chairman Howard McGrath denouncing the "British-Nazi-Mufti gangsters" and the [British Foreign Secretary Ernest] "Bevin-British Nazi government." Importantly, the arguments of partisans of Israel such as this rabbi and *The Nation* found their way into the general media in subtle ways. In *Life*, for example, shortly before Israel was established, the Mufti was "partition's most *rabid* foe" who was "surrounded by [Arab] league *politicos.*" *Life* coverage made it clear that he was an unsavory, irrational figure. In contrast, the war record of Jews in Palestine was celebrated: many "fought against the Axis in WWII," another article noted.[68]

Emphasis on the wartime ties between some Arabs and the Nazis was not the only way to demonize Israel's enemies. A corollary rhetorical formulation was talk of Arabs as a "fifth column." This was a common Cold War term whose use in this context located Americans on the Israeli side of the Middle East dispute. In Cold War discourse, a "fifth column" was a secret group of Communists working to subvert the American "way of life." If Israelis faced their own "fifth column" of Arabs, they seemed to be in the same situation as Americans, facing threats in a dangerous world, while the Arabs seemed to resemble devious Communists.

Such language was common. For example, one book review agreed with former Ambassador James McDonald's conclusion about Arab refugees who "comprised a potential fifth column."[69] Thus, this language, combined with other assumptions to write a narrative of Arab difference and alienation from Americans, while at the same time reinforcing American empathy for Israeli interests.

THE LEGACIES OF WAR: ARAB REFUGEES AND HOLOCAUST REFUGEES

The fate of the Arab refugees who had formerly lived within the borders of the Jewish state raised uncomfortable ironies for Americans in light of the argument that the creation of Israel had been necessary to give a haven and a modicum of justice to the Jewish refugees of World War II. How could those who had argued on behalf of Holocaust survivors now turn a deaf ear to the plight of a new set of refugees? American policymakers failed to push hard for a solution to the Arab refugee situation because both Israelis and Arabs resisted any compromise on the issue: Israel called for resettlement of the refugees in Arab countries, while Arabs called for repatriation of the refugees to their former homes in Israel. Yet, the uniqueness of the Holocaust also offers some clue to American policy as does the evolving political and cultural image of Jews which continued to depict them as victims deserving support.

The United Nations gave the responsibility for finding a solution to the refugee stand-off to the Palestine Conciliation Commission (PCC) established in December 1948 with representatives from three "neutral" countries, France, Turkey, and the United States. The United States was represented on the PCC by Mark Etheridge, who openly sided with the Arab League on the refugee question. He found little support in the White House for his position, although the State Department also tried to shift the American position. With the work at the PCC stalled, Etheridge resigned from it on 17 June 1949.[70]

Although the White House failed to press Israel hard on this issue, Harry Truman agreed with Etheridge, and Secretary of State George Marshall and Secretary of Defense James Forrestal among other advisors, that Israel had to be more flexible. Forrestal, for one, argued that helping the refugees was "consistent with the traditional humanitarian role of the U.S. in cases of major disaster."[71] Truman wrote to Etheridge in April 1949: "I am rather disgusted with the manner in which the Jews are approaching the refugee problem. I told the President of Israel in the presence of his Ambassador just exactly what I thought about it." Truman also wrote to Prime Minister Ben-Gurion directly.[72]

By the fall of 1949, it seemed that American policymakers (in a secret statement of regional U.S. policy, NSC 47/2) acknowledged the difficulty of moving on this issue or at least sought a compromise between the repatriation and resettlement positions, arguing that the Arab states should resettle a large number of refugees. By 1951, Truman still believed that the refugee issue was "the crux of the matter" in the Middle East, and continued to voice some criticism of Israel. But like the NSC report of two years earlier, Truman had moved closer to the *Israeli position* on refugees. The president speculated that the issue could be resolved by the actions of the *Arab* countries and with sufficient aid to the countries where the refugees were located. Eventually, Israel ended up repatriating a small number of dependents of those already living in Israel, totaling only about thirty-five thousand by 1956. There was no ignoring the obvious. As a State Department position paper in 1949 argued, with "existing realities . . . repatriation of Arab refugees to Israel is a dead issue."[73]

One reason that the repatriation of Arab refugees had become a "dead issue" was that Israeli officials were determined to bring as many Jews as possible to the country. Providing a haven for Holocaust survivors as well as a new home for any Jew who so desired one, a process of "ingathering," was considered by many Zionists and Israeli leaders to be a raison d'être for the state. In the first five years of the country's existence, the number of Jews doubled with three hundred forty thousand arriving in just the first year and a half.[74] Israeli officials assumed that Americans would understand the importance of resettling survivors of the Holocaust. American friends of Israel, such as Jacob Blaustein, also did their best to convince the White House that the continued resettlement of Jewish refugees was essential, while Israelis turned to the United States for financial help to achieve this goal. The Israelis argued that their immigration policy actually helped the United States by emptying the DP camps in Germany (thereby lifting from the United States "the burden of caring for the displaced persons"), "siphoning" manpower "from the Soviet reservoir to the Western reservoir," and "eliminating potential trouble spots" such as in Yemen where the whole Jewish community had been transported to Israel. Not surprisingly, in their fall 1950 request to Dean Acheson for U.S. aid to help absorb the Jewish refugees, Moshe Sharett and Abba Eban conflated the stories of Arab and Jewish refugees, implying that Israel could not be expected to care for the Arabs when it had its hands full with the Jews.[75]

Yet, despite American reluctance to agree with the priorities of the Israelis, the United States neither cut off aid to Israel in these years, nor tried to use strong political pressure against the country, and there were no American sanctions or resolutions passed against the Jewish state. Thus, Washington—by inaction—seemed to endorse the Israeli goal of in-gathering over the Arab goal of repatriation. To be sure, Americans had sometimes strongly criticized Israelis on this issue. Etheridge had been particularly indignant.[76] Israelis seemed to worry about the criticisms to the extent that their representatives, such as Eban, carefully tried to explain their position. Moreover, they prolonged negotiations instead of issuing a flat-out refusal of any repatriation.

Many Americans, as demonstrated in the press, were sympathetic with the Arab refugees' situation. *Time*, for example, referred to the refugees as the "New DPs" thus linking the plight of the Arabs to the DP story with which Americans were familiar. At the same time, the article was reluctant to assign blame for the condition of the refugees and noted that there were also seven thousand Jewish refugees from the 1948 war. Moreover, although *Time* clearly sympathized with the refugees, it is interesting to note that its figure of four hundred thousand refugees is closest to the *Israeli* estimate of their numbers; Arabs, the United Nations, and others argued that there were far more. As time went on, in press and policy circles, the situation of the refugees seems to have been divorced from the actions of the Israelis. For example, in a survey of news from November 1950, White House press officials concluded that "the Arab refugees ha[ve] continued to stir sympathy, as observers have hoped that *the U.N.* might renew its efforts to *resettle* them."[77] The assertion of UN responsibility and the reference to "resettlement" not "repatriation" is another example of how Americans were moving closer to the Israeli position.

If Israeli officials continued to assert that their country existed, in part, to provide a haven for Holocaust survivors and other persecuted Jews, they still had to find a way to pay for absorbing immigrants as well as establishing a viable state. In 1951, an economically unstable Israel turned to Germany for financial assistance, claiming $1.5 billion in reparations (the amount was to cover the costs of absorbing five hundred thousand survivors). After sometimes stormy negotiations, agreements were signed in September 1952. Israel was to receive $820 million (DM 3.45 billion) in reparations over the next fourteen years with $107 million earmarked for Jews outside of Israel. The agreement was ratified by both governments in March 1953, and the first shipments of goods reached Israel that summer.

In American public culture, the idea of German reparations had a certain moral appeal, symbolizing redemption and healing. For example, *Time* wrote of Chancellor Konrad Adenauer's 1951 speech before the Bundestag calling for reparations, "Speaking for the new Germany at its best, [Adenauer] offered a measure of atonement for old Germany at its worst."[78] Given widespread cultural images of Jewish victims of the Holocaust and condemnation of the Nazis, it is not surprising that many Americans would support the reparations payments. Meanwhile, the U.S. government's reaction was less enthusiastic, but the government was unwilling to publicly oppose the payments. In the spring of 1951, before direct negotiations had begun, Ben-Gurion and Eban approached Dean Acheson asking for American support on the issue. Acheson replied that the first priority for Israel should be peace in the Middle East. Moreover, he explained that he was not in favor of any reparations out of current German production since any deficit would have to be made good by the United States. Ben-Gurion responded that Germany was perfectly capable of making the payments since it had a higher standard of living than did Israel, and merely had to lower its standard of living to a comparable level.[79] Once negotiations were underway, Acheson made it clear in private that the United States wanted to see them continue, but that he would not make any public statements of support for reparations.[80]

Despite the reluctance of Acheson and other American policymakers to be publicly linked to the question of German reparations to Israel, the United States did have a material interest in the issue, since the U.S. was responsible for German debts in the early 1950s. Yet, more significantly, German payments to the Israelis would be a less controversial way of giving financial aid to the Jewish state. One State Department memo made the argument explicit: "there would be a definite political advantage to making a contribution to the Israeli economy indirectly through Germany. . . . Direct contributions gave rise to requests from neighboring Arab states."[81] The United States did not support German reparations for the Holocaust, because of the moral and emotional need to heal the wounds of this tragedy. If such reasoning had ever been part of American political thinking, it was nowhere in evidence by the early 1950s when easing Middle East and Cold War tensions seemed to be the most pressing issues. At the same time, what was also clear from the American policymakers' response to the reparations issue was a commitment to

Israel's well-being: if necessary financial aid could come through Germany, than that was a program worth supporting.

CONCLUSION

Many Americans who supported the creation of Israel argued that Jews were the particular victims of the Nazis and years of antisemitism, and deserved a state as reparation for their persecution. Such a view might have conflicted with the widespread cultural emphasis on universal values as a barometer of political decisions. But in the conflict between universal and particular understandings of Jews and Jewish suffering, Harry Truman and other Americans were able to take from both perspectives to justify the creation of Israel. Thus, in popular fiction such as *The Last Temptation*, in the press, and in the words of policymakers, Israel was both a demonstration of worldwide humanitarianism as well as justice for the Jewish survivors of World War II. Moreover, if we compare the discussion in this chapter with that of the cultural evolution of the "New Jew" in chapter one, it becomes clear that the domestic trends and foreign policy debates of the late 1940s had overlapping, mutually reinforcing narratives that drew on a shared set of images and principles.

In the debate over the establishment of Israel, although anti-Zionists such as Alfred Lilienthal may have been vocal, more significant for their political and cultural impact were those non-Jewish Americans such as Eleanor Roosevelt and Harry Truman who came to embrace Zionism and weave the story of the Holocaust into a public narrative of why Americans should support the creation of a Jewish state. Roosevelt's and Truman's attitudes toward Israel represent the trajectory that many Americans followed: their own antisemitism declined or disappeared in the postwar period; they were sympathetic with the victims of the Holocaust; and they came to admire Israel. Such admiration later became the mainstream position, as demonstrated by the historical narrative which overstated Roosevelt's and Truman's support for Zionism. (Both contributed to this narrative in their own memoirs.) Finally, these two figures are also representative of mainstream attitudes toward Israel to the extent that their views evolved in the late 1940s and early 1950s, responding to a changing American image of Jews. No longer shown as merely pitiful victims nor as dehumanized figures completely different from Americans, the Jews who survived the Holocaust and Israelis had seemingly transcended this fate, and, after 1948, began to embody what came to be called the "New Jew" in the American imagination.

In addition to shaping the images of Jews in the American imagination, popular understanding of the Holocaust and World War II also shaped the image of Arabs and their role in the founding of Israel. Arabs were linked to Nazis and, thus, became symbols of pro-Fascist and—in Cold War politics—pro-totalitarian forces. From the foundation of Israel, Arabs suffered from this cultural association, and seemed to be the natural antagonists of Jews, Holocaust victims, and Americans.

In policymaking circles, the significance of the Holocaust was not as clear as it had been in popular culture. While the Holocaust had evoked shock and sympathy, it did not seem to be—by itself—decisive in determining American policy toward the creation of a Jewish state. The Holocaust's limited effects on policy were most obviously demonstrated among American diplomats, those policymakers who strove to be aloof from popular sentiment. Nevertheless, it is significant to note that once Israel was established, diplomats also helped to bring the United States and Israel closer together, for example, by coming to accept the Israeli position on Jewish refugees, while letting the fate of Arab refugees remain an unresolved question.

3

Views of the New Jewish State

The "Americanization" of Israel

Israel was "a state sprung from the massacre of six million Jews and the desperate action of a small, poorly prepared, and ill-equipped army," Irwin Shaw wrote in his 1949 *Report on Israel*. Yet Shaw, and coauthor photographer Robert Capa did not depict Israelis as weak, pathetic Holocaust refugees. Instead, their book reflected an evolving American view of Israelis as pioneering, brave, and democratic.[1] The image of Jews as victims—of antisemitism and of the Holocaust—remained vivid in American culture and politics at least through 1967. But Israelis who overcame persecution to become tough, democratic pioneers in a harsh wilderness began to challenge that perception. At the same time, the persistent image of Jewish victims demanded an American moral commitment to the survival of these "new Jews," the Israelis. Indeed, their survival became one of the tenets of American foreign policy in the Middle East. That didn't mean, however, that Jews were fully accepted as "insiders" in American culture, or that the United States and Israel shared a close alliance during the late 1940s and early 1950s. Increasingly, Israelis came to be accepted as insiders once they were re-constructed as similar to Americans. Importantly, the Americanization of Israelis depended upon a simultaneous demonization of Arabs. The contrast between Arabs and Israelis underscored the similarity between Israelis and Americans and, thus, their mutual dependence in the face of Cold War challenges in the Middle East.

PIONEERS ON THE FRONTIER

Irwin Shaw, Robert Capa, and many other American observers were fascinated by the pioneering ideals of the "new Jews" of Israel.[2] Capa's photographs include numerous portraits of new arrivals hefting large suitcases or laboring in the bright sunshine. The photos and their captions celebrate diversity, noting when the subject is "native stock" or "imported" from Bulgaria, Turkey, or Hungary, among other countries. In his essays, Shaw fed a perception that a new culture of hardy citizens was emerging through shared labor and circumstance regardless of place of origin. For example, he writes that the population "dressed carelessly—partly because of the austerity brought about by the war, partly because of the rigors of the hot climate, and partly, too, as a semiconscious expression of disdain for the effete values of the civilizations left behind." The pioneer style began with the prime minister. David Ben-Gurion appeared at the country's first anniversary parade, "tieless, with his collar open in deference to the sartorial demands of a country that must survive through the sweat of its manual workers."[3]

The Israel described by Shaw and Capa was pioneering in deed as well as in appearance. Israelis were building roads, aqueducts, and settlements in the desert, clearing malarial swamps, planting trees, and successfully harvesting wheat and other crops. Shaw and Capa also observed approvingly that these pioneering Jews were eager to learn from Americans. Israelis were implementing "European or American standards of energy and efficiency." The caption under one photo of an American immigrant perched atop a tractor reads that he "was naturally put in charge of a machine."[4]

Another American novelist who also wrote nonfiction portraits of Israel was John Hersey. In a 1952 article for *The New Yorker*, he focused on the most visible symbol of the pioneer ideal in Israel, the *kibbutz*. Hersey's essay was—ostensibly—critical, examining the many problems that faced this once "pure and ideal socialis[t]" enterprise. Yet, his admiring portrait celebrates the farms, and their members whom he calls, "magnificent people . . . visionaries, able somehow to look through the dust around them and see phantasms of future plenty." Shaw and Capa were similarly in awe of the *kibbutz* ideal, "the creation of a moral life based on labor, in which no man employs another man, in which a small community of men and women work for each other."[5]

Perhaps the greatest challenge to *kibbutzim*, according to Hersey, was human nature which, he argued, is individualistic, necessarily making uniformity and equality elusive. Moreover, he concludes that the roughly eight thousand American immigrants to Israel helped reawaken people's "natural" instincts. For example, some *kibbutzim*, especially where there were many American members, voted to do away with the practice of housing children separately from their parents. In Hersey's description, then, Israelis were becoming more Americanized by moving toward a more "natural" social organization clearly defined by the ideal in postwar America. Israelis were also embracing the American ideals of success, individuality, and mechanical know-how. Other journalists agreed. For example, one article tells of a California cotton grower who came to Israel in 1954 with modern machinery, promoting the intensive, large scale farming he practiced on his own tracts in the United States.[6]

Hersey concludes that disaffection with *kibbutz* life was increasing, because "the zest for pioneering is partly gone now that Israel is a state." Yet, it is clear that the spirit of pioneering is simply redirected from agricultural settlements to other forms of building the new state, such as improving cities and establishing industries. Moreover, Hersey seemed to agree with one Canadian *kibbutznik* about the lasting value of the settlements for all of the nation's endeavors: "Anyone who can succeed here can succeed at anything anywhere in the world."[7]

Attention to the pioneer ideal in Israel was widespread in the American press during the late 1940s and early 1950s. For instance, one writer observed in the *Atlantic* "[On *kibbutzim*] you see the faces, lean, hard, tanned, self-reliant, intelligent, sober; yet full of faith, hope, and confidence—[they] explain the success" of the new country.[8] Press accounts frequently attributed the success of Israeli pioneering to both an elemental dedication and the exploitation of the latest technology. A *Life* portrait of the state in 1951 observed: "Developing the desert is a job Israel has tackled with biblical fervor and machine-age tools."[9] The article made it clear that pioneering was also found in new industrial plants, "gleaming" apartment buildings, new modern medical labs.

Similarly, a 1954 *New York Times Magazine* article celebrated Israeli pioneering in the form of agriculture and road building, the planting of forests, and the extraction of minerals from the Dead Sea. The accompanying photographs included images of young women picking crops, road crews building a highway, workers joining water pipes across the desert, and men at work in factories. The pioneer ideal was based in the wilderness and in agricultural settlement projects, but since Israelis were building their state from nothing, as the phrase went, their urban and industrial endeavors were also great acts of creation and, thus, of pioneering. Beyond the obvious hardships of their lives, what made the Israelis true pioneers in the eyes of many Americans was their spirit of adventure and determination. Henry Wallace noted in *The New Republic* "the magnificent efforts of the Jewish settlers." John Hersey observed,

"The Israelis seem feverish yet unhysterical. They meet their plentiful hardships stubbornly." Hersey and other journalists believed that Americans had influenced such spirit.[10]

Journalists weren't the only ones admiring Israel's pioneering. The Congress of Industrial Organizations (CIO) published in 1949 a glowing report on the new state and the efforts of its pioneers. (Union members felt a special kinship with the state, because Histadrut, the General Federation of Labor, had an impact upon almost all aspects of Israeli life.) In fact, the report overemphasized the role of the pioneers, averring that most Jewish immigrants had come to work the land in cooperative settlements. The report described a drive and a determination in all aspects of state building, from greeting new immigrants, to constructing houses, hospitals, and convalescent homes, to embarking on reforestation projects. "At every point," the authors observe, "we found intense activity." The CIO reserved the greatest praise for Histadrut, comparing it to the CIO, thus, reinforcing the idea that Israeli and American workers were similar.[11]

From the White House, Truman had also looked admiringly on the pioneering enterprise. The administration's announcement of the first Export-Import Bank loan to Israel in early 1949 praised the state's agriculture methods and output. Truman's focus on pioneering remained central to his image of the Jewish state. Six months before he left office the Jewish National Fund started a *kibbutz*, "Kfar Truman," in the American president's honor. Truman accepted this tribute, saying, "The growth and progress of the new state of Israel are a source of great satisfaction to me."[12]

The intensive state building remade Israelis, and molded their characters. The quintessential pioneers were the native born, known as *sabras*. The term became ubiquitous in American journalism and fiction; it refers to a desert cactus that is tough and prickly on the outside, sweet and tender on the inside. Many Americans seemed to feel an identification with the *sabras*, as one article in *The New Republic* (October 1949) observed, they, "like Americans, are aggressive, competent and impatient to get things done." In his November 1951 *New Yorker* article, John Hersey made comparisons between *sabras* and Americans clearer: "Israeli children are regular Californians—sturdy, open-faced, sun-coppered kids, potentially bigger, it seems, than their parents, and perhaps bolder, too." In its 1949 report, the CIO noted that the farm families were "well-tanned" and "jaunty," the industrial workers "healthy-looking" and "sturdy."[13]

American images of the new Jewish state made it clear that Israelis were "tough," masculine figures in a dangerous world. By the cultural politics of the 1950s which made Israelis similar to Americans and helped define American-Israeli relations during those years, "masculine" men dominated, and took responsibility for women. In popular fiction, media, and American foreign policy, gender categories were applied to nations as well as individuals which naturalized traditional roles.[14] The United States was a masculine country that took responsibility for other, "weaker" nations. Thus, U.S. Cold War policies were, in part, presented in and shaped by gendered terms.

Inevitably, traditional masculinity represented the norm in politics and in culture. That which was seen as unmasculine was, therefore, alien to the accepted parameters of action and behavior. Gendered discourse is useful for understanding American attitudes and policy toward Israel, because social values and ideology during the early years of the Cold War were treated as legitimate concerns in the success or failure of American diplomacy. Foreign policies, such as the 1947 Truman Doctrine which committed the United States to oppose the power of "armed minorities" everywhere and the 1950 planning document NSC–68 which made the fight against Communism a military enterprise, defined the Cold War as a contest between "two ways of life" in which the United States would demonstrate its moral and social superiority. In the 1940s and 1950s, the American "way of life" included clearly defined gender roles. In addition, Cold War political alliances often implied a certain degree of cultural similarity and kinship. Therefore, the cultural components of national identity are highly relevant to an understanding of international relations in this period.

Israel and Jews came to be perceived as masculine, ready to fight the Cold War alongside America. Images emphasizing Jewish masculinity and similarity to other American men began to displace the old stereotypes of Jews as weak victims. As a result, Americans began to perceive Jews as insiders with similar political and social ideals. Moreover, the emergence of Israelis as "insiders" had a powerful effect on the political assumptions of U.S. policymakers.

By contrast, Arabs were increasingly stigmatized as non-Western, undemocratic, racially darker, unmasculine outsiders. Israel's enemy, in other words, was alien to Americans, too. That contrast helped reinforce the view that Israelis were like Americans. Beginning with the founding of the Jewish state, the sympathies of many Americans lay with the Israelis, whose leaders were considered fellow Westerners. Nevertheless, in the late 1940s and early 1950s, American policy as well as media coverage of the Middle East reflected ambivalence about the Arab-Israeli dispute. That ambivalence disappeared by the late 1950s as Arabs became outsiders and Israelis became insiders. In American public culture, the difference in status between Arabs and Israelis was defined most clearly by measures of masculinity.

Images of masculine pioneers resonated with the mythic heritage of the American West. Leonard Finder, a friend of Dwight D. Eisenhower, invoked that heritage in a 1957 letter to the president defending Israel's policy in the Suez War: "Israel's predicament is reminiscent of that of American pioneers a century ago when confronted with hostile Indians." By reminding Americans of their own rugged past, images of Israeli pioneers helped to salve anxiety that postwar American society was becoming "soft." That anxiety was expressed in books such as David Riesman's *The Lonely Crowd* and William Whyte's *The Organization Man.* Both authors asserted that white-collar men, under the weight of bureaucratic conformity and the temptation of wealth and an easy lifestyle, were losing their individualism, initiative, and ambition. Riesman argued that Americans (meaning men) were becoming "other-directed" as opposed to "inner-directed." Riesman's observations really concerned the future of American masculinity, according to Barbara Ehrenreich: "The inner-directed were 'hard' and confronted 'hard' things; the other-directed were 'soft,' even 'limp' . . ." Riesman's argument resonated deeply, adds sociologist Rupert Wilkinson, because it articulated the historical pull between conformity and individual assertiveness in American culture.[15] Within that context, the picture of Israeli pioneers was a comforting reminder for Americans of their own mythic past and a reaffirmation of their own possibilities.

The image of Israeli pioneers both reflected and reinforced similarities with and close relations to Americans. Prime Minister David Ben-Gurion asserted this mutual identity in a 1951 speech to the National Press Club: "the character of your pioneering struggle . . . [was] similar in essence to [our pioneering]."[16] The pioneer paradigm of both cultures is made up of a number of components. First, a modern people set out to tame a wilderness of "savages"—Indians in North America, Arabs in the Middle East. Second, the settlers, whether Israelis or Americans, had to succeed for their own survival. That made their pioneering a crusading mission and an act of self-defense, since the settlers were besieged by the primitive inhabitants of the land. Third, the pioneers are imbued with a spiritual conviction; they are the "chosen people." Fourth, the pioneers are a tough, independent lot, reluctant to submit to civilization's strictures or give in to its excesses. In American pioneer ideology, those characteristics are manifest in the lone tough cowboy and the family man settler alike. The Israelis' dedication to the community, unpretentious lifestyle, and egalitarianism also bolstered their pioneer credentials in the eyes of Americans. In short, the two cultures were kin.

In the American press, Ben-Gurion was the very model of an Israeli pioneer. Journalists emphasized his "tough past" and frequently mentioned his plain clothes, frugal habits, and long workdays. When he was first elected, one magazine noted, "The roughened hands of a laborer will hold the reins of government." His temporary retirement to a *kibbutz* in 1953 was considered symbolic: "a constant reminder to the rest of the country, and presumably the world, that this desert must be opened, and is being opened to development." Clearly, Ben-Gurion did not lead a "soft" life. As a symbol for all Jews, Ben-Gurion's "tough past" was emphasized, and he was quoted saying, "Suffering makes a people greater." Eventually, the American media turned him into a larger-than-life father figure of the State of Israel. In 1956, for instance, *Time* described him as "look[ing] like an Old Testament patriarch" and "a prophet who packs a pistol." Another *Time* article on Ben-Gurion quoted from the Bible, "Behold he that keepeth Israel shall neither slumber nor sleep." Photographs often showed him in majestic profile.[17]

Images of Israel's masculine pioneers permeated popular fiction as much as they permeated the news media. Like Ben-Gurion, the fictional characters are frugal, egalitarian, practical, and tough. The Zionist leader in the film *The Sword in the Desert* refuses to endanger his soldiers, and so leads a dangerous mission through enemy territory. Joseph Viertel's novel *The Last Temptation* is full of such noble characters. One gives up a career as a dancer to work in a hospital. The *kibbutz* dwellers in the film *The Juggler* entertain themselves by singing and dancing around a campfire. The residents cooperate and make do with few supplies and primitive conditions, surrounded by dangerous enemies. And the movie gives the impression that most Israelis lived just like its characters, even though only a small percentage of Israelis lived on *kibbutzim*. Israelis weren't austere for its own sake, but for the goal of nation building. Their success is illustrated by facilities such as state-of-the-art hospitals. One of the characters in John Hersey's *The Wall* argues that the Jews have an ability to build a civilization out of nothing. The Israeli professionalism, intellectual prowess, and mastery of technology portrayed in books and movies resonated with Americans who prided themselves on their own pragmatism.

In both fictional and press accounts, the story of Palestine and Israel echoes the story of American pioneering, settlement, and success in a "virgin land." Palestine was, in the words of Hersey's Rachel, a "bright, unexploited landscape." The Puritans' vision of the American continent, as described by historian Perry Miller, was similar: "a bare land, devoid of already established (and corrupt) institutions . . . where they could start *de novo.*" *The Juggler,* the first American film to be shot in Israel, highlights the beauty and wildness, and critics praised the vistas of the new nation. A 1953 *Variety* review noted that the film was about "the pioneering of a new republic by brave people. . . . It is rather inspirational." Similarly, press accounts argued that the frontier environment shaped Israeli character just as it had done in the United States. One article reflected how "physical environment . . . can create type." The significance of pioneering and the West in American culture is deep-rooted. Political scientist James Combs wrote that "the West is a mythic reference point, a standard by which we judge the conduct of people and society in the present." Israelis measured up, because they were hardy pioneers.[18]

The pioneering efforts of the Israelis and their economic development were often contrasted in American politics and media with the *lack of* development among Arabs. The failure of Arabs to develop economically by Western standards was often coupled with the problem of refugees from Palestine, living in squalid conditions in camps bordering Israel. While attention to those two issues reflected American concern, that attention simultaneously strengthened the image of Arab weakness and incompetence.

Images of Jewish suffering had helped to galvanize support for the creation of Israel, but there were crucial differences underlying the views of Jews and Arabs. First, awareness of the Holocaust coincided with American efforts to overcome prejudice at home—especially anti-semitism—reflecting the idea that all Americans were similar to each other. Second, Americans (and Westerners in general) felt some guilt for the Holocaust. Americans may have felt sorry for the Arab refugees, but did not feel guilty for their plight. Third, Jewish victimhood was almost always depicted as part of a story of rehabilitation and redemption after the war. Jewish efforts to overcome their victim status were celebrated as heroism. Fourth, while all European Jews had been victims of the Holocaust, only a small minority of Arabs were refugees. The majority had their own land and countries, and were unaffected by the refugee problem. Yet, Arab countries remained undeveloped in the eyes of the West. Westerners attributed the conditions to poor decisions, incompetence, or the fact that Arabs weren't Western. Moreover, Arab development was compared to that of Israel which was making strides against long odds.

Of course, oil linked Arabs to the economy of the developed world. But, the oil industry was dominated by Western countries which only helped strengthen perceptions of Arab incompetence. And oil heightened the contrast between Israel and her Arab neighbors, since Israeli development was rooted in idealism and self-sufficiency, while oil evoked images of profiteering by Western corporations. As one review put it:

> Instead of the Indian chiefs, fur, cattle, and railroads, the Middle East provides equally spectacular sheiks and kings, oil and pipelines. In both areas, France and Great Britain, Russia, and the United States, or their government-supported corporate enterprises, were the main contenders for fabulous wealth.[19]

Moreover, the partnership between the U.S. government and oil companies had important cultural implications. That partnership went beyond the imperative to help Europe recover from World War II; the Middle East presented an opportunity for oil exploitation. As one 1945 State Department report noted, Saudi Arabia was "in a fair way to becoming an American frontier."[20] If Saudi Arabia was prized for its abundant natural resource and pictured as a territory to be conquered, its inhabitants were, like Native Americans, subjects for domination.

While the oil industry encouraged only selective development in Arab countries, the United States and the United Nations took some high profile initiatives to promote economic growth and solve the problem of the Arab refugees. But those efforts failed. They also revealed a patronizing attitude toward Arabs. One international initiative—with a strong American involvement—was the United Nations Economic Survey Mission for the Middle East. It was begun in September 1949 to devise solutions to economic problems. The countries studied were Iraq, Lebanon, Israel, Jordan, Arab-Palestine, Syria, and Egypt. The immediate impetus for the mission was to find an alternative to indefinite relief programs for Arab refugees. The mission was chaired by American Chairman of the Board of the Tennessee Valley Authority Gordon Clapp. His three deputy chiefs were from Turkey, France, and the United Kingdom; significantly, there were no Arabs among them. That revealed the lack of respect Western reformers had for Arabs, and turned out to be one of the key problems with the Economic Survey Mission (ESM). The structure of Arab aid programs also implied that the recipients were unable to care for themselves. It was not until 1953 that Arab representatives were placed on the advisory commission to the United Nations Relief and Works Administration (UNRWA).

The ESM report, adopted by the General Assembly in December 1949, recommended a work-relief program for refugees over the next eighteen months.[21] Clapp had asserted at the outset that the mission's immediate task was to help jobless refugees. Projects would include terracing for new crops, irrigation works, road building, reforestation, and construction of two small dams. The emphasis was on small projects, because Arabs were not ready for more ambitious ones: "The important first step is . . . to break with the habit of inertia." Arabs also lacked capital and skilled labor necessary for large projects. Eventually, ESM predicted that industry would develop in the Arab countries, but the "area is, and for a long time to come will remain, agricultural." Overall, ESM's recommendations were based upon the principle of limited outside assistance in order to foster "self-help" for Arabs. The final report noted with a patronizing air: "The highly developed nations of the world did not make their way by wishing. . . . They worked, they invented, they educated and trained their children." Arabs, in other words, had nothing but their own lack of enterprise to blame for their plight.

Clapp and U.S. officials emphasized that they were undertaking an economic enterprise, not a political one. Nevertheless, there were political assumptions and recommendations embedded in the report. Officials clearly had sympathy for Arab refugees who were "unable to return to their homes." Yet, the White House and the ESM were decidedly ambiguous about the *cause* of the refugee problem. Moreover, ESM tempered sympathy for the specific plight of the Arab refugees by comparing them to refugees everywhere, and tying their existence to the chain of events begun by Hitler.

Following a call from the United Nations for money to pay for the recommended development projects, Truman asked Congress to appropriate $27,450,000, which was half of the total needed. The State Department, too, recommended that ESM projects were in the financial interest of the United States, since they were designed to facilitate the phasing out of direct relief payments to refugees.[22] Concerned about public reaction to the Clapp mission, the State Department carefully monitored the press. From the point of view of the department, coverage was disappointingly light, although generally positive. Three papers carried editorials which were supportive of long-term development plans although skeptical of short-term public works programs.[23] The editorials endorsed the report's emphasis on self-help. One cautioned that this might take some time, although it would "appeal to those with any knowledge of the primitive feudalism of the Middle East." Clearly, the editorial writer viewed the Arabs as "backward."

Meanwhile, press stories generally endorsed the idea that limited, small pilot projects would work better than ambitious economic goals for the undeveloped world. On 10 January 1950, the *New York Times*, for example, noted that development must start "modestly and realistically." A month later, the *New York Herald Tribune* endorsed most of the assumptions in the report, but criticized the tone: "the report adds up to a stern sermon to those who need and want help." Nevertheless, the article seemed confident about the prospects for the success of the recommendations, since all that was needed for economic development was "capital, know-how, and enterprise." Press reports also noted the "realism" and "hard-headed" aspect of ESM recommendations. During the Cold War, those amounted to words of praise, connoting a pragmatic spirit as well as a masculine response to difficulty. Amid the general praise, criticism came from I. F. Stone who wrote that the report was a "disappointing anticlimax" and "a sanctimonious sermon" about self-help.[24]

Although Arab refugees became a lower priority for Washington policymakers after the ESM report and the formation of the United Nations Relief and Work Administration, the political and economic issues refugees faced were still unresolved. In fact, the formation of UNRWA turned care for the refugees from a temporary operation into a permanent UN function. Truman made another attempt to tackle some of these issues when, in November 1951, he charged Edwin Locke Jr. with coordinating American economic and technical assistance to the Middle East as a Special Assistant to the President and a Special Representative of the Secretary of State. Arguing that refugee aid programs had been ineffective, Locke wanted to reinvigorate them. But after months working in the region, Locke became more pessimistic, complaining to Truman that the refugees were "becoming increasingly desperate" and UNRWA was clearly not the answer. Moreover, he was worried about the Arabs' unfriendly opinions of the United States, which he considered unwarranted.[25]

By the time Locke was appointed, public attention was focused more on Cold War rivalries in the Middle East than on the plight of Arab refugees.

A few papers covered Locke's appointment, with most emphasizing that the primary goal of aid was to prevent growth of Communism in the region. For example, one editorial argued that the Locke mission was a "start on the political front in an area that is wide open to Moscow propaganda because of its technical backwardness and accompanying poverty."[26] Moreover, many of the stories attributed the lack of economic development to the Arabs themselves. The "real exploiters of the Middle East," concluded the *New York Times* in November 1951, "are not the Westerners but their own ruling classes" arousing "the passions of miserable people who have been led to seek redress in nationalistic and religious fanaticism." In the same month, *Business Week* used the example of Sheikh Mohammed Farghali, "boss of the fanatically nationalist Moslem Brotherhood in Egypt's canal zone," to demonstrate the dangers of "corrupt rulers" and "blind nationalism." The Arabs described here, and elsewhere, were not only vulnerable to the temptations of nationalism, but incapable of recognizing their exploiters. Arabs were increasingly seen as immature, fanatical, and irrational. In addition, much of the media accepted the Israeli view that the Jewish state had no special responsibility for the fate of the refugees. For example, one 1951 *Life* article observed that Israel "*shares* the unresolved *international* problem" of the Arab refugees.[27]

One reason Arabs fared so poorly in the press was because all of the countries of the region—except Israel—were treated as an undifferentiated mass. For example, various articles noted that the American aid at Locke's disposal ($160 million under the 1951 Mutual Security Act) would be divided in half between Israel on the one hand, and all the Arab states on the other. The term "Arab states," a couple of articles went on to explain, included Iran, Egypt, Greece, Turkey, Syria, Lebanon, Iraq, Jordan, and Saudi Arabia—three of which were not Arab. Thus, "Arab states" simply designated darker-skinned people of the Mediterranean and Middle East who were not Israeli. The automatic dichotomy in the language of "Arabs" and "Israelis" is an understandable shorthand given the political cleavages of the region, but it nevertheless weakens the rhetorical position of the Arabs by making them indistinguishable from each other. In one of the political ironies and cultural misunderstandings of Middle Easterners, Arabs who found strength and national identity through association among *all* their peoples clashed with American values which celebrated individualism and unique nationality. What Arabs saw as a sign of strength appeared to be weakness in the United States.

TOUGH JEWS AND WEAK ARABS IN THE COLD WAR

Locke was no more successful than Clapp had been at solving the refugee problem and bringing economic development to the region. While the situation of the Arab refugees seemed intractable to many, popular and political interest in the region remained keen. Increasingly, this interest centered on Israelis and their state—not on the Arabs and their refugees. For example, correspondence to the White House remained overwhelmingly supportive of the new state.[28] And American identification with Israelis began to extend beyond the pioneering metaphor to include Israel's military prowess. Israeli bravery and military ingenuity were popular themes in fiction of the late 1940s and early 1950s. Images of fighters were part of a broader picture of masculinity that shaped attitudes toward Israeli pioneering and development. During this period, the "tough Jew" was introduced to fiction as a character and a role model. Coined by Paul Breines, the term describes a fictional archetype prominent in American film and literature after the Six Day War in 1967 enhanced the Israeli military reputation to legendary proportions.[29] The ideal of a "tough Jew" was built on a set of traits long prized in American culture. Thus, tough Jews are "insiders" in American culture because they exemplify characteristics of ideal masculinity.

According to Paul Breines and other critics, Jewish characters with these traits appear in American fiction after Leon Uris created a Jewish superman in his 1958 novel *Exodus*. They argue that the tough guy is the direct heir of Uris' character. Although *Exodus* is a major cultural landmark in the image of Israel and Jews, images of tough Israelis and Jews are found throughout the decade before Uris wrote the novel. Their prevalence and acceptability paved the way for Uris and made *Exodus* a cultural touchstone. In 1947 and 1948, Irwin Shaw, Norman Mailer, and Laura Hobson created tough, honorable Jewish soldiers who were similar to Americans. The characters in the novels *The Wall*, *The Last Temptation*, and *My Glorious Brothers* by Howard Fast, and in the films *The Sword in the Desert* and *The Juggler* display even greater physical prowess and machismo.[30] Importantly, the fictional Jews are compelled to fight, and they only do so reluctantly. For example, a Haganah broadcast in *The Sword in the Desert* deplores the need for violence. Similarly, one of the characters in *The Juggler* says, "We don't kill people in cold blood." These are tough fighters who use violence only as a last resort.

Just as "*sabras*" held a special place in the image of Israeli pioneers, so they did in the fictional construction of tough Israeli fighters. Again, the heroism of individual Israelis came to stand for the character of the state. The dual image of the tough and tender *sabra* was the ideal response to the helpless victims of the Holocaust. Israelis would defend themselves when threatened, but they still embodied the traditional characteristics of tenderness, sentimentality, and moral righteousness. *The Sword in the Desert, The Juggler,* and *The Last Temptation* all have their share of *sabras*. By the end of the decade, Uris's *Exodus* presented a number of hypermasculine Israelis who summarized the virtues of the prototypical *sabras*.

In an apparent challenge to traditional gender roles in postwar fiction, not all *sabras* are men. Many women in these novels and films also prove themselves to be tough Jews. One *kibbutz* member in *The Juggler* easily carries a rifle, protecting her European male companion on a hike through the surrounding hills. The main character in Joseph Viertel's *The Last Temptation*, Deborah, survives her husband's wrongful execution and becomes a pioneer fighting for the State of Israel: "She was a gladiator now. She had slain dragons."[31] Similarly, a female *sabra* in *The Sword in the Desert*, confident of her own abilities and those of her fellow fighters, becomes the "voice of Israel" in a morale-boosting daily radio broadcast. Such strong women were also found in the Jewish resistance fighters of Europe; Rachel, in Hersey's *The Wall*, is the commander of one of the Warsaw Ghetto fighting groups. Despite the impression that "*sabra*" may be a unisex category, it does not break down traditional gender roles but reinforces them. These women characters are judged to be tough to the extent that they are masculinized. The tough women have to sacrifice some of their own femininity in order to fight for their country. Deborah, for example, turns down a proposal of marriage from her American lover after she unsuccessfully tries to picture herself as a housewife. The Israeli characters in this popular fiction were dichotomized into either masculinized fighters or resilient maternal figures. The maternal metaphor was part of the gendered construction of male and female roles in postwar America.

Importantly, the fictional counterparts to these tough Israelis, both male and female, were their cowardly, unmasculine Arab adversaries. In contrast to the brave, controlled, and heroic Jews, the Arabs "swarm[ed]," "shriek[ed]," had "unnatural fear[s]," and were driven into "frenz[ies]." The Arabs were almost always caricatures rather than characters. In short, Arabs were not only depicted as stupid and out of control, they were also peripheral to the main dramatic action. The impression given was that the Arabs and their political goals were unimportant in comparison with the struggle that the heroic Israelis were waging on behalf of their own independence.

Meanwhile, military images of tough Jews reinforced—surprisingly—the prevalent metaphor that Israel was an adolescent David fighting against a powerful Goliath. A common image of masculinity in American culture is that of the gutsy underdog. In fiction and in nonfiction, the remarkable aspect of Israel's independence struggle was that the Jews banded together against heavy odds to fight for their land. This idea was reflected in the myth that Jews had faced overwhelming odds in their independence struggle. Fictional descriptions of Jewish fighting abilities also highlighted Jewish resourcefulness in the face of unimaginative enemies. The Jews in *The Wall* learn to smuggle, organize clandestinely, and train themselves to fight. The Jews in *Desert* and *Temptation* overcome the better supplied British and more populous Arabs. The underground fighters in the film seem to outwit the whole British army with their daily radio broadcasts and their daring raid on a British military camp.

Press descriptions of Israeli military abilities paralleled those found in fiction; journalists frequently used phrases such as Israel's "tough little army." One July 1949 *Life* story on the new state, for example, made the David and Goliath image explicit: "Israel was born indeed, but the Jews would have need of the Shield of David to keep their nation alive." In addition, the article noted that the Jews were attacked and, at first, had only inadequate equipment until they were resupplied from abroad. Similarly, many stories used the population figures of all of the countries in question to emphasize that Israelis were, indeed, outnumbered. The 1948 war was described as an "assault of seven Arab states with 30 million people on the *newborn* Jewish state, with less than 700,000."[32] Such a comparison was, of course, deceptive since it didn't look at the size of the trained and mobilized forces. Israelis reinforced this David and Goliath story, such as when Ben-Gurion recalled to a wire service in New York that Israel had been short of arms in the 1948 war, "courage and faith were the principal weapons in our armoury."[33]

In the years after 1948, journalists and fiction writers continued to emphasize that the "young" Israel was continually threatened by its more numerous and brutal neighbors. Ironically, the image of Israel as a youthful David coexisted with the idea that the Jewish state and Turkey were the only viable allies in the region. Moreover, State Department officials argued by 1950 that Israel was not a beleaguered youth, but had established military superiority over all its neighbors. Although the country did not have a great quantity of arms, it had "qualitative superiority."[34]

Nevertheless, images of Israeli vulnerability persisted. For example, soon after Czechoslovakian arms deliveries to Egypt in 1955, *Time* mentioned how Israelis were "ringed by" Arabs and their "shiploads of arms from the Communists." Similarly, another *Time* story from early 1956 explaining Israeli retaliation for border raids noted that "Every Israeli sleeps within 20 miles of an Arab knife." A *US News and World Report* account of Israel's relationship with its neighbors argued that, "like the new kid in a rough neighborhood, Israel had to fight from the start." Many of the thousands of pro-Zionist letters to the White House drew the picture of a self-reliant state fighting against unfair circumstances and uneven odds.[35] Finally, fictional works that told the story of Israel's founding reiterated this David and Goliath story. These works included *The Last Temptation*, *The Sword in the Desert*, *The Juggler*, and *Exodus*.

For the many American writers who subscribed to a David and Goliath view of Israel's military situation, this understanding rested on a number of assumptions about Israelis. The first assumption was that they showed determination and confidence. One 1948 *Life* editorial, for example, argued that the state was created by "their defiant act of will." Another journalist explained the qualities of *sabra*s as "self-confidence, faith, manliness, and pride." Second, Israelis were successful in overcoming their underdog status because of the rigors of their training and their embodiment of the masculine ideal. George Biddle in *The Atlantic* observed of a liberation day parade that the soldiers were "tough and seasoned" like the best English or American troops, "yet different," with "a tremendous overflow of physical vitality." Historians also strengthened the image of Israeli masculinity through their language. Howard Sachar's 1957 survey saw Israel as "a virile, throbbing civilization, and it became a catalyst for the loyalty of vigorous, action-minded young people."[36]

Soon after the formation of the state, Israeli soldiers were described in the press as well-organized, especially the Haganah which had "shown itself a far better military organization than the so-called Arab Army of Liberation." A few years later, one *Time* critic praised the success of Israel's army, "a deadly machine of disciplined power . . . swiftly mobilized from the citizen soldier." By 1958, a *New York Times Book Review* reported that Israel, "surrounded by hostile enemies," relied on a "constantly alerted citizen-army." The repetition of the term "citizen soldier" and "citizen-army" not only stressed the idea that ordinary Israelis became extraordinary soldiers, but also strengthened the identification between Israelis fighting for their independence and the Americans' own story of independence more than one hundred fifty years earlier. The idea of citizen-soldiers had a nostalgic appeal, harking back to a simpler, less bureaucratic time of "self reliance." The image of *kibbutz*im surrounded by enemies reinforced that of ordinary Israelis at the mercy of numerous neighbors. *Time* in August 1948 noted, for example, that many of the collective settlements were "stockaded forts, built to protect pioneer settlers from Arab attacks." A third pillar of the David and Goliath paradigm was that Israelis were not only outnumbered by their neighbors, but also lived in a physically smaller country. Many articles mentioned Israel's size, often by way of comparison to an American state, "a country the size of Connecticut is ringed by hostile neighbors," reported *Life* in May 1948. Thus, "geography favor[ed] the Arabs."[37]

Images of extraordinary Israeli military ability also rested upon ideas of poor Arab abilities. First, the Arabs were deemed to lack courage. One journalist, for example, agreed with the views of his Jewish guide that "Arabs were . . . cowards, and ran at the least excuse." Another writer observed that when the Egyptians joined the fighting in 1948, they fought merely with "loud communiqués." Most journalists also focused on a second characteristic of Arab fighting: poor organization and discipline, and a certain degree of irrationality, for example, "embittered Arabs threw shells and bombs" as if there was no military reason for doing so. In addition, Arab leaders bickered and the forces had low morale. The Arab League, observed a May 1948 article in the *New York Times*, was "divided by internal dynastic rivalries and has yet to demonstrate military strength." A third characteristic of Arab fighting according to many American writers was that it was unfair as well as savage. For example, one November 1948 *Time* article noted the complaints of Israeli soldiers who had been engaged in hand to hand combat: the "Egyptian soldiers were biting them in the necks," they reported. Yet another characteristic of Arab fighting was primitivism. "Arabs were about as dangerous as so many North American Indians in modern mechanized war," observed one article.[38]

More subtle versions of these stereotypes could be found in the language of American policymakers. For example, the Chargé in Israel in early 1954 described border skirmishes as follows: on the one hand was "Arab infiltration and *marauding* and occasional murders," on the other hand were "Israel's *activities* in various demilitarized zones, unnecessarily harsh ambushing of Arabs crossing borders with non-aggressive intent."[39] The description of Arab deeds was more immediate and visceral, while that of Israeli actions was more antiseptic and analytical. One analyst on the Policy

Planning Staff observed, "The blunt fact is that the Jewish troops were more capable, more determined and better led than the Arabs."[40]

In addition to popular ideas about Arab military inferiority and Israeli military abilities, another set of political assumptions helped to strengthen an American identification with Israel in the first years of that country's existence: Israel was a democracy, depicted as similar in many ways to the United States. Right after the state was declared, *The Washington Post*, for example, noted approvingly that "Social and political equality are pledged to all citizens 'without distinction of race, creed or sex.'" The CIO affirmed in a report on the new state that it was a democratic nation with freedom of religion, speech, and the press. American democracy was, argued CIO leaders, "a welcome beacon-light" to Israelis. Discussion of Israel's democratic credentials was widespread in popular fiction. In *The Last Temptation*, for example, Israel's formation by a democratic process is described in detail. In a tense scene which was repeated in other fictional and press accounts, the Jews of Palestine crowd around the radio listening to the partition vote at the United Nations in 1947. Viertel pictures Israel as a modern democracy with principles similar to American ones; one character observes, "Behind everything we do, we know there must be justice for all."[41]

Popular fiction also highlighted Israel's democratic credentials by contrasting the moderate, reasonable leaders of the government with the minorities of right- and left-wing extremists in the country. Right-wing extremists were eager to seize more land outside of Israel's 1949 borders even if it meant sacrificing peace. Left-wing extremists were Communists, very different from mainstream Socialists. Deborah, the main character of *The Last Temptation*, is compared to an old friend who has become a cold, doctrinaire Communist advocating violence. Interestingly, the fictional image of politically moderate Israelis countered the stereotype that Jews might have more radical tendencies than other Americans.[42] Thus, there is no doubt on which side Israelis can be found in the global contest between Communism and democracy.

Viertel allows that Israel has its share of undemocratic elements, such as terrorists. But the majority of Israelis, the narrator insists, disavowed the attack on the King David Hotel in the summer of 1946, the April 1948 Deir Yassein massacre, and the assassination of UN mediator Count Bernadotte five months later. Nevertheless, when the stakes were high, even reasonable people were capable of irrational judgments. The circumstances of the 1948 war and the Holocaust background of many Israelis ("you can't lose your whole family in a gas chamber and remain calm and academic about these issues," one fictional character remarks) seemed to mitigate some of the extremism that surfaces. Justifications for undemocratic Israeli conduct were also found in the contemporary nonfiction rhetoric. For example, Edmund Wilson writes: "The terrorism of modern Israel was the result of the Nazi persecutions and of the policy of the British."[43]

Contemporary press accounts concurred that the majority of Israelis were "moderates." To counter worries that Israel's Socialist characteristics were similar to Communism, writers such as Henry Wallace stated emphatically that the Jews of Palestine were not Communists and had a "genuinely mixed economy." A few months after Israeli independence, one August 1948 article in *Time* explained that the *kibbutz*im were formed for practical reasons: "Socialist Zionists wanted to work the land as intensively as possible, with Jewish labor." The article was careful to point out that the collectives were not Communist. Similarly, the CIO leaders concluded that allegations of Soviet influence in Israel were completely false. Israelis opposed all totalitarianism, they concluded, as demonstrated in the last elections in which Communists received only 4 percent of the vote (with much of that small amount coming from the Arabs, they argued). Press articles also emphasized that Israel was increasingly moderate. For example, by 1953, Prime Minister David Ben-Gurion, once described "as a zealot of the left," was said to have become more of a centrist and political realist. Just as in the popular fiction, journalists were careful to distinguish those in the Israeli government from the terrorist groups.[44] During the Independence War, many press accounts discussed the power of the Jewish terrorist groups and the "helplessness" of the government in the face of them.

American policymakers also contrasted the Israeli government with the terrorist groups. The State Department considered the activities of the Irgun and Stern Gang "alarming," and argued that they had violated the truce terms by reinforcing their strategic positions in Jerusalem. (Both organizations used violent attacks and opposed the policies of the mainstream Jewish Agency and its Haganah.) Philip Jessup, the acting U.S. Representative to the United Nations, praised the Israeli government in the summer of 1948, because, it "had the courage and will to deal firmly with the Irgun and other dissident elements." In 1947, the CIA had also weighed in on the danger posed by the Irgun (committing "sabotage and terrorism") and Stern Gang (comprised of "extreme fanatics"). The inclination of U.S. policymakers to label these dissident groups as such was probably encouraged by the fact that they received assistance from the Soviets during the summer of 1948. The CIA also made a careful distinction between these small groups and the larger Haganah which "Because of its defensive work, its restraint, and its non-extremist intentions, . . . is supported by the majority of the Jewish community of Palestine and by most Zionists."[45] Later that year, U.S. officials were alarmed at the assassination of UN Mediator Count Folke Bernadotte and quickly surmised that it had been carried out "presumably" by the Stern Gang.[46]

Most pro-Zionist Americans also condemned the Irgun as a threat to Israel. UJA President Henry Morgenthau cautioned listeners at a Zionist Organization of America convention held in the summer of 1948 that if American Jews supported the Irgun, it was "a stab in the back for the State of Israel." The majority of the ZOA agreed with Morgenthau's assessment and passed a resolution condemning the Irgun.[47]

In the early years of the Cold War, whether or not a country was considered "democratic" had important political implications. As Jews demonstrated their dedication to democracy and proved their ability as fighters, both in fictional tales and in the 1948 war and assorted border skirmishes, they became more valuable as members of the Western, anti-Communist camp. Meanwhile, U.S. policy in the Middle East became increasingly concerned with Cold War rivalries. Even before Israel was formed, some observers—both Zionists and anti-Zionists—shared this worry. For example, one article in *The Nation* argued that if Truman did not "over rule the State Department" to support the partition resolution, "we will be courting what we say we want to avoid—Russian penetration of the Middle East." During the 1948 war, the National Security Council was worried about the introduction of Soviet forces into the region. This concern only increased after the war.[48]

Zionist supporters and Israelis saw the direction of U.S. policy and argued that Israel, unlike the Arab states, was a fellow democracy and would soon end its attempts to remain neutral in the Cold War. For example, UJA President Morgenthau, also a prominent Democrat and former cabinet secretary, assured Secretary of State Dean Acheson that Israel was "definitely on our side in the present East-West conflict." He cautioned that Israelis were reluctant to make their loyalties clear in public, because they did not want to hurt the prospects for immigration from eastern Europe and the Soviet Union. Similarly, president of the American Jewish Committee Jacob Blaustein assured Harry Truman in 1950 that Israel "can be counted on one hundred percent as an ally of the United States, . . . I am convinced the Israelis want democracy."[49] Israelis always emphasized the contrasts between their country and those of their neighbors, and the similarities between Israel and the United States. For example, one article in *Ha'aretz* argued, "In a world where totalitarianism is conquering territories and peoples and in the Middle East, where the word 'democracy' is deprived of its meaning, Israel shines to the Americans, as a state nearest to the Anglo-Saxon conception."[50]

Foreign Minister Moshe Sharett also assured Secretary of State Dean Acheson that, "By their nature and by their heritage the Jews were individualists and the theory of Communism was abhorrent to them." By 1951, Israel's first president, Chaim Weizmann, and Prime Minister, David Ben-Gurion, wrote to Truman celebrating American democracy and arguing that Israel had much in common with the United States. Ben-Gurion described "the remarkable community of ideals and interests which prevails between our two countries," adding "I appreciate your consistent belief in Israel's destiny as a bulwark of democracy and progress." Ben-Gurion made similar assertions in public, saying, for example, "we have created a vigorous outpost of democracy in the Middle East."[51] At the beginning of 1953, one Israeli *aide memoire* left no doubt about the country's political position and that of the Arabs:

> Democracy, which is the only sure moral foundation for a free world united against tyranny, had been increasingly set aside in the Arab States in favor of dictatorships, . . . [Arab governments] are in conflict with the policies of the free world, including Israel.[52]

The fact that Israel had just a few years earlier publicly professed its own neutralism in the Cold War seems to have been forgotten.

Many congressmen agreed with Israeli policymakers, having viewed Israel as a Cold War ally long before the White House did. For example, a group of thirty-two congressmen met with Secretary Acheson in early 1950 requesting that the United States send new arms supplies to Israel, one arguing that "Israel was the one state in the Near East upon which the United States could rely." Another congressman wrote to Acheson arguing for arms to Israel because of her "aggressive neighbors," and explaining that "the character of the government of Israel is so much in keeping with our own." For years, congressmen had referred to Israel as a "bastion" for "freedom and peace."[53]

A number of public statements from within the administration also highlighted Israel's democratic character—much to the disappointment of State Department diplomats. John Blanford, for example, complained that during the 1950 electoral season references to Israel as a "beachhead of democracy in a backward area" had succeeded in "arous[ing] intense opposition and feeling in the Arab countries." Edwin Wright strongly criticized the numerous speeches by Vice President Alben Barkley before

such groups as the United Jewish Appeal and Jewish National Fund prais-
ing Israel as "an oasis of democracy in a backward area of the world."
George McGhee compiled evidence of "adverse effects in the Arab countries" of statements from within the administration that seemed to favor
Israel. McGhee quoted one Syrian minister who argued that all U.S. actions were now suspect as "a camouflaged means of furthering Israel's interests." In addition, McGhee and Arab officials argued that U.S. policy
endangered a united front against Communism in the Middle East.[54]

Soon after the founding of Israel, some American officials asserted
that the Israeli government recognized the "disadvantages to it of too
close an association with the Soviet Union." Moreover, Israel saw the advantages of a closer association with the United States. The dominant
consensus among U.S. officials in the early 1950s seemed to be that Israel
was "pro-Western although not necessarily anti-Soviet." NSC 47, for example, accepted the distinction between private assurances that Israelis
gave to Americans and what the Jewish officials believed they had to state
publicly in order not to jeopardize Soviet support in the United Nations
and the possibility of increased emigration from eastern Europe and the
Soviet Union. The NSC observed that Israel was of great strategic importance because of its location, and recommended that the U.S. government
should remain cautious about Israel's policies: "Israel may become a danger or an asset depending upon the nature of her future relations with the
Soviets and with the Western Democracies." For their part, Israeli officials realized that American preoccupation with the Cold War, or "anti-
Soviet hysteria" in the words of Moshe Sharett, would increasingly affect
the American-Israeli relationship. Early in 1950, Sharett worried that Israel might be "written off" and that Israel should assure the Americas of
their "real stand" in the Cold War.[55]

Following the outbreak of the Korean War, Israeli leaders and their
supporters professed loyalty to the West more frequently than they had
before. Undoubtedly, American pressure on "friendly" nations throughout the world to support UN actions influenced the Israeli policy shift.
Jacob Blaustein told Truman that the Israelis had been "gratified" by U.S.
actions in Korea. Moreover, he argued that if there was any widening of
the war to the Near East, the only allies who could help the United States
would be Israel and Turkey. Sharett and other Israeli officials told Acheson that they were, indeed, worried about the possibility of a war between the east and west spreading to the Middle East. Ben-Gurion
praised U.S. actions in Korea, calling them a "bold and vital step to block
Communist expansion and hence may prove a turning point in history."[56]

American policymakers recognized the changing direction of Israeli policy. Acheson, for example, reported that Israelis said they understood the "fallaciousness of their policy of 'non-identification' and that they know the only hope of their salvation lies with the West." Assumptions about Israel's loyalty in the Cold War grew more common, while the Soviet Union was blamed in the early 1950s for wanting to encourage Arab-Israeli hostilities. Such views were expressed in 1953 by American Ambassador Davis (someone who had begun his tour of duty quite critical of Israel); he also concluded that while Israel wanted peace, Arabs did not. Media descriptions in the early 1950s consistently highlighted the similarity of political interests between Israel and America and the military value of the former to the latter. After Egypt accepted Soviet arms in 1955, positive descriptions of Israel's fighting ability became even more frequent.[57]

Israel's democratic image was increasingly strengthened by its masculine credentials. One 1948 magazine article made the following distinction between Israelis and Arabs: "The Jews were too tough, too smart, and too vigorous for the divided and debilitated Arab world to conquer." Masculinity was also linked with Western political orientation. "Both Israel and Turkey," read one article "were virile, modern and westward-looking inhabitants of an old, static and inward-looking region. . . . Turkey admires Israel's tough little army as the region's second best force . . . while Israelis see Turkey as the only other Middle East power of military significance." The article repeats what were by 1955, familiar political and cultural descriptions of Israel's tough army and country as an island in a hostile sea. Widely used descriptions of Israel as "a bastion or bulwark of democracy" in the Near East not only testified to the country's political views, but also reinforced its masculine characteristics.[58]

Similarly, press accounts that celebrated Israel's "realism" and "sobriety" attested to the state's masculine character. From the beginning of the state, many journalists viewed Israel as the "realistic" solution to the Palestine question. The *Washington Post*, for example, wrote approvingly of Harry Truman's judgment that quick recognition of Israel took account of the new reality of the region. Many U.S. officials, such as Deputy U.S. Representative on the Security Council Jessup, also concluded that the only realistic course after 14 May 1948 was the recognition of Israel and the establishment of a neighboring Arab Palestinian state.[59]

It should be noted that U.S. officials were sometimes very critical of Israelis and their decisions. Nevertheless, they seemed to expect more "realism" from the Israelis than from the Arabs, and assumed that Israelis had much in common with Americans. For example, Ambassador

Davis wrote back to Washington in September 1951 regarding the "Generally negative and irreconcilable attitude of Arabs on the one hand, and unconstructive, guarded, legalistic approach of the Israelis on the other." "Irreconcilable" assumes that no compromise can be made, while "unconstructive" indicates some flexibility. In addition, Davis wrote of the Israelis, "Given this country's able leadership and highly literate population, it should be expected to show more statesmanlike and less pettifogging approach." U.S. policymakers sometimes made it clear that the Israeli position on a particular issue was the "realistic" one. For example, Americans came to agree with Israelis regarding Palestinian refugees. As Deputy Secretary of State David Bruce said in late 1952, repatriation of refugees to Israel was "no longer feasible" and the "only possible solution" for most of the refugees was "resettlement in Arab States."[60]

In contrast to the descriptions of Israelis, Arabs were often described as "unrealistic" in the press. For example, once Israel had declared its independence, Arab calls for the abolition of the state were all dismissed. The *New York Times* noted, "such a position is not only unrealistic and unacceptable, but in effect amounts to a defiance of the United Nations." Other American journalists stressed the lack of responsibility among the Arabs, with one article from *The New Republic* concluding, Israel was "encircled by retarded states lacking in responsible leadership."[61]

Government officials often shared these views. NSC 47/2, a 1949 study on the Middle East, for example, used similar language to that found in the press. The report concluded that the Arabs had "retarded economic and social development," as well as a "generally inferior quality of . . . statesmanship." In addition, they suffered from "intense and competing nationalisms," were "incapable of working together," lacked "progressive or capable leadership," and were susceptible to extremists. Secretary Acheson, along with other U.S. officials, often assumed that Arab positions were extreme. He observed in 1950 that "past history had shown that the Arab League had taken extreme positions which it has not carried out." Even before the creation of Israel, the CIA had concluded that the Arabs were "inflamed by national and religious fervor," while many were "fanatical" and "irresponsible tribesmen."[62] A hallmark of fanaticism and irrationality in Arabs, according to some American observers, was their excessive emotion. For example, State Department officer Robert McClintock observed that Arab military commanders realized by the end of June 1948 that they would lose the war against Israel, and he worried that the Arabs would use the United States as a scapegoat in their frustration:

> they will seek to place the blame for their own bad judgment and emotion (which in statecraft amounts to bad judgment) on the United States.
>   It is . . . important to the interests of this country that these fanatical and overwrought people do not injure our strategic interests through reprisals against our oil investments and through recision of our air base rights in that area.[63]

Similarly, Philip Jessup, of the UN delegation, unfavorably compared Arab diplomacy with that of the Israelis: "In contrast on the whole with Arab representation they [Israelis] have shown dignity and strength in the U.N."[64] Secretary of State Marshall concurred that the Arabs were, indeed, overly-emotional. He explained that his job was to deal with the Arab-Israeli conflict "on a realistic basis, as free as possible from the emotionalism which surrounds the issue. . . . The emotionalism of the issue had caught up the Arab peoples to such an extent that Arab leaders are not able to make concessions which otherwise they might be willing to make."[65] Not coincidentally, great emotion and irrationality were considered in postwar social understanding to be indications of a lack of masculinity.

In addition to dispassion and realism, another sign of masculinity was "maturity." As Barbara Ehrenreich argues, in early Cold War parlance, "maturity" was a measure of masculinity. "Immaturity" was to be guarded against. Jessup observed of the Arab states in the summer of 1948: "The immaturity of Arabs is revealed in [the] blindspot which prevents even more moderate Arabs from recognizing existence of Israel as a political fact." He concedes that Arab moderates "recognize the intelligence and ability of Jews," but since the Jews are still seen as "evil," any benefits the Jews might bring to the area are obscured. These ideas of the unmasculine Arab character also shaped the image of Arab leaders. For example, Egyptian "dictator" Gamal Abdel Nasser, in the early and mid–1950s, was deemed "immature" by journalists.[66]

The suitability of Arabs as Cold War allies was compromised by a whole set of images—revealed in fiction and nonfiction—that set off Arabs as outsiders and challenged their masculinity. The references to Arab cowardice in *The Sword in the Desert* and, later, in *The Last Temptation* and *Exodus* reinforced the construction of an image of Jewish masculinity. Israelis became more valuable as democratic allies in the Middle East as they proved their mettle as fighters in opposition—both militarily and rhetorically—to the cowardly Arab fighters. One contemporary critic concluded that Communism might come to power because there was "nothing virile enough to resist it." A group of congressmen argued that the United States could not count on the Arabs, who "had proved themselves thoroughly unreliable during the last war." Moreover, Arabs were considered by some to be unprincipled fighters, described as "marauders," "irregulars," "devious," and willing to engage in "ambush[es]."[67]

Aside from their image as poor fighters, Arabs lacked a democratic political tradition and had failed to develop their economies—a sure sign that they were lacking democratic inclinations. Some American diplomats observed that Arab states were hopelessly weak. Moreover, as Clapp and Locke had worried in their economic missions to the region, the Arabs were especially vulnerable to Communist pressure due to their lack of development. Journalists concurred with this assessment; for example, on a visit to the Arab town of Nazareth, George Biddle wrote: "Half the Nazarenes are Communists, easily propagandized on account of their present, unhappy economic plight." Many Americans described Arab society as "feudal" and, therefore, antithetical to Western societies. Similar judgments of Arab political and economic characteristics were also found in policymaking circles, such as the NSC, which referred to the "semifeudal leadership" of the region.[68]

RELUCTANT PARTNERS: THE EISENHOWER ADMINISTRATION LOOKS AT ISRAEL

The increasingly cohesive cultural images of Israel which focused upon the country's pioneering, military ability, and democratic structure were not readily accepted by all American policymakers. This seemed especially true in the early years of the Republican Eisenhower administration usually portrayed in the histories of the period as being particularly critical of Israel, in contrast to its Democratic predecessor. Yet, while the administration did inject a new tone into relations with Israel, there was a remarkable continuity in attitudes and policies, and indications that policymakers were internalizing many of the popular cultural and political assumptions about Israel.

At the start of their administration, Dwight D. Eisenhower and his Secretary of State John Foster Dulles wanted to project a Middle Eastern policy that was fair to both Israeli and Arab interests. Following a twelve country trip to the region in the spring of 1953, the secretary emphasized that the United States was impartial in the Arab-Israeli conflict, while supporting "orderly" self-government as opposed to "extreme nationalism" which the Kremlin might use to "capture" dependent peoples. Dulles called for concessions on both sides of the conflict, but he earned himself the criticism of Israel's supporters when he challenged Israel to "cease to look upon itself . . . as alien in the" Middle East. Zionists countered that Israel was alienated by Arab economic and military threats against it.[69]

The fears of Israel's supporters were confirmed in September 1953 when the United States temporarily suspended aid to the Jewish state—the only time American aid had been suspended in these years. The suspension of aid came in response to Israel's planned construction of a canal that would divert water from the Jordan River shared by Israel, Jordan, and Syria. After Israel defied the order of the United Nations Truce Supervising Organization to halt work on the project (which was located in the demilitarized zone with Syria), Dulles ordered the suspension of $26 million in economic aid. While the suspension was still in effect, on 14–15 October, Israeli forces retaliated for a raid that killed a mother and her two children in a village near the Jordanian border; soldiers attacked the West Bank village of Kibya, killing sixty-nine men, women, and children. The United States strongly protested the Israeli action and made public the suspension of aid. By 27 October, Israel announced that work on the hydroelectric project would cease; the next day, Dulles announced resumption of U.S. aid to the country.[70]

The administration's suspension of aid had been greeted by a storm of protest in the United States. The secretary was visited by a delegation, including Senator Irving Ives and Representative Jacob Javits, and representatives from a number of Jewish organizations, that protested what it saw as unequal treatment of Israel and the Arab states. Dulles stressed that the suspension was temporary, and in a public statement following the meeting, asserted that there was "no change in the basic friendship of the United States to Israel." In addition, he told the press that the technical aid in question was part of monies allocated to many countries none of which had yet been disbursed. Finally, he noted that there were no such allocations to the Arab states.[71] Thus, Dulles tried to backtrack from his criticisms of Israel and suspension of aid.

Although he was criticized by Israel's supporters for his "harsh" tone, Dulles argued publicly that Israelis genuinely wanted peace. Moreover, of all the countries in the region, he stressed the possibilities for economic growth and development in the Jewish state. Using the idealistic language already widespread in popular rhetoric about Israel, the secretary said: "We were impressed by [their] vision and supporting energy. . . . Inspired by a great faith, they are now doing an impressive work of creation." In contrast, Dulles did not praise the "vision" or "impressive work" of the Arab peoples.

Following the controversy over Israel's Jordan River project and the Kibya massacre, Eisenhower, like his predecessor, decided to tackle the issue of regional economic development. He appointed Eric Johnston, head of the Motion Picture Association of America and former chairman of the International Advisory Board of the Tennessee Valley Authority (TVA), to establish a Jordan River development project. The mission was designed to develop the valley's water resources as well as provide irrigated land for Palestinian refugees, diffuse Arab-Israeli tensions by building economic cooperation, and demonstrate American willingness to be a fair broker among the parties. Johnston negotiated with officials from Israel, Egypt, Jordan, Syria, and Lebanon from October 1953 to October 1955 over a proposal to use Lake Tiberias as a reservoir from which water would be distributed by canals with electricity generating plants along the way. The water network would be overseen by an international agency, probably under UN auspices. By fall 1955, an agreement seemed near, but fell apart when the Arab League Council postponed consideration of the plan, effectively killing it.

For a number of reasons, Eisenhower's efforts to revisit the thorny issue of economic development and refugee resettlement met the same fate as the initiatives undertaken by Truman. Although the Johnston plan addressed much more than the fate of the refugees, there was no hiding the fact that irrigation of the Jordan Valley would enable the permanent settlement of refugees outside of Israel. Arab states could neither set aside the goal of repatriation, nor recognize Israel's existence by collaborating in such a project. Dulles acknowledged this stumbling block but told Eisenhower that there was no way to avoid it: "We should not let [the Arab] attitude deter us from supporting proposals which we honestly consider to be fair."[72] Israel was also unwilling to concede on a number of points; it demanded more water, dams, and hydroelectric plants than its allocation, and objected to the international operation authority.[73] Finally, Johnston's past association with the pro-Zionist American Christian Palestine Committee seemed to belie—at least in the eyes of a number of Arabs—Eisenhower's and Dulles' efforts to be a fair broker in the region.[74]

Through the mission, the secretary and the president intended to correct what they thought to be Truman's mistakes and regain flexibility for U.S. policy in the region. Other members of the adminstration also articulated this theme in their pubic statements. For example, Assistant Secretary for the Bureau of Near Eastern, South Asian, and African Affairs Henry Byroade made a high profile speech recommending a limit on immigration into Israel, an assurance from Israel that it had no expansionist intentions, Arab abandonment of "negativism toward Israel," and a "realistic" approach of both sides toward the refugee issue, including Israeli compensation for abandoned property. A year later, Dulles gave a speech before the Council on Foreign Relations that sounded similar themes.[75] He emphasized U.S. neutrality in the Arab-Israeli conflict, and argued that the most important problems remaining between the two sides were the refugees and a lack of permanent borders.

Although Eisenhower and Dulles did their best to affirm publicly American neutrality in the Arab-Israeli conflict, they could not ignore the fact that Israel had been strongly asserting its pro-Western orientation since the start of the Korean War. Indeed, Israel's original "non-identification" policy ceased to exist after mid-1950, and the country's diplomats had been working hard to obtain U.S. territorial and political guarantees, a treaty of alliance, and a supply of modern weapons. Although the United States provided aid to Israel in the first half of the 1950s, and looked the other way when Israel acquired additional arms from other countries, Eisenhower and Dulles refused to enter into the sort of close political and military relationship that Israel desired. Nevertheless, American economic aid to Israel continued, the two countries consulted on regional issues, and favorable political views of the Jewish state predominated public and private discourse. Thus, Israel's growing identification with the West in the Cold War and the cultural and political "Americanization" of Israel in these years did not bring all of the concrete political results sought by the Jewish state, but it had both a short-term and long-term influence on U.S.-Israeli relations.

American arms policy in the late 1940s and early 1950s represented most clearly U.S. efforts to maintain neutrality and avoid getting too deeply involved in the Arab-Israeli dispute, as well as growing American ties to Israel in a Cold War world. Arms policy also illustrated the continuity between the two administrations. Long before Eisenhower came to office and the Korean War intensified Truman's concern about U.S. strategic positions in different areas of the Third World, the basic framework of American arms policy in the Middle East was set with the founding of Israel. During the heaviest fighting in 1948, the United States abided by an arms embargo to Israel and the Arab states in an effort to contain the war and limit its duration. The CIA, at the time, predicted that neither side had adequate arms for prolonged fighting, with Israel stronger in light weapons and the Arabs better supplied in heavy equipment. Most of Israel's arms came from eastern Europe; the principal supplier for the Arabs was the United Kingdom.[76]

Once the United Nations embargo was lifted in August 1949, U.S. policymakers wanted to guard against an arms race in the region, yet permit the export of arms "deemed necessary for internal security and self defense." Thus, Israeli leaders and their supporters who wanted increased arms sales continued to speak of an "existing arms embargo" against the country, although the United States had sent defensive equipment to Israel. Secretary of State Dean Acheson was sensitive about this distinction, asserting that the arms embargo no longer existed. Demands from Israel and her supporters increased in early 1950 with news of new British arms shipments to Egypt (as well as Iraq and Jordan). Acheson and State Department officials deflected the requests with the argument that the arms were for defensive purposes, and the United States had already sent more arms to Israel than to any Arab country. Acheson reminded congressmen who came to him to plead the Israeli case that the defense of the eastern Mediterranean was of great strategic importance to the United States. Some defensive forces were therefore necessary in the region. Interestingly, although Acheson disagreed with the congressmen's entreaties, he seemed to agree with their assessments of which country in the region made the best ally: "I thought that the Egyptians were not thoroughly reliable."[77]

American journalists agreed with policymakers that the Cold War should be an important concern for their country in the Middle East, but that the United States should not contribute to an arms race in the region. Nevertheless, most seemed to believe that providing Israel with the arms she requested would not create an arms race. For example, one *New York Times* editorial written soon after Israel was formed called for lifting the arms embargo as a matter of *justice* for the Jewish state: "[the U.S.] can do no less than recognize Israel's right to fight for its life." Within a few years, some journalists concluded that arms should not be given to the Arabs because they were less trustworthy Cold War partners: "On two previous occasions the Arabs have turned against the West," argued the *Ohio Plain Dealer*. "To give the Arabs arms now would be to play the Russian game. If they did not use them against the Western outposts in the Near East they would be inclined, after a bit of rabble rousing by their leaders, to resume the war against Israel. Either eventuality would delight no one more than the Russians."[78]

CONCLUSION

The sympathy that many American journalists felt for Israel in its quest to obtain more arms was just one example of the growing support for and identification with the Jewish state. The focus in popular and political culture upon Israel's pioneering, military abilities, and democratic credentials built upon a foundation of good will toward Israel that had been in place since 1947. This support was clear to both press and political observers. For example, a week after the formation of Israel, the *Washington Star* noted that "the dramatic action of the Palestine Jews . . . fired the imagination of many an American." Upon Israel's formation, *Life* noted that many Americans wished the endeavor good luck and wishes. In addition, a number of journalists made it clear that they identified with Israel during the 1948 war. One critic, for example, later wrote of the war, "this was a fearful, dangerous moment for Israel. The Arabian [*sic*] armies attack . . . and the nights are filled with gunfire and the blasts of bombs."[79] In popular fiction written after the war, there was an even stronger identification with Israelis. An American journalist in *The Last Temptation*, for example, had already decided which side to take in the 1948 war: "Those are enemy—well, Arab—emplacements right there," he says looking out from his hotel.[80] From the formation of the state, most politicians agreed that there was at least some public support for Israel. As Democratic Party chairman Howard McGrath told the Herald Tribune Forum: "Israel is supported by the great mass of people in the United States in her right to exist, in her right to prosper."[81]

Such benevolent American attitudes toward Israel grew stronger and more widespread after 1948 through a cultural "Americanization" of the state. The images of Israeli pioneering, military abilities, and democratic characteristics resonated in the press and popular fiction as well as in Washington's halls of power. In the context of a Cold War that seemed increasingly global, Israel's democratic government and assertions of Western kinship became even more crucial for policymakers, including Republicans Eisenhower and Dulles who had tried to fashion a policy "neutral" in the Arab-Israeli dispute. Greater sympathy for Israel was also encouraged by images of Arabs that stressed their economic incompetence, poor fighting abilities, political instability, and overt aggressiveness. Interestingly, the idea that Israel was an innocent nation beset by hostile neighbors reflected Americans' perceptions of their own country's situation in the Cold War threatened by expansionist Communism.

Ironically, while political and cultural sympathy with Israel increased after 1948, American political attention to Israel and the other problems of the Middle East decreased in the late 1940s and early 1950s. Truman, for one, was inclined to let Israel make its own way, writing, "It is now up to the new state to make good on its own and I am of the opinion that it will."[82] Truman was able to take such a stand in regional politics, because the dire consequences of U.S. recognition of Israel predicted by the State Department (including severe damage to American-Arab relations and the cut off of oil supplies to the United States) had not come about. Similarly, the Truman and Eisenhower administrations planned for *potential* Soviet threats to the region, but there were not any immediate ones that required American intervention. The primary political problems in the Middle East with which policymakers dealt were instability caused by "anti-Western nationalism" and Arab-Israeli tensions which could lead, over the long run, to "disorder and eventually to regimes oriented toward" the Soviets.[83] Yet, with Western "responsibility" for the Middle East resting mainly on Britain through the early 1950s, U.S. policymakers were hesitant to become too deeply involved in the political problems of the region. They seemed to be guided by the advice of Defense Secretary Forrestal who observed of the Middle East at an NSC meeting in late 1948: "the area as a whole was like a piece of flypaper. Getting stuck on any one part would get us stuck on all."[84]

Thus, while popular and political sympathy with Israel grew in the first years after that country's independence, concrete American political commitments to the state were more limited. Meanwhile, images of Israeli pioneering, military prowess, and democratic characteristics built upon the foundation of support for Israel that emerged from the Holocaust and the American quest to erase discrimination against its own Jews. This increasingly cohesive image of Israel continued to evolve through the 1950s, finally contributing to greater policy changes in the 1960s.

4

The 1950s Religious Revival and "Christianizing" the Image of Israel and Jews

In early 1954, Reverend George Docherty of the New York Avenue Presbyterian Church in Washington DC—a church attended by many congressmen as well as the president of the United States—told his congregation that "under God" should be inserted into the Pledge of Allegiance to the Flag. He argued that such a change would reflect distinct American values, since "An atheistic American is a contradiction in terms." Congress agreed with the assessment and rewrote the pledge. Two years later, Congress adopted In God We Trust by unanimous vote as the official motto of the United States. Yet, lawmakers were not just calling for new slogans; they professed personal religious belief as well.[1] Religious affiliation was also widespread among ordinary Americans. According to one survey, church membership climbed from 44 percent in 1940, to 55 percent in 1950, and reached a peak of 69 percent in 1959. Another survey reported that 73 percent of Americans were church members in 1952.[2] Religious resurgence was also seen in the nation's bible sales. *The Holy Bible, The Revised Standard Version* was the nonfiction best seller in 1952, 1953, and 1954.[3]

On the surface, at least, the United States was experiencing a religious revival in the 1950s that reverberated widely. Dwight D. Eisenhower's assertion, "our form of government has no sense unless it is founded in a deeply felt religious faith, and I don't care what it is," captured the urgency of the revival.[4] Newfound concern with religion, particularly its perceived function as the glue of modern American society, affected political and cultural discourse in various ways. Issues that many might have previously defined as secular, were seen anew in religious terms. Paradoxically, then, religion became "secularized." Many agreed with the influential Protestant theologian Reinhold Niebuhr who asserted that "faith contains everything from the preference for good plumbing to the insistence on the dignity of man, the free enterprise system and the virtues of America as a nation."[5] Hence, religion offered a framework to understand not just the spiritual world, but the political world and foreign policy as well.

Americans used religious values not only to judge whether a policy was moral or immoral, good or bad. They also used those values to create a narrative about the nature of American society and culture, the mission of the United States in the world, and the character of non-Christians. For instance, the contrast between believing Americans and atheistic Communists carried a political message in the Cold War, which many Americans came to view as a religious war.[6] Not surprisingly, the surge in piety that many Americans reported was one factor that influenced attitudes toward the Jewish State of Israel. There was an emphasis on close ties between Jews and Christians as partners in a "Judeo-Christian" civilization, a recent cultural designation. Moreover, the biblical roots of the Jewish state elevated it to a special status. In the popular and political imagination, Israel was formed by the "Chosen People" and populated by prophets, warriors, and simple folk like those in Bible stories. The popular celebration of Israel also romanticized its people at the expense of their Arab (mainly Muslim) neighbors. Battling foes outside of the Judeo-Christian family, Israelis seemed just like Americans.

FROM CHRISTIANITY TO JUDEO-CHRISTIANITY

Religion—particularly Christianity—was, of course, integral to national culture before the Cold War. For example, in the early twentieth century, tens of thousands of Jewish immigrants were arrested for violating the Sunday Sabbath laws; the cases that reached court were usually upheld. In 1931, the Supreme Court stated that the United States was a "Christian nation." In his seminal World War II era study on race in America, Gunnar Myrdal asserted that Christianity was an "important ideological root of the American Creed."[7] Such assumptions continued into the Cold War. For instance, Eleanor Roosevelt observed in 1952, "it seems to me . . . we are a Protestant country."[8] Some foreign policymakers made similar assertions. For example, Assistant Secretary of State for Near Eastern Affairs George McGhee said in 1950 that the United States was a Christian nation.[9] Moreover, the majority of Americans affirmed the country's Christian character: nine out of ten surveyed in 1954 said they believed in the divinity of Jesus.[10]

The dominance of Christianity was nothing new. What was new was the celebration of "universalism" in the public culture beginning with World War II. From a universalist perspective, Americans had to reach beyond their own church. That imperative encouraged ecumenical alliances. As one religion scholar has observed, the mid-twentieth century was a time of "formal ecumenical advance unmatched in previous centuries."[11] The National Association of Evangelicals was formed in 1942, the World Council of Churches in 1948, and the National Council of Churches in 1950. The ecumenicism of the postwar years and the belief in the universality of Christian values convinced Protestant leaders that their religion could be the blueprint for an international postwar order. Prominent among them was Presbyterian lawyer John Foster Dulles who had helped to plan the World Council of Churches. He brought his Christian ideals to his positions as chairman of the wartime Commission to Study the Basis of a Just and Durable Peace and as counsel for the first United Nations conference. Dulles observed that Christians bore the greatest responsibility for a peaceful world after the war, since "Moral law may point the way to peace, but Christ, we believe, showed the way with the greatest clarity." He asserted that internationalism "gr[e]w out of the practice by the nations of the simple things Christ taught." Dulles' belief in the importance of Christianity in world diplomacy avoided sentimentalizing the religion; he, and others such as Reinhold Niebuhr, argued that Christ's message was "realistic."[12]

Dulles and Niebuhr were not alone in this faith in "Christian realism." For example, one contemporary observer of religion concluded that "only Christianity could create a humane 'world community, a universal *modus vivendi*'." Belief that Jesus' message was realistic reflected and was reinforced by postwar gender views that realism was masculine. Thus, postwar Protestantism was celebrated as masculine. Dulles observed that "Moral forces, too, are mighty. . . . Christians are not negative, supine people." Former President of the Federal Council of Churches Charles Taft wrote in *The Protestant Panorama*: "The *tough fiber* of Protestantism must be recovered from much of the soft sentimentality that has sometimes engulfed us." In the same book, *Christian Herald* editor Clarence Hall asserted: "The United States today . . . is the largest and *most virile* Protestant nation on the face of the globe."[13] This gendered understanding of Christianity helps demonstrate how religious identity came to stand for political values and characteristics, how the vocabulary of politics and religion overlapped.

The expansive view of an activist, global Christianity was encouraged not only by the dangers posed by Communists, but also by the fears that twentieth-century rationalism and scientific culture would de-Christianize America.[14] This was an unwelcome proposition, especially when the links between political character, morality, and religion solidified in Cold War America. Americans were on guard against the twin threats of secularism and communism. FBI Chief J. Edgar Hoover, for example, blamed crime on secularism and Communism. A dozen states barred atheists and agnostics from adopting children or being notary publics.[15] Joseph McCarthy's dramatic 1950 speech in Wheeling, West Virginia which charged that the State Department was riddled with Communists was notable for its religious message and "biblical tone." He asserted: "Today we are engaged in a final, all-out battle between communistic atheism and Christianity."[16]

Like McCarthy, many Americans, found affirmation of their political values in a religious identification. During the Cold War, they reassured themselves of Western virtue and moral superiority over "godless Communists." Rising evangelist Billy Graham, for example, asserted that Communism "is masterminded by Satan."[17] Seen through a Cold War lens, such views led to the conclusion that Christianity was a universal standard of morality and spirituality. Yet, since postwar dangers seemed so great, many Americans were motivated to seek religious alliances outside of the Protestant faith. In particular, the increasing emphasis on the "Judeo-Christian" heritage was furthered by the Cold War climate of fear, and an ideology that equated goodness with the West. In fact, the adoption of the Judeo-Christian heritage as synonymous with Western values helped to legitimate and broaden the Cold War ideology of superiority over the Communist world. For politicians the Judeo-Christian label described political as well as spiritual characteristics. Eisenhower, for instance, concluded that "the ideal of peace" was "another noble concept of our Judeo-Christian civilization."[18]

The idea of a Judeo-Christian identity took on new importance in the 1950s. The move to turn American spiritual values into universal moral values rested on an assumed triad of religious identity, "Protestant-Catholic-Jew." Sociologist Will Herberg explains the label in his popular 1955 book of the same name; the three religions, he argues, were "three diverse, but equally legitimate, equally American expressions of an overall American religion standing for essentially the same 'moral ideals' and 'spiritual values.'"[19] Reinhold Niebuhr explained how the faiths unified the country's culture:

> The religious community allows the new Americans to rid themselves of their foreignness and yet at the same time to preserve contact with

the European culture of their past. But they do not feel these religious communities to be European, for to be Protestant, Catholic, or Jew [*sic*] is very definitely a part of the American way of life.[20]

Political leaders, such as Harry S. Truman, believed that the three groups were "bound together in the American unity of brotherhood." And religious leaders such as Willard Johnson of the National Council of Christians and Jews emphasized the brotherhood inherent in the Judeo-Christian tradition which included "many denominations within one broad pattern, . . . [with] a remarkable degree of community of belief and purpose."[21]

The idea of a Judeo-Christian heritage predated the Cold War. In the 1930s, the term was a social and political description used mainly by intellectuals and social critics after Fascists and antisemites appropriated the term "Christian" to describe themselves.[22] Historian Deborah Dash Moore argues that it was the armed forces during World War II that led the way in making Judeo-Christian identity a common assumption. Equality in the treatment of Protestantism, Catholicism, and Judaism, and an effort by chaplains to reach out to people of all faiths became "standard operating procedure." Training for chaplains emphasized ecumenism, with the clergy bunking together and learning about other religions. Soldiers were required, for example, to attend ecumenical programs on their bases or to celebrate religious holidays that might otherwise have been ignored. Moore argues that through its wartime practices, the military strongly encouraged the idea of a Judeo-Christian heritage and, consequently, "a new understanding of American Jewish identity."[23] It's important to note that instances of antisemitism remained common in the army. Nevertheless, the wartime military led the way to embracing Judeo-Christianity, though it would not be until the postwar period that such cultural assumptions became widely accepted.

The inclusion of Jews in the Judeo-Christian brotherhood was surprising, considering that the antisemitism of the early twentieth century was based on religious (as well as economic, political, and racial) prejudice. Before the 1950s, Christian leaders and movements usually mirrored the cultural emphasis on assimilation and sometimes shared the antisemitic beliefs of many Americans. Antisemitism could be found among all religious groups, including liberal Protestants who preached tolerance but hoped for general assimilation and accommodation.

Evangelical Protestant beliefs probably changed the most from the prewar to the postwar period. Historian Robert Ellwood observes that with the Cold War many evangelicals "shift[ed] . . . the central Antichrist focus from Jews, modernism, or Catholicism to Communism, in the process making alliances with conservative, McCarthyist Roman Catholics and, in conjunction with the prophetic importance of the state of Israel, with Judaism." Thus, evangelicals who believed Communism to be the greatest danger facing the world affirmed their Judeo-Christian identity and the special meaning of the 1948 creation of Israel. Ellwood notes that the Jewish state was

> Universally regarded in prophecy-oriented conservative Christian cir-
> cles as a supernatural sign of immense importance. . . . The children
> of Abraham now had a new and tremendously significant role, in
> which they needed to be supported by Christians, as the doomsday
> clock ticked toward the consummation of all things.[24]

Even during the postwar period, some Jewish-Christian tensions remained. For example, the differing religious perspectives of popular preachers and writers such as Jewish Rabbi Joshua Loth Liebman, Protestant preacher Billy Graham, and Catholic leader Monsignor Fulton Sheen were explicit in their broadcasts and books.[25] Each asserted the superiority of his religion and its ability to help people find answers to the important questions of life. Thus, for these men and others, the cultural flourishing of Judeo-Christianity did not mean an abandonment of one's own faith. Nevertheless, theological disputations were not necessarily seen as unbridgeable chasms between the religions. It is unlikely that the tremendous 1946 best seller by Joshua Liebman *Peace of Mind* was read by the majority of people as a mean-spirited insult to Christianity even as it argued that Judaism could bring people true contentment.

In the 1950s, then, the universalist theme in American culture and the call for ecumenism, along with anti-Communism and the creation of Israel were strong enough—all together—to overcome antisemitism and embrace Judeo-Christianity. Thus, many Americans—the majority of whom were Protestant—came to identify with a broader "heritage" or "civilization" that included Jewish religion and history.

OUTSIDE OF THE JUDEO-CHRISTIAN BROTHERHOOD: MUSLIMS

While Americans celebrated their Judeo-Christian heritage, they also used it to distinguish themselves. Along with "atheistic Communists," Muslims were obvious "outsiders." That stigma, in the midst of the 1950s spiritual revival, had profound implications for American attitudes toward Israelis and the Arab-Israeli conflict. The image of Arab Muslims is part of a long-standing European narrative that stigmatized the "Orient" as outside the bounds of Western culture.[26] Orientalism depicted people of the East as irrational, depraved, childlike, and different, while Westerners were rational, virtuous, mature, and normal. East and West religious differences have probably been most responsible for the staying power of Orientalism; Islam remains demonic and monolithic in the Western imagination to the present-day. In America, Orientalism reflected the idea of choseness and millenarianism. The expansion of the nineteenth and twentieth centuries opened up new vistas for American influence, including the "benighted" and "degraded" Middle East. Many millenarianist sects believed their missionary work in the Holy Land could prepare the way for the end of days. Missionary work among the Arabs, moreover, was spurred by the belief that Christians had a prior claim on the biblical lands. Many Christians, then, resented Muslim physical control of the land.[27]

Americans perceived a gulf between themselves and Muslims not just because of the doctrinal differences, but because Muslims seemed to be "mired in religion and primitivism," while the West, including Israel, surpassed religion, and was "greater than the sum of its parts."[28] This judgment was certainly ironic in the climate of the 1950s religious revival. Nevertheless, the "primitive" status of Muslims and Islam was widely assumed. For example, in 1951, Eleanor Roosevelt waited with anticipation for the "Moslum" (*sic*) women of Belgrade to take off their veils and, thus, join the twentieth century.[29] American journalists were also patronizing. The *New York Times Magazine* concluded, for instance, that Arabs "lived in a world of literary darkness and ignorance" because of high illiteracy rates. And it wrote on another occasion, "The Arab is fundamentally a child of nature. His life is primitively dramatic in a way that the Occidental has almost forgotten. Blood feuds and terrorism are never far under the surface."[30]

The label "Moslem" became a shorthand reference for all sorts of political opinions that seemed irrational by American standards. For example, one article in *Businessweek* about anti-Israel opinion in the Arab world noted that in Lebanon, "which has a large Christian population, businessmen talk openly of the need for peace." In contrast, "Moslem opinion" was holding back Arab countries; Arab governments had to be cautious "lest they upset diehard Moslems." The State Department made similar assumptions about the character of Lebanon. As the most Western of the Arab states, it was practical and its large Christian population was "privately not unhappy at [the] establishment of another enclave

against the Moslem world." Nevertheless, the same potential for irrationality remained because the Lebanese were Arab: "the emotions of the
street can arise . . . as easily as in more fanatical countries," while any
pressure from outsiders for peace with Israel "is like waving a red flag to
a bull."[31]

Assumptions that Muslims encouraged the Arab-Israeli conflict, reminded readers with whom they should identify. For example, a
Newsweek article noted, "As Mohammed II slew Christians five centuries
ago, modern Arabs with Koran and pistol talk holy war on Jews." Moreover, reports of Arab aggression toward the United States after the UN
vote in 1947 to partition Palestine encouraged Americans to side with the
Jews. For example, "Mobs rioted through Damascus, smashed windows
of the United States legation and engaged in bloody battle with Syrian
Communists. And in Beirut, Lebanon, . . . Arabs attacked offices of the
American owned Trans-Arabian Oil Co., and caused the American military attaché to set up machine guns to protect the legation."[32] Arabs did
not just veer out of control in the midst of hostilities, but their day-to-day
political life was seen as unstable and inscrutable. Common press descriptions of Arab politics included, "seething," "mysterious," "strange,"
"enigma[tic]," full of "intrigue" and "guile," "restless," and "feudalis-
tic."[33] Try as they might, Americans had a difficult time relating to Arabs,
because "A veil of the finest oriental gossamer . . . shrouds the whole understanding."[34] The contrasts to Israel were sometimes explicit and sometimes implicit, but common in government circles and the press. For
example in a State Department analysis on the Arab-Israeli conflict, the
authors noted, "the Israelis are highly literate, industrious, and relatively
free of the diseases which handicap other peoples of the area."[35]

Thus, while Jews were increasingly seen as religious brothers, Muslims were stigmatized and held at arm's length. The images of primitivism
had political implications. One State Department position paper observed
that "the general negative nature of Arab mentality" affected the political
future of the region.[36] And while Jews seemed enriched by their heritage,
many observers found little relation between modern Arabs and their ancestors: "How can one explain [Arab] architecture and achievements in
mathematics, war, medicine, and the humanities in terms of the apathy,
filth, disease, degradation, and laziness of their descendents?"[37] Further,
the description of Arabs as "unrealistic" carried feminine gender associations in Cold War rhetoric. Finally, in their popular image, Arabs were
merely the source of Western oil. For example, in a 1956 commencement
address, John Foster Dulles referred to "those four Middle Eastern coun-

tries" that stood between the United States and oil.[38] He was discussing the importance of oil for Western industry and military, and didn't bother to name the four countries in question.

It would be a mistake to end this brief survey of images of Muslims and Arabs by giving the impression that they were uniformly negative or even hostile. There were certainly examples in the public culture of respectful or sympathetic descriptions of Islam and its adherents.[39] This is especially true in an era when many Americans were fascinated by religion, even those faiths outside of their own experience. Cultural narratives are not always consistent. Nevertheless, what predominated in the public culture of the 1950s was an image of Muslims as different from most Americans.

THE JUDEO-CHRISTIAN HERITAGE, ISRAELIS, AND THE POLITICS OF JERUSALEM

The stigmatization of "outsiders," such as Muslims, helped cement the bonds of those who considered themselves heirs to Judeo-Christian civilization. Moreover, newfound fascination with Judaism and Jewish history reflected the conviction that the Judeo-Christian heritage was the cultural glue for postwar America. In particular, many new books and articles cited the qualities of Jews as unique. One critic, for example, wrote that "the ethnoreligious system of Judaism expresses the particular genius of a people." At the same time, the attention to Jews was predicated on their place within the Judeo-Christian heritage, and the legacy which great Jewish thinkers bequeathed to the modern world: "the wisdom which the Arabs had inherited from the Persians and through them from the Greeks, and ultimately came to Western Europe, and led to the Renaissance, was due in large part to a group of forgotten Jewish rabbis."[40] Although references to Jewish particularity or "genius" were not new, they stand out at a time of increased fascination with Jews and their religious heritage.

Popular books emphasized the continuity between Judaism and Christianity. Edmund Wilson's best-selling 1955 book on the newly discovered Dead Sea Scrolls was one example. The Scrolls raised the question of whether Jesus was a member of the Jewish apocalyptic Essene sect. Wilson argued that the Scrolls proved the continuity between Judaism and Christianity. It is doubtful that many Christians lost faith in the divine origin of their religion, because of Wilson's book or the controversy over the Scrolls. Nevertheless, the popularity of Wilson's account reflected a cultural fascination with religious subjects, and emphasized the idea of a general Judeo-Christian heritage. There were many other popular books about religion written during these years. The *New York Times Book Review* started a section called "In the Field of Religion" in response to the many new works. A number of books examined the history of Jews and Judaism, and emphasized the connections between ancient and modern Jews. For example, in *Red, Black, Blond and Olive*, Edmund Wilson begins his discussion of modern Israel with an examination of the biblical origins of Hebrew. He writes of "Jewish genius—the development of the moral consciousness, of man's relations with God."[41]

Despite their biblical connections, Israelis were seen as modern "European intellectuals and idealists" and coinheritors of the Judeo-Christian tradition. The Jewish state was animated by its religion, but most Israelis were pragmatic moderns rather than ultrareligious, and they were far from parochial. As one visiting journalist noted with approval, "one has the impression that religion here has less hold on the people than in any Catholic community in America." Another article describing the debate over whether "God" was to be in the Israeli proclamation of independence argued "Very clear was the fact that modern Israel bore little relation to the biblical Jewish theocracy."[42]

At the center of the modern State of Israel was the ancient capital of Jerusalem—a city in which many Americans had a special interest. John Foster Dulles, for example, observed that "the world religious community has claims in Jerusalem which take precedence over the political claims of any particular nation." For many, too, Jerusalem touched off a spirit of idealism that made them hope for peace in the "Holy Land." Adlai Stevenson wrote of such feelings in *Look* following a trip to the region in the summer of 1953. He recalled: "I thought . . . how much in common have the Arabs, Jews, and Christians who have shared the Sacred City for so long; how their common inspiration—faith in one God—sprang from these same rocky hills and deserts." (Stevenson's thoughts illustrate that cultural images were not monolithic; he emphasizes the religious brotherhood of "Arabs, Jews, and Christians.") Journalists were also in awe of the city; one reported, "the sweet, clear, dry, cool winds of Jerusalem were unction and balm, full of grace. And the hills: where does any land rise and fall more gloriously?"[43]

Many Americans felt that—as Christians—the Bible gave them a stake in the Holy City. Stevenson reflected that, writing: "There by the gate where Saul strode off toward Damascus, I wondered for a moment who speaks for Christianity in Jerusalem."[44] Similarly, in a 1953 television portrait of Jerusalem, Edward R. Murrow framed the story as one about a city made holy by Jesus' presence almost two thousand years before. And journalists frequently used biblical references to Jerusalem, thus emphasizing the connection between the biblical land and the territory disputed in the twentieth century. For example, stories refer to Jerusalem as the ancient capital of the Jews.[45] Articles often quoted from Psalm 137, "If I forget thee O Jerusalem, let my right hand forget her cunning."[46] The easy acceptance of the biblical paradigm strengthened the narrative of Judeo-Christian unity which connected Israelis and Americans. In Jerusalem, many Americans saw the Arab-Israeli dispute in microcosm, the tragedy of the conflict most dramatically illustrated in the division of the city. Indeed, numerous press accounts described the "divided Jerusalem" with its "two worlds."[47]

The question of sovereignty over Jerusalem was one of the most difficult disputes of the Arab-Israeli conflict. According to the United Nations partition plan of 1947 Jerusalem and its surrounding area was to be under international control. During the 1948–1949 fighting, Jewish forces took the western part of the city and Jordanian forces occupied the eastern and old city (that division remained until Israel occupied the entire city in the 1967 war). Officials such as Prime Minister David Ben-Gurion argued that Jerusalem was without question the capital of the Jewish state, saying, "Israel without Jerusalem is like Zionism without Zion." Mainstream American media usually accepted the Israeli view of the dispute, highlighting the Jews's initial willingness to accept internationalization and guarantees of access to holy places. In contrast, the press noted the Arabs' rejection of "compromise" and usually labeled territorial internationalization as "unworkable." In addition, some observers wrote of Arab aggression against the city. For instance, American Federation of Labor President William Green, described tough Israelis who had earned the right to the city: "[Jerusalem] had been sanctified by the heroic defense which was made against the Arab attacks."[48]

Control of Jerusalem was a sensitive issue for most Americans who felt some claim to the Holy City. But with the two occupying powers refusing to relinquish the city to international control, the United States failed to press the issue. When internationalization was raised anew in the United Nations in 1952, U.S. officials ducked out of the discussion. Undersecretary of State David Bruce told the American embassy in Israel that "no purpose would be served" to discuss the issue at that time.[49] The

American press tacitly supported the administration's position, and applied little pressure for resolution to the dispute.[50] Furthermore, among Americans in general there was not any groundswell of popular opposition to Jewish annexation of half of the city.[51]

For U.S. officials, there was certainly a political appeal to sidestepping a messy international confrontation in favor of a de facto calm. It is reasonable to assume that there were other factors contributing to American inaction. Moreover, for many Americans, newly conscious of their Judeo-Christian heritage, there must have been a sense of fulfillment to see the Jews reestablishing their biblical capital. Modern political circumstances did not just remind Americans of the religious places of their Sunday school lessons. They brought the Bible and its prophecies to life.

The connection that Christian leaders felt to the Jerusalem issue was even deeper and more complicated than that of most Americans. Moreover, opinions about Jerusalem varied among different groups of Christians, and were tied to attitudes regarding the creation of a Jewish state. Many fundamentalist church groups supported the Jewish claims to the city because they believed that the Jewish return to the Holy Land was the necessary prelude to the Second Coming. Many liberal Protestant groups, such as the American Christian Palestine Committee, supported Zionism and a Jewish Jerusalem with international control of the holy places.[52] But other liberal Protestants, such as the editors of the nondenominational weekly *Christian Century*, opposed Zionism and favored an international Jerusalem. Some of the anti-Zionist Protestant leaders based their views on a missionary background and work with Arab educational institutions or oil companies. Meanwhile, Catholics supported the internationalization of Jerusalem most strongly, believing that it would strengthen the Vatican's influence in the area. Thus, it is fair to say that most American Christians felt a connection to Jerusalem, but not all agreed who should hold sovereignty over the city. Nevertheless, while some Christian missionaries or publications might have remained anti-Zionist, what dominates in the mainstream public culture is the assumption that the political problems of Jerusalem and Zionism were religious issues; this perspective privileged the ties between Christians and Jews as members in the Judeo-Christian family.

JUDEO-CHRISTIANITY AND POPULAR FICTION

Paralleling the political debates over the status of Jerusalem, movies and books also reinforced the Judeo-Christian bond for many Americans by retelling Old and New Testament stories with embellished drama and romance. The spate of biblical novels and films from the 1950s are often dismissed by critics as shallow, literal, and preachy melodramas.[53] But the films and novels were popular, and they offer a fascinating portrait of ancient Jews who bear a close resemblance to modern Americans, Jews, and Israelis. The religious implications of this fiction were clear: they imbue the Bible stories with a new meaning for modern society. Some of the artists included introductions explaining the importance of the biblical stories in contemporary American life. Significantly, as the stories showed similarities between modern Americans and ancient Israelis, they "Christianized" the image of Jews. The fiction was also political, drawing parallels between ancient Judeo-Christian values and modern political values in the United States and the Middle East. In particular, the stories underscored the relevance of Israel's story to the regional Cold War contest.

The urge to recreate biblical stories reflects the increased popularity of American history and folk culture after World War II. Attendance at museums and historic sites rose dramatically after the war, and popular and political language became laced with references to the nation's "heritage," according to historian Michael Kammen. He cites Cold War anxiety as a possible explanation: Americans sought a "timelessness" that would offset the uncertainties of change and international threats.[54] In this atmosphere, the retelling of Bible stories familiar from one's youth would be comforting. The biblical fiction of the 1950s made the mythical literal, the ephemeral concrete; the popular works satisfied a thirst for the past and reinforced a sense of shared history. The inclusion of Jews in this shared heritage was ironic. Previously, the Christian image of Jews was dominated by negative views of their religion and unflattering social stereotypes. In the 1950s, that image was superceded by the idea that the Jews were the founders of Western monotheism. Moreover, the identification between the modern American audience and ancient Hebrews carried over to modern Jews and Israelis, because of the underlying message that modern Jews embodied ancient values.

The fundamental theme in the biblical fiction of the 1950s was the importance of monotheism in any meaningful moral system. Works which highlighted the story of monotheism included Frank Slaughter's novel *The Song of Ruth: A Love Story of the Old Testament* (1954), and such films as *Samson and Delilah* (1949), *The Ten Commandments* (1956), and *The Prodigal* (1955). The monotheistism of Jews gives them a special place in an ancient world of pagans. In *The Prodigal*, for example, adapted from the story told in Luke 15, Micah is threatened by pagan worshippers, but strengthened by his Judaism which is contrasted with immoral vapid idol worship. The faith of the pagans rests on materialism, physical pleasures, and dramatic spectacles—including human sacrifices. The contrast between paganism and monotheism here drew on Cold War assumptions about the differences between the Communist world and the West. The Judaism of *The Prodigal*, like Judeo-Christianity in the twentieth century, appeared to be based on true spirituality, while the pagans of the film—and the modern Soviets—reduced everything to a physical, materialist equation.

The reasons for the moral superiority of Judaism are not always explicit since few details of the religion are given. In *Samson and Delilah*, for example, the superiority of the religion rests on Samson's brute strength. The lack of specificity about the nature of Judaism invites Christian audiences to identify with the heroes. Monotheism is presented as a universal good, as the voice-over introduction by director Cecil B. de Mille illustrates: "Ever since the dawn of history, man has fought against fear and superstition." *The Ten Commandments* succeeds in weaving together the struggle for monotheism and the struggle of the Hebrews to free themselves from bondage; so that their exodus from Egypt is also a vindication of their faith in one God. Moreover, the triumph of political freedom, perceived to be a universal goal in 1950s America, affirms the moral superiority of monotheism. Anticipating many of the themes of the best-selling fiction during the 1950s, Howard Fast's 1947 novel *My Glorious Brothers* retells the Chanukah story as a parable of the universal quest for freedom. It too invites readers to find Cold War political lessons in the biblical-era struggles. The parallels between Fast's story of ancient Jews and modern Israel are clear. One review, for example, notes that "the Maccabees were winning and losing against incredible odds as the homemade army of Israel is doing today." The Jews of Fast's novel were successful in their struggle against their Syrian-Greek conquerors because they held to Jewish ideals and religious values, here depicted as equality and democracy.[55]

More than any other work, de Mille's *Ten Commandments* sets out to tell "the story of the birth of freedom" on a grand scale. De Mille intertwines the story of freedom and slavery with elements of morality, law, and spirituality, creating a narrative with contemporary resonances. Indeed, the filmmaker appears on screen at the beginning of the film to explain that the story is about whether man should be "ruled by God's law or by the whims of a dictator . . . [and] this same battle continues throughout the world today." Importantly, the liberation of the Hebrew slaves in this film is synonymous with freedom for all, not just for the Jews. As the multitude of slaves leaves Egypt, the narrator says, "A nation arose and freedom was born into the world."

Yet, in this fiction, monotheism seemed to be "universal" to the extent that it was Christianized. Thus, New Testament themes and language can be found in the stories from the Hebrew Bible. In *The Ten Commandments*, for example, the Hebrews await deliverance by "God's chosen one." The story of the messianic Moses turns out to have many parallels with the story of Jesus.[56] In addition, Moses describes his encounter with the burning bush using language from the Book of John: "and the Word was God. . . . He is not flesh but Spirit, the Light of Eternal Mind. . . . His light is in every man." In the 1960 film *The Story of Ruth*, the tale of the loyal Moabite differs from that in the Bible. Naomi is visited by an angel who tells her that from her daughter-in-law will issue a great people including a king [David] and one whom many will worship as the Messiah [Jesus]. Among other fiction, the novels of Sholem Asch are notable for their focus on the Christian aspects of the Judeo-Christian heritage. In Asch's work, Judaism evolved into the more inclusive, progressive Christianity. In *The Prophet*, for example, Isaiah is a foreshadow of Jesus and his teachings of love and redemption; one contemporary critic noted that "in spirit and time, Isaiah is midway between the Ten Commandments of Moses and the teachings of Christ."[57] In *Mary*, animal sacrifices are a metaphor for the primitive aspects of Judaism in contrast to the progressive teachings of Jesus. Asch presents an explicitly Christianized Judaism which invites his American readers to identify with the Jews. His link between Jewish and Christian understanding appealed to some critics—and we can assume to many readers; one review noted, Asch's "noble design of the Messiah as the bridge from Judaism to Christianity deserved respect."[58]

One particularly Christian element of the messianic tradition explored by Asch is the need for suffering to achieve spiritual redemption. The theme of martyrdom is strongest in *Mary* with its climatic crucifixion. But it is found in the other books as well. Asch's Moses doubts his own spiritual value, because he left suffering back in Egypt: "Only he who can suffer as they suffer, and in the midst of suffering remain strong in faith, can await redemption."[59] Asch's Jews are a chosen people, because of their mission to suffer throughout the ages. And the author finds the meaning of this suffering in the redemption of Christianity. Nevertheless, the strength that Jews derived from their faith in the face of their suffering led to their survival as a people. For Asch and other authors, that survival was manifest in the State of Israel.

Asch's emphasis on the chosen status of the Jews and the universality of moral codes made him the most popular writer who championed Judeo-Christian culture. In 1955, he told one interviewer that ever since a visit to Jerusalem, "I have never thought of Judaism and Christianity separately. For me it is one culture and one civilization, on which all our peace, our security, and our freedom are dependent." A Polish-born Jew, Asch faced charges of apostasy and rumors that he had converted to Catholicism, because of his outspoken Christian ideals. In an interview in the *New York Times Book Review*, he answered the charges by explaining, "My attitude towards Jesus was that I felt he was a part of us. . . . I consider myself to be a very good Jew. . . . But why should it be forbidden me to have the joy of creation from our rich spiritual heritage?" Asch's celebration of a joint culture was significant, because the popular author seemed to be speaking for many people. He published many novels and stories—both in Yiddish and English. The biblical series of five novels which he started in 1939 led one critic to call him "the world's greatest living Jewish author."[60] Throughout the series—*The Nazarene* (1939), *The Apostle* (1943), *Mary* (1949), *Moses* (1951), *The Prophet* (1955)— Asch focused on the continuity between the Hebrew and Christian Bibles.

In addition to celebrating the Jewish roots of Judeo-Christian monotheism, biblical fiction authors of the 1950s celebrated the spiritual heritage of Jews and their status as the "chosen people." The narrative of the "chosen people," common to both American and Jewish culture, posited the idea that Jews and Americans were kindred peoples. It also reinforced, for Americans, Israel's divine claim to its parcel of land in the Middle East. Importantly, the narrative of the chosen peoples was not just a religious idea. In the United States, it had long since been naturalized as part of the cultural and political foundation of the country. Starting in 1630 with John Winthrop's "A Model of Christian Charity," it was clear that the Puritans— who would have a prominent role in shaping American culture—believed that they were "a city upon a hill" and the new chosen people who had formed a covenant with God just as the ancient Jews had done.

The biblical fiction encouraged the identification of Americans with Jews and Israelis in another way. An important theme in the fiction was the extent to which Jews conformed to the dominant American gender roles of the 1950s. The characters filled the iconographic contours of non-Jewish, American male heroes, and the genre placed heavy emphasis on the physical prowess and battle skills of its heroes. The physically powerful, masculine Jewish heroes were drawn in sharp contrast to the non-Jewish men around them. For example, in *Samson and Delilah*, the effeminate Philistine governor appears at a hunt in an outfit with gold baubles, a neatly trimmed beard and mustache, and speaks with a British accent. Asch's Moses had a "powerful neck and . . . broad shoulders, and . . . arms like two hammers, [he] looked like a slave giant." Pharaoh is described in opposite terms: "His fleshy body fell into folds, rising and falling as he breathed." Similarly, Boaz, in *The Song of Ruth*, had a "magnificent body . . . [and] was a far more regal figure than the puny youth who had been elevated to kingship." Victor Mature's Samson and Charlton Heston's Moses are similarly muscular, traditionally masculine specimens.[61] The masculinization of the Jewish heroes challenged the stereotypes about Jewish men and created a closer identification between Americans and Israelis.

The biblical stories often include a subplot of a steadfast Jewish man tempted and hence threatened by the wiles of a beautiful, usually pagan, woman. This scenario, is at the center of *The Prodigal* and *The Ten Commandments*. The Jewish men seem powerless to resist the attractions of the pagan women at first. The connection between evil and paganism is made explicit by the sexual threat posed to the hero. For example, in *The Prodigal*, the priestess and female servants of the goddess turn out to be prostitutes, while the narrator warns the audience that these gods are "of the flesh, not of the spirit." In this film, as well as in *The Song of Ruth* and *The Ten Commandments*, pagan rites are sexualized with worshippers reaching symbolic orgasm at the height of religious devotion. Thus, idolatry equals sex and sin, and is the antithesis of Jewish identity. For example, in harvest festivals, Slaughter's Jews dance in "joyful abandon with nothing of sensuality about it."[62] Similarly, the Jewish male heroes become less sexual as they triumph over pagan temptations. In *The Ten Commandments*, once Moses is exiled from Egypt, his costumes slowly cover more and more of his body, and his hair and beard grow. The desexualization of Moses, like that of Asch's characters, echoes the qualities of Jesus and, thus, reinforces the image of a Christianized Judaism.

The dangers of sexuality and the virtues of chastity are also depicted in relationships between Jewish men and women. In *Samson and Delilah* and *The Prodigal*, the heroes return to plain, but steadfast Jewish women. In *The Ten Commandments*, Moses marries Sephra (a pious, monotheist, although not a Jew), but all of the scenes between them are chaste. Even the adulterous relationship between David and Bathsheba is mitigated by the love the two feel for each other, and their repentance for having broken the law. The pious Jewish women are also mothers or mother figures. The inviolable maternal icon is the corollary to the iconographically masculine hero and the sexual temptress. Jews—dominating this triangle—are the characters with whom the audience identifies.

In addition to their physical attributes and ability to withstand temptations, the Jews of biblical films demonstrate masculinity through spiritual strength, a strength with which many Americans identified. The Judeo-Christian heritage was for many a source of strength in the face of "godless" Communism and Soviet materialism. *The Ten Commandments* links the struggle for freedom by the Hebrews and the American struggle against the "slave system" of Communism. Asch describes Egypt as having a "totalitarian system" and de Mille's pharaoh seems to have a lot in common with Soviet revisionist historians when he commands that the name of Moses "be stricken" from the monuments and histories of Egypt.

The dialectic of freedom and slavery was a powerful symbol during the Cold War, since the terms overlapped with modern political parlance. The Jews represented freedom and were perceived to be a part of the West, "the free world." The strength of the Jews and their ability to fight becomes an important test of their capacity to be "free men." Sholem Asch asks of the Jews in *Moses*, "Would the Israelites acquit themselves like free men and stand up to the enemy without waiting to be rescued?" Freedom and the harsh conditions of the desert soon transform the former Jewish slaves: "Their limbs were as of molten steel, their bodies molded by storm, their faces brown, like polished bronze: their thick-curled locks and beards had been combed by the iron combs of the desert wind."[63] Masculine individualism in conquering the wilderness is, of course, a familiar theme in American culture.

One of the real-life "tough Jews" of the American imagination in the 1950s was Prime Minister David Ben-Gurion. U.S. officials observed that Ben-Gurion resembled biblical figures (in his own imagination as well as in the minds of others). American Chargé d'Affaires in Tel Aviv Richard Ford said Ben-Gurion was a "profound student of Old Testament miracles, [who] seemed [to] enjoy being bracketed with Joshua."[64] Often dubbed a prophet and patriarch, Ben-Gurion was for the American press a living embodiment of biblical history who resembled forebearers such as "Moses and Ezra . . . his own immediate ancestors in the cycle of Jewish wandering and homecoming." The prime minister's image was built upon his political position and power as "the lawgiver" as well as upon his legendary knowledge of the Bible. Ben-Gurion frequently referred to biblical history in his speeches, including those for American audiences. For example, before the National Press Club in Washington in 1951, he discussed the four-thousand-year-old history of Israel whose great events "live on in the memory of the Jewish people and have also become the heritage of the Christian world."[65] As prime minister of the country, Ben-Gurion created the impression that the Bible was alive and well in modern Israel, even in the world of secular politics.

Another image which strengthened the American identification with Israelis fighting for independence was that of "citizen-soldiers"—also prevalent in the narratives of the American Revolution. For example, in the *Song of Ruth*, readers learn of citizen-soldiers ready to defend their country: "every man in Judah who could wield a spear was busy training himself." The press also promoted the image of citizen-soldiers. For example, one review of a book about Israeli pioneers quotes from the Book of Nehemiah, "every one with one of his hands in the work, and with the other hand held a weapon."[66]

Finally, biblical fiction emphasizes another parallel between the two cultures—adherence to the rule of law. As Boaz in *The Song of Ruth* explains, "to an Israelite the Law is above everything else . . . the Law is from God."[67] In *David and Bathsheba*, David is punished when he is tempted to think that he was above the law. Law, the fiction preaches, is essential to Jews, because with it they are rational human beings with free will. As the original people of the Bible, the Jews are defined by this struggle to uphold the law and, thereby, achieve freedom.

JUDEO-CHRISTIANITY, AMERICAN POLITICS, AND MODERN ISRAEL

The pieties of popular fiction and the views of the mainstream press contributed to a political atmosphere celebrating religion. National politicians similarly contributed by professing their faith. Harry Truman readily admitted that religion affected his outlook and decisions. His readiness to support the creation of Israel on moral grounds was also based on his religious convictions. The president later recalled that "I've always done considerable reading in the Bible, I'd read it at least twice before I went to school." Arguing that Truman treated the book seriously, Michael J. Cohen writes in *Truman and Israel*: "For Truman the Bible was neither legend nor myth but literally the story of everyday, God-fearing people." A Baptist who attended church regularly before he was president, Truman believed that the United States had a religious mission since the "fundamental basis of American law was given to Moses on Mount Sinai."[68] Moreover, he believed in the brotherhood and equality of all religions. He said at a meeting of the National Conference of Christians and Jews that all faiths in the United States had as a "common heritage the great thoughts of the Hebrew prophets."[69] The president's White House assistant Clark Clifford understood Truman's views. In a White House-State Department meeting on whether the United States should recognize Israel, Clifford argued for recognition with the biblical quotation, "Behold, I have given up the land before you; go in and take possession of the land which the Lord hath sworn unto your fathers, to Abraham, to Isaac, and to Jacob" (Deut. 1:8). Truman, indeed, believed that the Bible dictated that Jews would have their own land in Palestine.[70]

Eisenhower and Dulles set out to separate their foreign policy from such "irrational" factors and to forge a policy based on "realistic," "rational" interests, but they were nevertheless strongly affected by the contemporary religious currents in American society. Eisenhower recognized the political and social value of religion when he confessed to the very popular Billy Graham in 1952 that his religious worship had lapsed during his military career and "Americans won't support anyone who's not a member of a church." Candidate Eisenhower did make some well-publicized appearances at religious services during the campaign and often spoke of the importance of religion in his speeches. He joined a church in 1953, kept a Bible from Graham on his bedside table for the eight years he was in office, his cabinet voted to open all its meetings with a prayer, and he told Graham, "I believe one reason I was elected president was to lead America in a religious revival."[71]

Eisenhower, whom the Republican National Committee called "the spiritual leader of our times," had a powerful effect on the importance of religion in contemporary American culture.[72] He stressed that all religions should be valued equally, because "this country is a spiritual organism." He found what he called the "spiritual foundation" of the United States in the struggle of the Revolution and words of the Declaration of Independence. "All of us should become constantly more aware of our dependence upon the Almighty for guidance in the vast affairs of humanity," he stated in 1958.[73]

Eisenhower's religious ideas affected his Cold War views. He argued on a 1959 trip to the Middle East that there was a "need for continuing strong adherence by all of us in the free world to spiritual values, . . . support for the dignity of man and his search for a better life without falling subject to Communist political domination." One year earlier, he said at the American Jewish Tercentenary Dinner that all Americans were united in the "noble concept[s] of our common Judeo-Christian civilization": "faith in human dignity" and the "ideal of peace." Eisenhower argued that Jews had a particular spiritual legacy for America, who "through the Old Testament, g[a]ve new dimensions of meaning to the concepts of freedom and justice, mercy and righteousness, kindness and understanding." And, as Jews shared a Judeo-Christian heritage with their brethren, they were engaged in a common spiritual and political struggle: "In this faith in human dignity is the major difference between our own concept of life and that of enemies of freedom. . . . Today the Communist conspiracy is the principal influence that derides the truth of human worth." Eisenhower concluded the speech (which had mainly been on foreign affairs) with the assertion that America was fulfilling biblical prophecy: "Yes, my friends, we know, with the prophet Isaiah, that the work of righteousness shall be peace." Eisenhower's spiritual view of politics, also affected his opinion of Israel. The president, for example, observed that "The peoples of Israel, like those of the United States are imbued with a religious faith and a sense of moral values."[74]

Since in Eisenhower's view the Judeo-Christian heritage defined Western civilization, Muslims were clearly outsiders to the United States. Speaking before an audience of Muslims in Washington, he observed that Islamic culture, although not part of the spiritual foundation of civilization, *added* "some of its most important tools and achievements." Eisenhower also failed to acknowledge that there were Muslim Americans: "thousands of Americans, both private individuals and government officials, live and work—and grow in understanding—among the peoples of Islam . . . and many from Muslim lands are in our country too."[75] Although he acknowledged the presence of Muslims in the United States, they appear apart from the rest of the country, excluded from the "our" of which he speaks.

Eisenhower's Secretary of State, John Foster Dulles, always held strong beliefs about the importance of spiritual leadership in American foreign policy. Samuel Flagg Bemis describes Dulles as "the only religious leader lay or clerical, ever to become Secretary of State."[76] Dulles prided himself on his adherence to moral law in diplomacy.[77] Like Eisenhower, Dulles believed that the founders of the United States "were deeply religious people" who created a country that sought to do God's will on Earth and he argued the nation "existed not merely for itself, but for mankind." Speaking at the 150th anniversary of the Presbyterian church at which his father preached, Dulles reiterated his conviction that Americans were a chosen people, "heirs to a noble heritage." He believed that this religious foundation differentiated the United States from the "materialistic" Soviet

Union where political and social practices had been separated from spiritual content. He assured Americans that "your President, your Cabinet, your Congress recognize the priority of spiritual forces."[78] Since Dulles described the Cold War as a contest between the forces of good and evil, he dismissed as "immoral" those countries that attempted to remain neutral.[79] Dulles spoke of the importance of spirituality in general, although he likened the American mission to the Christian one: "Jesus told the disciples to go out into all the world and to preach the gospel to all the nations. Any nation which bases its institutions on Christian principles cannot but be a dynamic nation." Nevertheless, he argued that the Judeo-Christian heritage as a *whole* was valuable: "Our American history, like Hebrew history, is also rich in the story of men who through faith, wrought mightily."

Dulles believed that there was a close relationship between Christianity and Judaism, explaining that his own (Christian) background had given him an understanding of Judaism and therefore special insight into matters affecting Israel.[80] Dulles also found insight into modern politics in his study of the Bible. He told one of his assistant secretaries of state in early 1957 that the Old Testament revealed that the ancient Middle East had the same political problems as in the twentieth century, asking how "he could solve problems which Moses and Joshua with Divine guidance could not solve."[81] Thus, the hard-nosed Cold Warrior believed that spiritual factors affected strategic considerations. After his tour of the Middle East in 1953, he gave three reasons for the importance of the area, the first two were strategic realities and oil. But, the third, he said was the "Most important of all, the Near East is the source of three great religions—the Jewish, the Christian, and the Moslem. . . . Surely we cannot ignore the fate of the peoples who have first perceived and then passed on to us the great spiritual truths from which our own society derives its inner strength."[82] From an Israeli perspective, Dulles's religious convictions held open the possibility of influencing the diplomat who came into office professing that the United States should not be biased in favor of either side in the Arab-Israeli conflict. Israeli ambassador Abba Eban saw in the secretary "a curious strain of Protestant mysticism which led him to give the Israel question a larger importance than its geopolitical weight would indicate."[83]

Other Americans, such as Reinhold Niebuhr, were also guided by their religious beliefs when they looked at modern politics in the Middle East. As an influential theologian and philosopher, Niebuhr articulated a spiritual justification for the Cold War. Moreover, his stress on the unity of Judeo-Christian culture inspired many: "At his best," wrote Sidney Hook: "Niebuhr writes with the intensity of a Hebrew prophet, and a prophetic Judaism or Christianity is essentially a moral rather than a theological attitude toward life."[84] When he learned of the Holocaust, Niebuhr became a Zionist. He argued that Jews must have their own country, in part, because assimilation was a form of death, and Jews had the moral right to survive as a people. In late 1942, he was one of the founders of the Christian Council on Palestine, and continued to be active in the successor organization, the American Christian Palestine Committee formed in 1946. He used his political influence in Washington testifying on behalf of Zionists before the Anglo-American Committee of Inquiry in 1946. A decade later, Niebuhr argued that the United States should resupply Israel during the Sinai war. He supported Israel's refusal to evacuate the Sinai after the war, and criticized the "anti-Israel posture of the United Nations."[85]

The prominence of Reinhold Niebuhr in the culture of the 1950s reveals much about how the religious revival affected foreign policy narratives. Niebuhr was both a symbol of the 1950s and a spokesman for an era that celebrated religion and normalized the Judeo-Christian union. Yet, the postwar interest in religion did not necessarily mean a resurgence in religious beliefs, nor was it incompatible with the secularist strain in American history. Historian Paul Carter notes that many Americans subscribed to what Niebuhr said without believing in his theology.[86]

CONCLUSION

Given its pervasiveness, the 1950s religious revival with assertions of Judeo-Christian unity could not but affect how Americans viewed the State of Israel. Images of Jews and Israel changed markedly in these years and had important political consequences. The Jewish state of the popular and political imagination was one of modern day prophets and simple folk like those who filled the pages of Bible stories. Americans treated the political problems of the Middle East differently from those in other parts of the world because of the religious significance of the "Holy Land." A man such as John Foster Dulles, who combined views of hard-nosed "realpolitik" with religious piety, acknowledged the special status of the Middle East by virtue of the religions based there. While Dulles and others paid lip service to the region being the home of three great religions, most of the indications in American public culture stressed that Christianity was the culmination of this religious heritage. Judaism, part of the "Judeo-Christian civilization" benefited from this association while Islam remained a religion and culture apart.

Thus, the Cold War cultural narrative of religious revival and Judeo-Christian unity influenced attitudes toward Israel. Eisenhower and Dulles were contributors to this narrative, championing the importance of spiritual values in the Cold War. Israel came to have a clear place in this typology, not just in the popular culture but in the halls of power. Numerous policymakers, critics, and popular writers and artists increasingly saw Israelis as religious brothers, sharing an understanding of moral values and, subsequently, political values in a Cold War world.

5

Acceptance and Assimilation

Jews in 1950s American Culture and Politics

At a meeting of the National Security Council in 1958, Secretary of State John Foster Dulles blamed Jews for the Eisenhower administration's foreign policy difficulties in the Middle East. He was worried about the excessive private American monies that flowed into Israel while few donations went to the Arab countries. To diplomat George Allen's suggestion that the United States end tax exemptions for American contributions in support of Israel, Dulles answered that there was no possibility of it passing Congress. He complained that "the State of Israel was in fact the darling of Jewry throughout the world, and world Jewry was a formidable force indeed." He added that even the Soviet Union, long split from the Jewish state, would not challenge it in any substantive way.[1] Dulles was clearly resentful of what he perceived to be the illegitimate power of "world Jewry."

This episode reveals much regarding the contradictory cultural narratives about Jews in postwar America and the changing perception of Jews in American society. On the one hand, there was a growing acceptance of Jews in American society in the mid- to late-1950s, in politics and culture. On the other hand, some, such as Dulles, were critical of the power of American Jews that they deemed to be illegitimate. Yet, Dulles' resentment doesn't seem to be in keeping with his invocation of the Judeo-Christian values and identity described in the previous chapter. In the following chapter, we will look at how a set of seemingly contradictory cultural narratives not only coexisted with this religious narrative, but also reinforced it. We will shift our focus away from the Judeo-Christian paradigm to look at how Jews were increasingly viewed as similar to other Americans in secular affairs and how they gained more domestic political power in the 1950s. Attention to Jews as a politically powerful interest group fueled resentment among some policymakers such as Dulles, while it was counterbalanced by the growing perception in the public culture that Jews were all-American. Here, as in other examples, superficially contradictory narratives can coexist as well as strengthen each other. Nevertheless, it would be a mistake to assume that there is a perfect balance that smoothes out the rough edges of contradiction. As we look at the political successes of American Jews with respect to Israel, the very real limitations on the group's growing political power will also be examined. In particular, this chapter will look at the U.S. positions on the contentious issues of immigration to Israel, cross-border strife, and arms shipments to Israel, and to what extent they seemed to be affected by the changing images of Jews and Israel.

THE AMERICAN JEWISH SUCCESS STORY IN POPULAR FICTION

The cultural narrative of the 1950s that depicted Jews as just like their fellow Americans was, in some ways, a continuation of the universalist narrative of the immediate postwar years. In the press, in politics, in fiction, Jews were seen to be similar to their fellow citizens in behavior, outlook, and values. Yet, in this period of declining antisemitism and growing assimilation for American Jews, there was a difference from the earlier, universalist ideals. Jews were very much like Americans, but their particular identity was acknowledged not erased. Thus, this revised view of Jews invoked a Cold War discourse which emphasized that diverse peoples throughout the world could all adopt similar values and build partnerships in a dangerous world.

   The struggles of assimilation were vividly played out in the popular fiction of the 1950s. One of the best known examples of twentieth-century Jewish American literature was Philip Roth's 1959 *Goodbye, Columbus*. Roth's successful, middle-class Jews were a touchstone in the image of American Jews. Roth's characters entered the public culture as assimilated Jews who struggled with the meaning of their own identity in the modern United States.[2] Yet, Roth's stories had been preceded by a number of literary attempts to grapple with the place of Jews in modern American life. In some of the popular fiction of the mid-1950s, Jewish characters moved beyond stereotypical victims and symbols of the biblical past. They were full-fledged actors in contemporary social dramas who were distinctive from other Americans, but still shared much in values, goals, and loyalty. Here, they were accepted as full members of the nation as long as their American identity was dominant over their Jewish identity. This fiction drew on Cold War values to depict an American way of life in which a modified pluralism was celebrated. The issue of conflicting loyalties was a very real dilemma in the 1950s. Socially, the dominant culture stressed homogeneity and conformity. Politically, Americans were supposed to demonstrate unquestioned loyalty in a world of subversives and fifth columns.

The fiction about American Jews answered these dilemmas in a number of ways. First, the central theme of this fiction was the reenactment of the story of the American Dream, from poor immigrant to successful, assimilated citizen. At the center of this drama, Jews stood for all Americans. Second, this fiction explored the possible costs on the road to that dream—a loss of morality, roots, family values, and a sense of identity—and provided solutions to avert these consequences. Third, it sanctioned small cultural differences which did not challenge the status quo. Fourth, like earlier fiction about Jews and Israelis, in these stories, masculinity and protection of the patriarchal line were demonstrations of affinity between Americans and Jews. Finally, the fiction depicted lingering examples of antisemitism. But unlike the films and books of the mid-1940s, the Jews were not helpless victims who were defined by discrimination. They were upright citizens who sometimes faced anachronistic thinking.

Importantly, many of the popular stories of American Jews in this period were penned by Jewish writers who were concerned with assimilation, separatism, and success in modern America. For many Jewish writers, these cultural ideologies dominated their horizons, and they wrote about themselves fitting into the American landscape. Yet, Jewish writers and artists were not just telling Jewish stories. Through their now prominent roles in American film and letters, Jewish writers and artists helped to reinvent postwar American cultural ideology, and did so in a way that shaped their own identity in the country. Thus, the Jewish characters in this fiction redefined the iconographic modern American hero to include their particular ethnic story.

These popular works of fiction drew on a long-standing cultural ideology that America was the promised land, imbued with a sense of mission, and in which anyone could achieve Horatio Alger success. The material and social achievements of these characters makes them archetypal immigrants and exemplars of the American success story. By mid-century, Jews indeed, seemed to have fulfilled the mythical dream of success. The majority of American Jews—ranging from 75 percent to 96 percent in more than a dozen sample communities across the United

States—worked in nonmanual professions. In contrast, just 38 percent of the American population as a whole worked in nonmanual positions. And, a declining proportion of Jews worked in lower level white-collar jobs, such as clerks and salesmen. Further, Jews by midcentury were better educated than their non-Jewish counterparts with a higher percentage of Jews going to college than non-Jews. Those Jews who did go to college, usually had incomes that exceeded noncollege graduates, as well as non-Jewish graduates.[3] Thus, by many social and economic measures, Jews came to be embraced as "insiders" in American culture.

Popular fiction of the period reflected these trends of Jewish achievement. Novels and films contained a rich collection of Jewish Horatio Algers rising from new immigrants to middle-class businessmen and professionals. The stories which told about the climb up the American ladder of success usually began with the ghetto origins of the immigrant Jews. The Jewish authors have a nostalgia for the ethnic flavor and religious culture of the ghetto that betrays their contradictory feelings about assimilation. Jews were not the only ones with this nostalgia. As discussed in chapter four, in the postwar United States, many Americans, felt a yearning for their "heritage."

In many ways, the fiction celebrates the world of the immigrants. For example, although Sholem Asch's character of Isaac Grossman in *A Passage in the Night* grew up in a cramped tenement apartment, it was transformed on Fridays "by the magic of his mother's Sabbath."[4] The "old neighborhood" in other novels such as Gerald Green's *The Last Angry Man*, Jerome Weidman's *The Enemy Camp*, Saul Bellow's *The Adventures of Augie March*, and Herman Wouk's *Marjorie Morningstar* are peopled by colorful characters, especially parochial, older relatives. The young title character of Wouk's novel feels both affection and distance from the old world relatives, as she describes her uncle: "Samson-Aaron had always been the soul, the visible symbol, of that group of vague people called The Family. . . . They had peculiar Yiddish names—Aunt Shosha, Aunt Dvosha, Uncle Shmulka, Uncle Avromka."[5] In addition to embodying the image of a pure ethnic past, these older relatives are the ones who encourage their grandchildren, nieces, and nephews to reach for their dream, to climb the American ladder to success.

These examples of popular fiction also depicted the ghetto as a place to escape. The immigrants, such as the protagonists in *The Enemy Camp* and *A Passage in the Night*, who were able to overcome the ghetto's disadvantages and leave its confines were heroic embodiments of the Horatio Alger story. Asch's main character moves from rags to riches with just twenty-seven dollars which he propels into a real estate empire, but he firmly believes that all could achieve what he did, "This is America. Everyone has the right to get ahead." Critics and others endorsed these sentiments about the possibility of mobility for all in the postwar United States, even as they noted the particular success of the Jews. One review, for example, called the Jewish Lower East Side, "one of the most familiar starting points of the great American success story." Jews, thus, embody *the* American story.[6] For the characters and the authors who created them, the story of economic climbing becomes intertwined with ethnic identity. Lower class automatically signals "more" ethnic.[7]

The most notable of the 1950s intergenerational immigrant stories was *Marjorie Morningstar*, a book that symbolized the dramatic changes in the images of American Jews. Wouk's book was a bestseller from September 1955 to March 1956, and was the biggest seller of all fiction books in 1955.[8] Herman Wouk and a drawing of his character Marjorie even made it to the cover of *Time* magazine in November 1955. Wouk's story of coming of age, ascendance to the middle class, and valuing one's heritage told Jews that they were just like other Americans. Young Jewish—and non-Jewish—girls modeled themselves on Wouk's heroine.[9] One review described the appeal of the story to non-Jews as a "triumph that this intensely particular background is integral to the American scene." Marjorie was hailed as "a classic American heroine" and "a typical American girl."[10] Such praise summed up the novel's impact: redefining Jews as typical Americans, as cultural insiders. The advertisements for the book apparently took their cue from the reviews: they highlighted the coming of age aspect of the story and the dilemmas of an American teenager, "It's the *American* story that everyone is talking about" gushed one ad from early 1956. "There's a little of Marjorie in *every* American girl," it continued. Yet, neither the reviews nor the ads omitted the Jewish content of the novel, and sometimes found a redeeming social value in the story. One pious ad quoted a *New York Daily News* editorial: "In this city where millions of Jews and Gentiles live and work together, it seems to us that *Marjorie Morningstar* can contribute more to interracial sympathy and understanding than any number of sociological studies."[11]

One reason that Wouk's novel seemed to resonate so powerfully with many Americans in this period of the Cold War was that while it celebrated the ideal of success and a certain amount of assimilation, it was a cautionary tale against leaving behind too much of one's history for the temptations of materialism. One of the frequent criticisms made of the Soviets and the Communist system was their emphasis on materialism

and economic determinism. Wouk shows the danger of chasing after economic success to the exclusion of other values. Marjorie wants to assimilate and succeed in modern American society and, yet, she clings to her
ethnic origins, as do most of the young Jewish characters in these novels.
As Richard Amsterdam observes in *Remember Me to God*, "Richard's
family, and all the Jewish families he knew, accepted as a matter of course
their nearness to immigrant origin."[12]

Some of the characters seem to succeed in distancing themselves
from their immigrant origins, but in so doing, they pay a heavy price. For
example, when Sholem Asch's Isaac Grossman is nearing death, he has a
spiritual crisis because he ran away from his Judaism. Moreover, he believes that he has sinned because he built his own success on money that
he found in a wallet and failed to return to the owner. His efforts to make
restitution to the heirs of the man are met with scorn by his secular son
who worries that his "kike" father will disgrace the family. The elder
Grossman, although living a nonobservant life, regrets that his son has
left Judaism behind, and pathetically affirms, "he knew he would be prepared to die rather than deny his Jewishness."[13] The son turns aside his
father's dilemmas and has him placed in a mental institution for wanting
to reclaim his Jewish morality.

Other fathers in these novels, such as in *Marjorie Morningstar* and
Remember Me to God, also find themselves dismayed by their children's
move away from Judaism. In part, they blame their own ambition to assimilate and achieve financial success. Kaufmann's Adam Amsterdam, for
example, is uncomfortable with his choice to leave behind orthodoxy and
become a Reform Jew. In contrast, his Harvard son who is enamoured
with the lives of elite, New England Protestants finds the Orthodox service "so vulgar and low class." The senior Amsterdam tries to convince
his son that there is value in the family heritage: "I say the same prayers
that my father did, [and] I feel a little bit of my father's exact enjoyment
living in me."[14]

The Jews of popular fiction also proved themselves to be insiders in
American culture through their image as sage fathers. Conforming to a
gendered understanding of family roles and affirming their role as pro-
genitors, Jews were depicted as strong fathers in their own right and in-
heritors of a patrilineal bond that they shared with the next generation.
In *A Passage in the Night* and *Remember Me to God*, two male rabbis fill
the role of wise counselors to their youthful, rebellious charges. These
rabbis make it clear that the young men's identity is based on the heritage
that they received from their own fathers. The ideal father is not only

wise, but he wants to protect his family. He demonstrates the essential qualities of masculinity: maturity and responsibility.

While fathers such as Adam Amsterdam protect their families and preserve their religious heritage, they adapt to modern America by changing the nature of their Judaism. The Amsterdams' change of denomination was common in the postwar United States. Many of the wealthiest Jews were Reform, ancestors of the German wave of immigrants from the mid-nineteenth century. Increasingly the children of east European immigrants from the turn of the century abandoned Orthodoxy as part of their assimilation into mainstream society. The greatest number of new congregations in the postwar period were Conservative, representing what many saw as a compromise between Reform and Orthodox. Certainly, the denominational changes did not mean that Jews deserted organized religion. Moreover, with the general revival of civic religion, Jews found that they had to demonstrate their religious values in order to be accepted in the mainstream. The mainstream press responded not only to the interest in religion in general, but also to Jews in particular by printing a number of explanatory articles about Judaism, its traditions and rituals. The articles stressed that Jews were just another group in the American family.[15]

Yet, even while some Jews affirmed their civic religion and new-found Reformed values under the American umbrella, many worried that Jews were in danger of losing their particular identity entirely. This possibility loomed largest in the middle-class enclaves of Cold War America, the suburbs. Social commentators wrote about what had become the clichéd suburbanization of Jews in the 1950s. Nathan Glazer, like the fictional Adam Amsterdam, worried that the assimilationist pull of middle-class communities might overwhelm particular identity: "[the suburbs] simultaneously strengthened Judaism and weakened Jewishness."[16] Most of all, the suburbs posed a symbiotic danger to traditional spiritual values. To Glazer and other observers, assimilation and material comforts could turn into shallowness and mere social climbing. One effort to counteract the loss of Jewishness was the formation of "federations" established in almost every sizable Jewish community throughout the country. These organizations became the center of Jewish life for the less religious, assimilated Jews. Many suburban communities combined much of their secular and religious activities in "synagogue-centers" which were religious houses along with community centers organizing educational, social, and cultural programs. A number of rabbis found themselves dismayed by a Jewish identity that seemed less and less dependent on a spiritually enriched religious life. Moreover, they distrusted the motives of some of their congregants who "wanted an easy, relaxed kind of country club atmosphere, rather than a house of worship with a positive philosophy for Jewish life."[17]

Following gendered assumptions about social roles in an era when "Momism" was perceived as a real threat to the future of America's children, the male authors writing of Jewish American life tended to indict their female characters for leading Jews away from their heritage. Kaufman, Wouk, and Asch draw a sharp distinction between the fathers who try to preserve the religious heritage for their children and the mothers whose vain social grasping threatens the heart of Jewish identity. In contrast to the fathers who seek to blend ethnic identity and success in the American mainstream, the brash, stereotyped Jewish mothers appear ready to throw over thousands of years of culture for quick social acceptance. Thus, the male heroes represent stable moral values and the ideals of the American socioeconomic system. A corollary assumption was that women were often ambitious, morally and physically weak, and manipulative. As argued in previous chapters, this gendered understanding of sexual roles pervaded contemporary images of Jews, and forged an identification between American and Israeli and Jewish male heroes. In addition, given the centrality of the family as a symbol of all that was good in Cold War America, it seems natural that the moral struggle within these novels is over the sanctity of the family.

Kaufman's and Asch's Jewish mothers have unrelenting ambition and are determined to see their children fit into the Gentile world. They have lost any feeling for Judaism, joining congregations for appearance's sake, although they do not participate in services or carry on traditions at home. Yet, while they seem to push away their religion and their ethnic identity, they are territorial. The mother in *Remember Me to God* is shocked to hear that her son plans to marry a Gentile. One review of the novel likened the characters' Jewish identity to "a familiar garment, shabby, despised even, but dear."[18] Wouk's materialistic Jewish mother has much in common with the other mothers, but she is more complex. She is determined to push her family up the social ladder, but she remains sincere in her Jewish beliefs.

The folly of Jews trying to escape completely from their heritage is also revealed in the self-hatred of some of the young Jews. Wouk's Marjorie who is embarrassed by her parents' background finds herself disgusted by the old neighborhood and its working-class life. While most of the characters rush headlong away from their history, they are also aware of the selfish downside of such a quest. Marjorie's boyfriend Noel (formerly Saul) explains his disdain for middle-class Jewish "Shirleys": "The mother of the next generation, all tricked out to appear gay and girlish and carefree, but with a terrible threatening dullness jutting through. . . . Behind her . . . would loom the mother. . . . Smug, self-righteousness, mixed with climbing eagerness." Marjorie, in turn, tells him of "Sidney" who tries to escape his Judaism by disdaining the middle-class ethic of success: he "wants to be a writer or a forest ranger or a composer or anything except what his father is, because he's ashamed of his father being a Jew . . . and he ends up in his father's business just the same."[19]

The life of Jerome Weidman's hero George Hurst is also shaped by the character's insecurity about his Jewish identity. He marries a wealthy Protestant woman and feels that he is forever an outsider in his marriage. The most extreme example of self-hatred is found in *Remember Me to God*. The young Richard Amsterdam comes to believe that the wealthy Protestants whom he meets at Harvard are superior in every way to Jews. He conflates class and ethnic identity, assuming that the Jewish lower-class world from which he came is uncivilized. He tries to emulate the manners and lifestyle of his "betters," even writing an antisemitic tract "How to Be a Gentleman" which explains how to disguise one's Jewishness and to put on airs of being upper class. He finally decides that he can't be both an American and a Jew and that what he really wants is to be a "plain human being," a Christian.[20]

Kaufman, Wouk, Weidman, Asch and other postwar Jews affirm that the young Jews who wrestle with the feeling of what one of them terms a "split personality" between Jewish and American identities should reaffirm their Jewish heritage, values, and identity and, at the same time, recommit to American society and the success ethic. In addition to fiction writers, many Jewish intellectuals probed the questions of Jewish identity, alienation, and assimilation.[21] The conclusion of most writers was that American Jews should recognize that their American and Jewish identities were really compatible, and if they were to give up religion and their Jewish heritage, they would be losing something valuable for which there is no replacement. For example, when Isaac Grossman of *A Passage in the Night* tries to find a solution to his moral crisis and atone for his deception of years earlier, it is a compassionate rabbi who uses Jewish law and common sense psychology to find a solution to the dilemma. The characters in *Remember Me to God* are also helped by the wisdom of a modern rabbi and a perceptive minister who explain that it is not a contradiction to be an American and a Jew.

Marjorie Morningstar learns these lessons as she discovers that the way to be at peace with herself is to reaffirm both her Jewish and her American identities. Although Wouk ridicules the excesses of materialistic climbing and Jewish mothers, he argues ultimately that Jewish-American, middle-class culture holds within it a rich tradition of spirituality and affection, and that there is no better alternative for Jews. In contrast to her friends, Marjorie settles down to what appears to be a happy life, because, we are led to believe, she follows the traditional American Dream *and* holds on to her Jewish identity. Her choices were shared by many middle-class Americans in the 1950s: she marries, moves to the suburbs, stops working outside the home, raises children, and becomes active in her congregation and community organizations. Wouk criticizes excessive conformity and rigidity, as do the other authors, but he endorses Marjorie's choices.

Saul Bellow's *The Adventures of Augie March* and Gerald Green's *The Last Angry Man* examine the dilemmas of assimilation and success which face American Jews, but they differ from some other popular novels of the era, because they question the American success ethic.[22] Saul Bellow's *Augie March* turns the middle-class values of the postwar period on their head as the aimless young title character grows up under the influence of the local crime boss and a money-hungry, deceitful older brother. Augie tries to fit into the mainstream, but is unable to conform to social expectations. Although Bellow's novel challenges social conventions, it, like many other popular novels about American Jews, is what one critic described as a "dialogue between alienation and accommodation."[23] *The Last Angry Man* also challenges 1950s middle-class conventions. The title character is sixty-eight year old Dr. Samuel Abelman who has been practicing in a multiethnic neighborhood of Brooklyn for forty years. The acerbic, though dedicated, practitioner, like Augie, is unable to conform to the model of middle-class success. His colleagues have all moved out to the suburbs to set up large practices, but the "ethnic" Abelman does not fit in the genteel world of the suburbs. An advertising producer who encounters the doctor decides to do a television series on "real" (read ethnic, working-class) people such as Abelman.

In part, Sam Abelman's anger stems from the antisemitism which he experienced in Romania as well as on the playgrounds of New York. But the reader soon learns that a more subtle form of antisemitism is alive in middle-class suburbs where residents recoil at the idea that ethnic working-class people might move into their neighborhood. As one Connecticut woman observes, "I don't mind the bright creative people. . . . But these cloak and suiters! . . . I'd dislike them even if they were Episcopalians and behaved the way they did." Characters in other novels, such as *Augie*

March and *Enemy Camp* also experience antisemitism. Kaufman's novel, full of caricatures, provides the most extreme examples of antisemitism, from assumptions that all Jews have long hook noses and funny black clothes to the judgment that after Jews "denied the Savior . . . [the] religion went stale . . . that's part of your punishment."[24]

Many of the 1950s Hollywood films about American Jews also address the issue of antisemitism, but it is an isolated, lingering problem which the Jewish characters overcome when the need arises. Moreover, for the few Jewish characters who were included in films before 1958 (when adaptions from Jewish novelists were put on film), their ethnic identity is minimized. The scant attention to ethnic identity was part of a continuing pattern in Hollywood begun in the 1930s when films began to de-semitize and de-Judaize images of Jews. Bland characterizations seemed even more prevalent in the 1950s when many filmmakers and artists did their best to avoid challenges to a homogeneous view of American life. The inattention to Jewish identity is reflected in the reviews of the films: some of the reviews do not even mention the Jewish subjects or antisemitism.[25] The Jews rise above the discrimination because they are just like everyone else, and because they are brave and dignified. Unlike the characters in the 1947 films about antisemitism, the Jews are not *defined* by their status as victims. For example, in the 1958 film *Home Before Dark*, an assistant professor at a liberal arts college moves to a small town where he experiences intolerance from many who are worried about "an influx" of Jews. Although he is ostracized by most, he is befriended by a non-Jewish woman who is also alienated from the townspeople. By the end of the film, they drive off to Boston together, and the man's Jewishness becomes a nonissue. The blandness of Hollywood's ethnic depictions extended to the film version of Herman Wouk's *Marjorie Morningstar* from which the ethnic flavor is removed to turn it into what the advertisements for the book had promised: an "all-American" story.[26]

In many films, lip service is paid to a character's Jewish identity, although there is nothing distinctive that sets him apart from other Americans. *Three Brave Men* tells the "basically true" story of a Jewish naval officer accused of being a security risk. The film centers on the patriotic man's attempt to clear his name and the triumph of the American system.[27] The image of the loyal Bernie Goldsmith in this film reflected the declining association in popular belief between Jews and radicalism and communism.[28] Goldsmith is loyal and brave throughout the ordeal. Further, the man's dignity through an experience that "separate[d] the men from the boys" affirmed his masculinity.

The protagonist of the film is also just like other Americans to the extent that he shares in the Judeo-Christian heritage. When the crisis breaks, the man's rabbi is sick, so the local Presbyterian minister offers to counsel the family; the pastor becomes the Jew's greatest defender. Similarly, in a meeting to plan defense strategy, the minister leads an ecumenical prayer of the assembled friends: "We're several different faiths here, but I'm sure none of us will deny the wisdom and mercy of God." Aside from the pastor's benign observation of difference, the only characters who mention the man's Jewish identity are anonymous crackpots who accuse him of disloyalty, because he is Jewish. Antisemitism is also depicted as a minority position in a film made soon after *Three Brave Men*. *I Accuse!* focuses on a Jew accused of disloyalty by his country's military establishment, who triumphs over the charges with great dignity.[29] While this retelling of the Alfred Dreyfus story in turn of the century France lingers on the problem of antisemitism, it sanitizes general complicity and scapegoats a few virulently antisemitic officers. As in the other films of the period, there is no outward manifestation that Dreyfus is Jewish, and he appears to be like most other French officers, only more dedicated and honorable than most.

In 1958, Irwin Shaw's and Norman Mailer's novels about World War II (*The Young Lions* and *The Naked and the Dead*) came to the screen. They, too, looked at the difficulties faced by Jewish soldiers in a sometimes hostile military establishment.[30] Yet the Hollywood versions of these novels were very different than the best-selling books that had appeared more than a decade before. The films played down the pervasiveness of antisemitism, focused on the abusive conduct of only a few characters, and made little distinction between Jews and other soldiers. The film version of *The Young Lions* also reduces the problem of prejudice to one character's simple confession, "I never knew a Jew before. . . . Someone jolts you and you have to look inside yourself." In addition, in Shaw's novel, the main Jewish character is the ultimate victim, shot and killed. Here, the Jew returns home to rebuild a life with his American Christian wife. A third film of 1958 looked back on World War II and featured a prominent Jewish character: *Me and the Colonel*. In this farce, the role of Jews as victims is also minimized. The character most threatened by Nazis is not the Jewish protagonist, but a Polish officer in disguise.

In most of the popular fiction about American Jews, the mission of World War II and the Israeli independence war are conflated. Yet, the ties between the Jewish characters, Zionism, and the State of Israel are not always clear, and are not discussed at great length. Israel forms an accepted backdrop to the lives of American Jews, but it is certainly not a dominant theme in any of these popular works. At times, Zionist work is merely a pleasant cultural activity for Jews. In *Marjorie Morningstar* and other books, the characters socialize through Zionist committees and parents look for mates for their children among the volunteers. Admiration for Zionists is accepted as the norm in the world of these Jews. Nevertheless, the depiction of Israel and its relationship to Diaspora Jews remains sketchy, at best. For example, in the 1955 film *Good Morning Miss Dove*, a young Jewish war refugee who arrives in the United States in the 1930s is teased by his classmates because he is different.[31] His teacher Miss Dove decides to educate her class about Jews, and so teaches a geography lesson about Palestine and arranges for the children to go to the new boy's house for a "traditional Jewish feast." Thus, she ignores the Arabs who are the majority in Palestine, and equates east European culture and identity with the culture of the Middle Eastern territory.

The enthusiasm for Zionism found in the characters of fictional works mirrored the views of many contemporary Americans. Not surprisingly, the drama of Israel's story appealed to many American Jews in particular. Years earlier, Horace Kallen had pointed to Zionism as the source of his own renewed Jewish identity: "Zionism became a replacement and reevaluation of Judaism which enabled me to respect it."[32] As Arthur Hertzberg and many others have argued, the relationship between American Jews and Israel even strengthened their national identity. For example, Hertzberg writes that in the years of the Marshall Plan and the rebuilding of Japan, "The creation of Israel was the equivalent task for American Jews." Moreover, as Israel moved to the center of Jewish community life and identity, Hertzberg concluded that "Support for Israel, and not learning Hebrew, was the 'spiritual content' of the relationship." "Support for Israel" covered many activities as well as sentiments, and eventually helped spawn a Jewish political and philanthropic network. Jewish philanthropy focused on Israel, and the new state stood as a symbol of Jewish power within the United States.[33]

For many American Jews, then, supporting Israel became one way of affirming their "Americaness." Historian Howard Sachar writing in 1957, celebrated the importance of the "doughty and courageous little state" to American Jews:

> [the Israeli spirit] was a spirit of complete, unselfconscious, thoroughly affirmative Jewishness. Without this spirit Jewish life in America with all its wealth, security, community democracy, and pragmatic realism, would hardly signify more than the dissipation of

an unprecedented opportunity for corporate self-expression. With this spirit, the American Jewish community bade fair to create a civilization of such enduring vitality as to pre-empt from medieval Spain the title of "Golden Age."[34]

For Sachar and other Jews, there was a symbiotic relationship between the United States and Israel. Even before 1948, many American Jews had envisioned the projected Jewish state as similar to the United States. Thus, observes Jonathan Sarna, American Jews could "defuse the sensitive issue of dual loyalty" and "boast of their own patriotic efforts to spread the American Dream outward."[35] Importantly, American Jews were not ready to give up their nationality. From 1948–1967, an average of 600–1,200 American Jews moved to Israel each year, but most of them returned to the United States.[36] Emigration numbers not withstanding, given the importance of Israel for American Jews, it is interesting how little the subject is mentioned in the popular fiction about the lives of American Jews. In the portraits of contemporary Jewish life, American identity was paramount and, perhaps, ties to a foreign country would have threatened that image. It was apparently safer to relegate stories about Israel to the symbolic realm of biblical fiction or heroic tales of Israel's "birth."

Although most American Jews agreed with the view put forward by historians and social observers that the story of Jews in the United States was "wholly unprecedented even in the millennial annals of the Jewish people," they could not escape from the pull of Israel, the place one critic described as the "ancestral home of the Jews." At the same time, Jewish writers, anxious to affirm their own national identity, put American Jews in a different category from European Jews who were described as "always in exile."[37] In *Remember Me to God*, the rabbi emphatically denies that he is not at home in the United States: "in spite of this grand concept of exile from the Promised Land, the fact is that no Jew is in exile until he's exiled from the Jews."[38] Kaufman and many other American Jews had long before accepted Horace Kallen's early-twentieth-century ideas about pluralism as an explanation for the "multiplicity of elements" that made up America.[39]

THE LIMITS OF ASSIMILATION

As discussed in chapter one, after World War II, Jews felt, and were seen as, increasingly part of the American pluralistic landscape. One piece of evidence of this acceptance and confidence was the widespread Jewish celebrations in 1954 of the three hundreth anniversary of their ancestors' arrival in New Amsterdam. Prominent politicians took the occasion to affirm a bond between Jews and other Americans. For example, Adlai Stevenson, addressing one of the gala celebrations, told his audience: "We are all descended from immigrants and from revolutionaries. And our strength is in large part due to the multiplicity of racial, religious, and cultural strands woven together into the fabric of American liberty."[40] Other indications that Jews felt at home in America and that non-Jewish Americans were reaching out to Jews were numerous articles detailing Jewish rituals and foods, often with the explicit goal of "help[ing] us to understand each other." Jewish leaders seemed to take it upon themselves—along with a receptive press—to educate all Americans about the tenets of Judaism. For example, the president of the Central Council of American Rabbis Philip Bernstein wrote an article for *Life* in 1950 called "What Jews Believe." Bernstein emphasizes the similarities between Jews and other Americans, asserting that the numerous, daily commandments which govern the lives of Orthodox Jews are really not that alien. They are best understood by Micah's summary "To do justly, to love mercy and to walk humbly before God." He also notes that liberal Jews accept that Jesus was a "loving teacher."[41]

In the fictional world created by American Jews, characters were increasingly at home in America, but the tension between their Jewish and American identities was a continuing theme. Unlike Sholem Asch, who professed that there was no conflict, most of the authors grappled with how these identities fit together. Even those characters who were assimilated were drawn to Jewish culture which cast "a spell that went back to the days of Abraham and Isaac."[42] Moreover, the religious and cultural accommodations made on the road to assimilation were seen as problematic. When the title character of Gerald Green's *Last Angry Man* dies, there are disagreements between the religious and the nonreligious at the funeral, with the religious asserting that they understand the man's *true* identity. In this and other novels, there is also a tension among the religious. The rise of Conservative and Reform adherents is at once ridiculed and celebrated. Reflecting their own ambivalence about assimilation, the authors imply that these denominations are less pure and, therefore, less Jewish than were the Orthodox.

Critics in the press also discussed the relationship between Jews and Christians, and among Jews, in a culture of assimilation. One liberal Congregationalist, for example, wrote in the Jewish magazine *Commentary* about the important connections between the Jewish and Christian traditions in a core of "ethical monotheism." Such "pro-assimilationist" views were countered by others who criticized the widespread emphasis on the

"Judeo-Christian" heritage as a threat to the unique tenets of Judaism. For example, British critic David Daiches said that American Jews were confused about whether to assimilate or cling to their religion; instead, they engaged in "a 'genteel' watering-down of Judaism to conform to U.S. cultural standards." He concluded that the American Jew further confused his assimilationist urge with Zionism: "He hopes that out of Zion will come forth good Rotarian Israelites and Hebrew-speaking hot-dog sellers."[43]

Others concurred that any effort to sweep away all differences between Judaism and Christianity with the Judeo-Christian broom represented a willful misunderstanding of Jewish distinctiveness.[44] Probably the most prevalent view embraced in the mainstream press was that Jews could assimilate to a certain extent, but should hold on to their Jewish identity and live "a Jewish life"—however they might define it.[45] Moreover, many assumed that Jews had a common identity, no matter how much they seemed to have assimilated.[46] Nevertheless, the assumption in the press and public culture was that Jews should be "modern" and embrace the political and cultural values of most other Americans. For example, one article in *Commentary* about the Hasidic Satmar community labeled its members "zealots," while the community as a whole was "characterized by an extremist intolerance toward opponents and causes."[47]

Early in the twentieth century, Horace Kallen had argued that modernization and assimilation would not be uncomplicated for American Jews: "Judaism is no longer identical with Jewishness and Jewishness is no longer identical with Judaism. . . . Judaism will have to be integrated with this secular, cultural form of community which is Jewishness if Judaism is to survive."[48] As demonstrated in this collection of popular fiction, many Jewish artists in the 1950s had not figured out how to reintegrate their Judaism and their Jewishness. Many were ambivalent about the whole enterprise of assimilation and the unresolved tensions between their particular (ethnic, Jewish,) and their "universal" (national, American, Western) identities. Nevertheless, these popular works projected a tidy coexistence for the contradictions and their characters asserted their status as full-fledged Americans.

Along with the celebratory images projected in popular fiction of the decade, social and political evidence also indicated that Jews were increasingly accepted as loyal Americans. In 1945, 67 percent of respondents to a public opinion poll believed that Jews held too much power. By 1962, the percentage of respondents who believed that Jews held too much power had fallen to 17 percent. Similarly, the number of survey respondents who reported that Jews represented a "menace" to the United States went from

24 percent in 1944 to 5 percent in 1950 to 1 percent in 1962.[49] The improved attitudes toward Jews were so strong that they could weather the highly publicized arrest in 1950 of Julius and Ethel Rosenberg as Communist spies. While the couple's trial went on for three years (culminating in their executions), it did nothing to reignite the stereotypes that Jews were more likely to be Communists or to be disloyal.

Yet, even if Jews were becoming normalized in cultural and political circles, some Americans, especially diplomats, continued to put American Jews in a separate category from other Americans. As described at the beginning of this chapter, John Foster Dulles was a case in point. The secretary complained about American Jews' vocal involvement in policy toward Israel. In mid-1954, he told a NSC meeting in exasperation that "it was utterly impossible to make public speeches on the subject of Israeli-Arab relations. . . . Assistant Secretary Byroade had recently . . . written and delivered a very sensible speech. However, it had been completely misunderstood in the United States and Middle East." Instead of trying to navigate Jewish public opinion, he recommended that the United States should make its policy known privately to Israel and the individual Arab states.[50]

Less than a year later, the United States collaborated with Britain to launch the initiative "Project Alpha" which was designed to bring a settlement in the Arab-Israeli conflict by, among other measures, connecting Egypt and Jordan through the Negev desert, repatriating a number of Arab refugees, and providing economic aid to all the participants. From the beginning of the Alpha proposal, Dulles remained resentful of the ability of American Jews to infringe on his delicate negotiations. He wondered how he and the other diplomats could "keep Jewish leaders . . . quiet during this period of preparation."[51] Dulles was not alone in his worries. Vice President Richard Nixon, for example, felt "disturbed by the heavy political pressure to subsidize an Israeli economy which could never balance itself."[52] And even with the general decline of antisemitism and slow dissolution of stereotypes about Jews, at least some American policymakers continued to view Israelis as "pushy." An example of these sentiments is found in a 1950 cable from Richard Ford, American chargé in Israel, who described Israelis as "These aggressively urgent people."[53] Whether or not such views reflected overt antisemitism on the part of Ford and others like him, or frustration with opposition to U.S. directives, the antisemitic resonance of the remarks cannot be missed.

Although Dulles professed numerous times that domestic politics should not determine foreign policy, throughout the negotiations over

Alpha, he kept congressional and presidential elections in mind. He believed that the administration had "rode out recent congressional elections at a sacrifice," but that might not be possible with the presidential election the following year. He argued that Project Alpha could only be successful if progress was made in 1955, because in 1956 Arab-Israeli relations would be "a political football. . . . This would undo the improvement in our relations with most of the states in the area during the past two years." Moreover, he concluded that if Republicans didn't make proposals that were acceptable to American Jews, the Democrats would step into the breech with proposals of their own. Further, 1955 was the optimal time for action, he concluded, because the administration had "deflat[ed]" Israel and the country was weaker than ever. He believed that the United States was thus in a good position to pressure Israelis who, if they rejected reasonable proposals, would risk losing financial support from American Jewry "not disposed to throw its money away recklessly on a bad venture." (Apparently, the secretary assumed that Jews were more calculating than idealistic regarding the disposition of their money.) Eisenhower shared Dulles' concern about domestic politics reiterating the importance of trying to get a settlement of the Arab-Israeli conflict before the 1956 elections.[54]

While some policymakers worried about the power of American Jews, others also understood that Jewish influence could be used to advantage for the United States in its negotiations with the Israelis. For example, in a 1955 memo prepared in the Bureau of Near Eastern, South Asian, and African Affairs strategizing about Project Alpha, diplomat Francis Russell noted that "United States Jewry could, at an appropriate time, play an important role in influencing the I.G. [Israeli Government] to cooperate." He concluded that American Jews would support any program that promised to bring peaceful conditions and, thus, "reduc[e] that high annual level of their contributions to Israel."[55] (Russell here echoes Dulles' conclusion that American Jews would be more concerned with the amount of money that they spent in Israel than with the political interests of the Israeli government.) American Jews were seen as potentially valuable influences on Israel to the extent that they were deemed to have real political power in the United States.

Evidence of Jewish political power, assimilation, and prosperity was found in many places. In addition to the stories of successful Jews that permeated popular fiction and the press, non-Jewish Americans could look around them and see the increased white collar and professional positions of American Jews, the great numbers of Jews going to college and moving to the suburbs, the decreased acceptance of antisemitism in the public culture, and the greater participation of Jews in politics. As discussed in chapter two, Jewish influence in politics was widely assumed to have swayed American policy toward Zionism and Israel in the late 1940s. Politicians became increasingly solicitous of Jewish supported causes in the 1950s, appearing at banquets and rallies such as those commemorating the Jewish tercentenary in America and United Jewish Appeal Annual dinners.[56] Some Jews carved out an active political role in both domestic politics and policy toward Israel. For example, Abraham Feinberg was a masterful fundraiser for both Israel and the Democratic Party. Meanwhile, he lobbied presidents and secretaries of state over the years on issues concerning Israel.[57]

Feinberg was not the only Jew who had influence in the Democratic Party. Indeed, over the years, Jews had a much closer relationship with Democrats than with Republicans. Democrats such as Adlai Stevenson maintained a close relationship with Jewish organizations and pro-Israeli groups. As a partisan of Israel, Stevenson publicly agreed with Jews who argued that support for the state was "above" politics. Speaking before bond rallies for Israel, Stevenson said that it was "refreshing to take time out [from his campaign] for a nonpartisan cause, such as the Israel Bond Drive" and that "the United States does not choose sides when it chooses peace."[58] The Jewish relationship with the Republican Party was very different than that with the Democrats. Rabbi Abba Hillel Silver was the most prominent of Zionist activists who was also a Republican. From his lonely political outpost, Silver frequently lobbied the White House on behalf of Israeli interests. Yet, in the midst of the debates over the formation of Israel, Silver's bombastic manner so completely alienated the Truman White House that he was barred from further visits. The outspoken activist did not win many friends in the Eisenhower administration either, and frequently lectured Dulles and other officials about which direction U.S. policy should take.[59]

The lack of prominent Jewish Republicans contributed to a perception among American Jews that an Eisenhower administration would be less approachable by them and less friendly to Israel. The Eisenhower campaign was well aware of these obstacles.[60] Only two months before the election of 1952, Jewish groups noted with worry that Eisenhower still had not made any position on Israel public.[61] The new administration got off on the wrong foot with Jewish groups when it proposed bringing Loy Henderson back from his ambassadorship in Iran to be Deputy Under Secretary of State for Administration; Henderson had strongly opposed the creation of Israel and some American Jews charged that he was antisemitic.[62] Charges of antisemitism even reached the president's brother, Milton Eisenhower, and, later in the 1950s, John Foster Dulles.[63] Eisenhower had no close Jewish friends, and throughout his years in the White House never reached out to Jewish acquaintances or other Jewish leaders. According to his biographer, he was "uncomfortable with Jews."[64]

Soon after Eisenhower took office, he received letters protesting that he had not appointed any Jews to important positions within the administration. His assistant answered such charges with the defense that he had, indeed, appointed Jews to sensitive positions: Max Rabb as an assistant to the president and secretary to the cabinet and Lewis Strauss as liaison with the atomic energy program. Such comments continued through the early part of the Eisenhower administration.[65]

Max Rabb, as the most prominent Jew in the White House became unofficial liaison to Jewish, ethnic, and civil rights groups. Rabb said at the time, and reiterated years later, that he just "stumbled upon" the position. He recalled that Eisenhower deliberately did not assign anyone to a position in charge of minority affairs: "he felt that ethnic groups should not be singled out with a caretaker in charge of them . . . any particular problem that arose should be handled quietly and unofficially." Given the premium that Eisenhower placed on universalism, this attitude is not surprising, but it does explain why some Jewish groups believed that Eisenhower was indifferent to their interests. Individual Jews and Jewish organizations addressed letters and entreaties to Rabb regarding American policy toward Israel. Rabb's responses were courteous, but made few commitments. He felt, at times, "overwhelmed from heads of Jewish organizations asking for my intervention . . . relative to their pet institution." Yet, it was also clear that Rabb shared the admiration for Israel felt by the Jewish constituents who wrote to him. An enthusiastic Rabb returned from a 1957 vacation in Israel exclaiming, "It is breathtaking to observe this new State and the rapid progress they are making." And describing a new arts center in the country, he wrote, "This is a magnificent project which certainly gives one the feeling that Israel has attained intellectual maturity."[66]

Another important Republican liaison to the Jewish community was Bernard Katzen who became Director of the Ethnic Division of the Republican National Committee and who was a friend of John Foster Dulles. Publicly, Katzen defended the administration against charges that it did not care about American Jews and that it was uninterested in the welfare of Israel. He argued that the Eisenhower administration's claim to be a "fair broker" in the Arab-Israeli conflict was the only sensible course during the Cold War when the greatest danger to the region was from threats of Soviet encroachments. Many American Jewish leaders continued to feel that whether it was intended to be or not, the impact of Eisenhower's policy was harmful to Israel.[67] Despite Katzen's efforts, many Republican Jews worried about electoral support in the 1956 election. One attendee at a party strategy meeting said that "person after person got up and stated that unless something was done about the Israelis [sic] situation all their efforts among Jewish groups would be in vain."[68]

The difficulty in which some Republican politicians found themselves with respect to Israel is illustrated by Congressman and, later, Senator Jacob Javits of New York. Javits was a loyal supporter of the Eisenhower administration and was also under pressure, especially as a Jew, to support Israel. He was not afraid to go against the administration—such as on the 1953 suspension of aid to Israel—but he preferred to work with the White House.[69] In the summer of 1956, Javits approached Dulles about his prospective senate candidacy saying that due to the Jewish voters in New York, he was not sure that he could run unless the administration changed its policy in the Middle East. Javits told Dulles that although he, personally, felt that the Middle East policy was going well, he said that the policy was not understood well.[70] While Dulles may have shared Javits' sensitivity to the political ramifications of U.S. policy, this did not necessarily mean that he was willing to change policy to conform to Jewish opinion.

Regardless of the party in power, and the influence of individuals such as Silver and Feinberg, Jewish organizations worked hard to establish political relationships in Washington that would benefit Israel. Leaders such as Jacob Blaustein of the American Jewish Committee and Philip Klutznick of B'nai B'rith remained in contact with the White House and State Department regarding policy toward Israel. Blaustein, for one, professed to the diplomats with whom he met that he was not in any way trying to use mass political pressure, implying that his meetings with State Department officials had nothing to do with such crude methods.[71] Indeed, Dulles viewed these contacts as useful, calling Klutznick, for example, "very helpful to the Department on Israeli matters and his organization has perhaps the strongest moderating influence on American Jewry."[72]

The easy Jewish access to the halls of power in Washington reflected the degree to which this small minority group had assimilated in the American mainstream and become accepted as ordinary Americans. Moreover, in the public culture of the press and popular fiction, Jews were not merely accepted, they symbolized the American success narrative par excellence, embodying the story of the immigrant's Horatio Alger climb to wealth, respectability, and patriotism. With this growing idealization and the decline of negative stereotypes about them, American Jews were in, what was for them, a position of potentially unprecedented political influence. Not surprisingly, Jewish organizations tried to use this new found power to influence American policy toward Israel.[73]

THE ACCEPTANCE OF JEWS AND ATTITUDES TOWARD ISRAEL

The usual story told in history books is that Jews failed to influence U.S. policy toward Israel during the Eisenhower years. But, what is actually remarkable is the extent to which an administration that had come into power professing that it would not play any favorites in the Arab-Israeli conflict, ended up supporting many of the positions of Israelis (and their American Jewish partisans). Whether this was by coincidence or design, it was clear that the cultural narrative of American Jewish assimilation and success overlapped with the image of Israel as a potential Cold War partner. Thus, Jews, in the United States or in Israel, seemed to resemble Americans in multiple ways.

Sympathy for and identification with Israeli interests is seen in some of the foreign policy dilemmas of the 1950s. In the middle of the decade, sources of international tension for Israel were the extent of Jewish and Arab immigration into the country, the final status of the state's borders, and Israel's acquisition of arms. On each of these three issues, the stated position of the U.S. government conflicted with that of Israel and its Jewish supporters in the United States. Nevertheless, what becomes clear through the decade is that U.S. policy, not withstanding the government's public position, increasingly reflected Israel's foreign policy interests and those of American Jews.

Potential Jewish and Arab immigration to Israel were controversial issues, yet ones on which U.S. policymakers, American Jews, and Israelis seemed largely to agree. American Jews were among some of the strongest emotional and financial supporters of massive Jewish immigration to Israel—although the national identification of American Jews was too strong to consider leaving the United States themselves. (In the first three years of the state's existence, only 1,711 of the 686,739 immigrants to Israel came from the United States.)[74]

The Israeli position on immigration stemmed from Zionist precepts that a Jewish state should be home for all Diaspora Jews. After World War II, Zionists were able to appeal to non-Jews throughout the world, because of the existence of thousands of European refugees living in squalid camps. But since Israeli leaders were not only concerned with saving survivors of Hitler's Holocaust, but also with encouraging all Jews to come to Israel, they codified their immigration policy in the 1950 Law of Return which gave Jews throughout the world the legal right to immigrate to Israel and the 1952 Nationality Law which conferred citizenship on as many Jews as possible, while excluding as many Arabs as possible. The 1952 law provided that citizenship came from immigration, birth, residence, or naturalization. Palestinian Arab refugees were excluded from the possibility of immigration (they didn't have a law of return), as well as from the definitions of residency (under which citizens had to be registered in Israel on 1 March 1952 and reside in Israel on 14 July 1952 when the law went into effect). Similarly, most Arab refugees were excluded from the remaining two categories; those born in Israel were entitled to citizenship only if one of their parents was an Israeli citizen and those who wanted to be naturalized had to have lived in Israel for at least three years, renounced their former citizenship, and learned some Hebrew. Thus, in contrast to the treatment of Arab refugees, Jews from around the world were welcomed to Israel with open arms. Indeed many Israelis, American Jewish supporters, and subsequent historians have called this mission of "ingathering" the "sine qua non" or "raison d'être" of the state.

The Israeli government took the goal seriously, welcoming an average of eighteen thousand Jews a month in the first three years of statehood. In its first five years of existence, the Jewish population of the state doubled. The first refugees to arrive came from displaced person camps in Europe, and soon from the Middle East as well. The expense of resettling the refugees was enormous, while the Israeli economy of the late 1940s and early 1950s remained precarious, ill equipped to absorb such huge numbers of people.[75]

Israeli policies that welcomed as many Jews as possible rankled with many, including some U.S. policymakers. In 1954, Assistant Secretary of State for Near Eastern Affairs Henry Byroade argued in a major policy speech that one of the most effective ways in which Israel could lower regional tension was to end immigration. Even in the midst of the Suez crisis, policymakers such as Dulles revisited this issue, calling in a national security meeting for the need to limit immigration. The director of the U.S. Information Agency (formerly Assistant Secretary for Near Eastern Affairs), George Allen, added the recommendation that the tax deductibility of private American contributions to Israel (then totaling $100 million) should be ended in order to pressure the country. In response, Atomic Energy Commission chair Lewis Strauss argued that Israel was the only country accepting Jews from Arab countries and that any infringement on U.S. philanthropy would be resented by all parties, religions, and nationalities.[76]

Strauss' caution acknowledged that there was broad American support for allowing persecuted refugees to find a new home. Indeed, such sentiments were a part of the basic narrative of American nationality in the twentieth century: the United States was a nation of immigrants, some persecuted, all coming to better their lives, experience freedom, and achieve economic success. Strauss thus reminded his fellow policymakers of the power of this immigration narrative and their unspoken nearness to immigrant origin. Even if Byroade, Allen, and others spoke out against continued Jewish immigration, the U.S. government, in the end, did little to pressure Israel to end it.

The American policy of continuing to give Israel aid (after 1950 averaging $40 to $60 million dollars a year),[77] which indirectly facilitated the absorption of Jewish refugees while at the same time calling for an end of Jewish immigration, contrasted sharply with the American position toward Arab refugees. There was no benign support for the return of the Arab refugees to their former homes. As discussed in chapter three, most U.S. officials supported a policy of Israel repatriating a few symbolic Arabs, while the majority would receive compensation and be resettled in Arab countries. The United States would fund this operation by reimbursing Israel for its payments to the refugees.

In contrast to the benevolent condemnation with which Americans greeted continuing immigration of Jews into Israel, the possibility of Arabs returning to their homes in the former Palestine was dismissed as a political impossibility. Since the formation of their state, Israelis had worked against repatriation of Palestinian Arabs, moving from discouragement to distraction to denunciation of the very idea. They explained the destructiveness of such a policy by describing returning Arabs as a "fifth column" that would destroy the state from within. The term was quickly adopted by Americans sympathetic with Israel, especially Jews, as well as mainstream journalists. Similarly, Israeli Arabs were described as a "security problem within the state." And at least two American ambassadors, under the Truman and Eisenhower administrations, adopted the Israeli perspective that Arabs were a fifth column.[78] Overall, U.S. diplomats continued to endorse most aspects of the Israeli position that repatriation was unrealistic, even if some refugees had to be allowed to return to Israel to placate the Arabs.[79]

While the press had previously celebrated the stories of destitute Jews rebuilding their lives in Israel, coverage of the Arab refugees revealed widespread American attitudes that the Arabs should not return to Israel. Press commentary, although infrequent, had much in common with the positions taken by U.S. policymakers. For example, one 1955 editorial in *Life* endorsed UN resolutions that promised refugees the right to return or to be reimbursed. Yet, the same editorial went on to assume that there wouldn't really be repatriation since "most of the homes are gone." The solution was thus simplified: "If the Arabs realized" that the homes no longer existed, most would not choose to return to Israel to live in refugee camps. From this view, Israelis needed only to pay lip service to the letter of UN resolutions, and, after most Arabs refused to return, pay compensation with loans from the United States and the United Nations. The editorial concluded by endorsing the U.S. government's economic development plans for the region which will "make the deserts bloom."[80] (This is the phrase used earlier to describe the results of Zionist and Israeli development efforts. *Life* editors seem to have been hoping that American efforts for Arabs would imitate the achievements of Israel.)

At the same time, the press celebrated the massive Jewish immigration to Israel. Common themes in the press stories about Israel, especially in 1952 and 1953, included descriptions of Israel's serious economic problems, dependence on foreign contributions, and difficulties of "ingathering." The heroic aspect of the immigration was highlighted, even when Israel's expenditure of vast sums of money was considered ill-advised. The press easily adopted the Israeli descriptions of the immigration policy, discussing the "ingathering of the exiles," reporting that the 1950 Law of Return was "sacred," and professing that all immigrants were treated alike. One 1951 *Life* article, among others, included a number of photos focusing on the diversity among the immigrants. Typical of the widespread celebration of a multiethnic state was a book review that found "unity in diversity" in Israel.[81] Such sentiments were expressed elsewhere in the public culture, including by Washington policymakers. Harry Truman, for one, articulated the assumption that the United States and Israel were alike because of their struggles for independence and their diverse populations: "We, too, once proclaimed our own independence in a ringing declaration which is still an inspiration to freedom-loving peoples. . . . We, too, are people of diverse origins who have gathered strength from many cultures."[82]

Press stories and political leaders may have said that they celebrated the multiethnic character of Jewish immigration, but their language and photos, in either subtle or obvious ways, asserted the message that Israel was a Western country. Accounts of the immigration stressed that all the groups, even the "near primitive savages from darkest Arabia [Yemenites]" socialized into the European norm that defined Israeli culture. Some stories were more blatant in their negative judgments about the "Oriental" Jews. For example, one account described the "Little dark-skinned Jews from the Yemen" who seemed "alien and anachronistic" compared to the rest of the Jews in a city like Tel Aviv. According to this author, the Yemenites (along with the "remnant of medievalism" represented by Hasids) would not quickly fuse with all of the other Jews who dominated the "melting pot." This author, as was often the case with other journalists, did not recognize the irony of his celebration of diversity at the same time that he was denigrating the non-European, nonassimilated Jews: "Other nations have professed but Israel is putting into practice, asylum, without prejudice as to origin." The irony grows thicker when one notes that the claim of an immigration policy without prejudice must be measured against the prohibition of Arab immigration.[83]

Back in the United States, American Jews were starring in a similar drama of acceptance and assimilation. In the same magazines and newspapers that celebrated the Israeli melting pot, Americans read stories about declining antisemitism and primers of Judaism. In these stories—as well as in best-selling novels and Hollywood fiction—American Jews were model immigrants, enacting the Horatio Alger myth for post World War II America. Thus, these narratives of Israeli and American immigration and assimilation were mutually supportive and comforting stories in a Cold War world.

Another major foreign policy issue for Israel in the mid-1950s—and a source of tension between the United States and Israeli governments—was the status of borders, and the consequent fighting across these de facto boundaries.[84] When Israel was created in 1948, many Palestinian Arabs who were forced out of or fled the Jewish state were separated from their land, houses, and crops. Soon, a number of Arab refugees crossed the border to reap crops, visit relatives, or steal from Jews; some also crossed accidentally before it was clear where the boundaries lay. The peak of infiltrations was in 1952 with sixteen thousand reported, and many that went unreported. Historian Benny Morris argues that less than 10 percent of the border crossings between 1949 and 1953 were by politically motivated agents or terrorists. And, even from 1954–1956 when the numbers in this last category might have changed slightly, the vast majority of infiltrators crossed for economic reasons. Nevertheless, some Israelis were killed by the intruders (peaking at 77 in 1953).

Israel had an unofficial, shoot-to-kill policy of infiltrators, used a variety of military means against them, and carried out retaliatory attacks in response to border crossings. The responses were out of proportion to most infiltrations, and often ended up punishing innocents who had not been involved. Following widespread international condemnation for its October 1953 attack on the village of Kibya in the West Bank, Israel shifted its focus to military and police targets, thus, increasing the scale of operations to larger companies of soldiers. This policy led eventually to the attack on an Egyptian army camp in Gaza in February 1955, killing thirty-eight and wounding thirty. In response, Egyptian leader Gamel Abdul Nasser began organizing *fedayeen* bands to carry out raids across Israel's borders and seeking a new source of arms. Thus, Israeli raids enjoyed a certain amount of political support at home, but worsened relations between Arabs and Israelis, and between Israel and the rest of the world.

The United States' position on the border conflicts was often critical of both sides. For example, Americans noted Jordan's responsibility for failing to prevent its "nationals" from crossing into Israel or to arrest upon their return those who had committed crimes in Israel. And, while sympathizing with Israel whose neighbors did not respect its borders, the United States denounced Israel's "aggressive policy" of "provocative brutality." Moreover, the United States was unwilling to give the guarantee of borders that Israel sought for fear that the country would not be willing to negotiate with the Arabs once it received such a guarantee.[85] The strongest stand that the United States took against the Israeli retaliation policy was following the Kibya raid: temporarily suspending aid. But, as discussed in chapter three, U.S. officials denied that the suspension had anything to do with Kibya. They instead argued that it was in reaction to Israel's violation of its armistice with the B'not Ya'akov water project.

U.S. policymakers tried to use political pressure to affect the situation, supporting the more moderate Israeli officials led by Moshe Sharett, and working against those who supported strong retaliation, led by David Ben-Gurion. Yet, the Israelis' defense of their policy probably also convinced some Americans and other Westerners that their actions were justified. For example, in remarks to Winston Churchill, the "moderate" Moshe Sharett explained why some retaliation was necessary: "Israel does not want war. . . . [it is] difficult . . . for a virile community to look on passively as its people are being murdered."[86] The argument that a country had to assert its masculinity would certainly have resonated with American policymakers in the Cold War. The United States failed to back up any of its criticisms with strong action. Thus, U.S. policymakers, in effect, looked the other way, encouraging Israel to continue the status quo.

On the issue of obtaining arms, Israel and the United States remained farther apart, in public statements and in policy decisions, than on other foreign policy issues in the mid-1950s. In part, this was because in order to have granted Israeli requests, the United States would have had to have taken a clear initiative, instead of merely ignoring or indirectly funding Israeli policies. The lack of American arms supplies to Israel was held up by many Jewish supporters of Israel as a key piece of evidence that the Eisenhower administration was biased against the Jewish state. On this issue, as on others, Dulles resented these criticisms and the efforts of American Jews to use domestic politics to interfere in foreign policy issues.[87] Anticipating the possibility of giving Israel some military assistance if, indeed, imbalances dangerous to the country developed, the secretary reminded Assistant Secretary Byroade in 1954 that "any steps we may take . . . [should] be done in such a manner that it will be clear that our actions are dictated purely by policy considerations."[88] Thus, Dulles was willing to entertain the possibility of arms sales, but felt strongly that no one should assume it was due to domestic political pressure. The secretary was equally sensitive to efforts by Israelis to manipulate U.S. domestic politics. Commenting on a trip by Moshe Sharett to the United States to sell Israeli bonds, Dulles charged that Sharett was not just selling bonds: "He was attempting to go over the head of the U.S. government in an effort to build up pressure here for Israel's demand for arms and a security guarantee."[89]

Israel had long been trying to obtain arms from the United States, but the requests took on a frantic quality after Egypt concluded a pivotal arms deal with Czechoslovakia in September 1955. In late 1955 and early 1956, repeated arms requests to the United States (including a personal appeal from Ben-Gurion to Eisenhower) went unanswered. While Americans stalled, both they and the British actually tied a new arms supply to the conclusion of an Arab-Israeli peace agreement. The French stepped in, concluding an arms deal with Israel in November 1955. The United States quietly encouraged the French shipments to Israel in late 1955 and early 1956, and Canadian shipments in 1956, although American policymakers wanted them to stop once there was an "equalization" of supplies between the Israelis and the Arabs. With these arms shipments, and Israel's military superiority to the Arab forces, Dulles remained unwilling to publicly supply Israel with any sizeable shipments of arms.[90]

Dulles and Eisenhower had other reasons to turn down Israeli requests. Both wanted to avoid a Middle East arms race tied to the Cold

War. Eisenhower wrote in his diary, "we would regard it as tragic if the USSR began to arm one where we undertook to defend the other with weapons and financial support." Moreover, although administration spokesmen donned a non-alarmist guise about the Czech arms sale, in private, officials were very fearful about the new leverage the Soviets now had in the Cold War. The administration did not want to risk provoking deeper Soviet involvement in the Middle East. Eisenhower was also reluctant to grant arms requests, because he believed that the Israelis were really looking for a security guarantee from the United States.[91] In addition, Eisenhower and Dulles were worried that any arms to Israel would endanger their ability to influence the Arabs. And, finally, since American officials did not believe that Israel was truly in danger and had sufficient weapons, selling the state more weapons made no sense.

For their part, Israeli officials had tried to convince the Americans that they needed the arms, *because of* Cold War dangers. Israelis and their American champions used the Czech sale to bolster the argument that they had been making all along: Israel was the true friend and ally of Western democracies. Ironically, then, leaders in both countries spoke of the Cold War dangers that threatened the Middle East, but came to radically different conclusions on the question of arms sales. Israelis went outside of the administration to make its case, telling members of Congress, the press, American Jews, and other prominent Americans that Communist arms in the Middle East threatened the West as a whole.[92]

Many American journalists came to the same conclusion that Israelis did. After the 1955 Czech arms deliveries, the press frequently mentioned how Israelis were "ringed by" Arabs and their "shiploads of arms from the Communists."[93] Israeli retaliation for border raids was once described as heavy-handed. Now, the Israelis were said to have "behaved with restraint," because "Every Israeli sleeps within 20 miles of an Arab knife."[94] Lobbying from American Jewish organizations for arms shipments shared these dramatic descriptions of the danger that the small state faced from its neighbors. For example, Jacob Blaustein told Dulles that an arms race was already underway: "the Arabs are running fast and far ahead, while the legs and arms of Israel are being tied."[95] Throughout the negotiations, American Jewish leaders established a working relationship with Washington officials, even if they could not sway the final policy outcome.

The lack of American arms shipments to Israel is usually discussed as a great defeat for Israel and a sign of poor relations between the Eisenhower administration and the Jewish state. Moreover, several interpretations of this period highlight the dangers that Israel faced from the east European arms.[96] While it is true that the requests of the Israeli government and its supporters were not met, Eisenhower administration officials continued to discuss the issue with Israeli representatives and American Jewish leaders, encouraged France and Canada to supply Israel with weapons, and remained convinced that the small state was in a strong military position.[97] Officials were concerned with Israel's welfare, but were unwilling to give Israel too much power in the making of U.S. policy or to anger the Arabs unnecessarily. In this context and in light of other policies toward Israel, one could say that the United States—while not acceding to Israel's requests—was certainly not harming the country. American policies toward Israel in the mid-1950s, just as Jews in general were becoming more accepted in popular and political culture, were benign at worst and favorable at best.

CONCLUSION

Irrespective of the outcome of any one policy debate, during the 1950s, American Jews became not only more accepted in the halls of power, but also throughout public culture in the United States. While antisemitism declined in the United States, American Jews also found themselves the beneficiaries of the increased emphasis on international, multiethnic alliances in the Cold War. Such an emphasis addressed the tension between universal and particular identities. American Jews and other ethnic groups did not have to choose between these identities; they could have both, as long as the particular was subsumed under the universal (now redefined by the Cold War yardstick as a Western identity). This shift in cultural images was found throughout the public culture, including in popular fiction. But in contrast to the values espoused in the universalist fiction of the mid-1940s, a distinct ethnic identity did not now threaten American identity if that ethnicity was part of a pluralistic society. Lawrence Levine concludes that the pluralism of the 1950s was actually quite shallow: "pluralist ideas were overwhelmed by the certainty that ethnic distinctions were in the process of inevitable extinction."[98] Yet, despite the apparent weakness of ethnicity, many Americans in the 1950s became convinced of the value of the immigrant heritage of their country in which, as described by historian Lawrence Moore, "outsiderhood is a characteristic way of inventing one's Americaness."[99] An apparently contradictory paradigm is at work here. In the popular fiction of this period, Jews become consummate insiders in American culture, because they were posited as outsiders and resourceful Horatio Algers.

This image, of course, had a profound effect on the image of Israelis who were intimately associated with American Jews in cultural discourse. For example, in 1951, the popular television show *The Toast of the Town*, ran a special entitled "The Israel Anniversary Show" to celebrate what host Ed Sullivan called "the very glorious third anniversary of the founding of the young but powerful State of Israel." The show, before an audience of twenty thousand assembled by the Zionist Organization of America, contained a mixture of American and Israeli songs, a variety of well-known performers, testimonials about Israel from politicians and American Jewish leaders, and vaudeville comedy skits playing on Yiddish expressions and accents. The message throughout was that a celebration of Israel was really like a celebration of American Jews, and that all Americans, Jew and non-Jew alike, could identify with Israel. Host Ed Sullivan observed: "The cause of Israel is particularly close to the heart of anyone of Irish extraction, because the Irish and the Jew, their struggles were so much alike in the characteristics of their populace, their people was so much alike."[100]

In other contexts, American Jews celebrated their identification with Israel. The creation of local and national Jewish organizations in the postwar period exemplified a new Jewish confidence at home as well as loyalty to Israel. The first president of the Israel Community Center congregation in Levittown, NY described how the founding of the Jewish state was an imperative to him and his neighbors: "We just *had* to organize a synagogue and center . . . and that we *must* call it Israel Synagogue Center in honor of the new State of Israel. . . . I felt that if people in Israel [were] . . . saying 'We are Jews and we're going to create something worth while,' then I, too, wanted to stand up and really belong to the Jewish people."[101] Such identifications only grew stronger and more prevalent in the 1950s, helping to shape the political role of American Jews, and the perception among non-Jews that Americans and Israelis had shared political interests.

6

The Cold War, Suez, and Beyond

Cultural Images and Changing American-Israeli Relations in the Late 1950s

Soon after Egyptian forces seized the Suez Canal Company properties in July 1956 and Gamal Abdel Nasser decided to nationalize the company, Secretary of State John Foster Dulles met with European allies, and spoke out against Nasser's actions and the threat they posed to the countries that used the canal: "it is one thing for a nation to defy just one or two other nations. But it is quite a different thing to defy the considered and sober judgment of many nations." Six months later, Dwight D. Eisenhower voiced similar opinions about the importance of respecting international opinion when he called on Israel to withdraw completely from the Egyptian territory it had occupied in the October 1956 Suez invasion. The president praised Israel's partners in the invasion, Britain and France, for their withdrawal from occupied territories, "they showed respect for the opinions of mankind as expressed [by] . . . the United Nations." He called on Israel to do likewise and uphold the will of the UN and the principle of not using force to settle political disputes.[1]

In these two examples, Dulles and Eisenhower seemed to use a similar principle to criticize both Egypt and Israel. Yet, what is remarkable about these speeches at the beginning and end of the Suez crisis is not that they indicated a similarity in American views of the two countries, but that they masked very different attitudes toward the two countries. If we look beyond these speeches and the immediate policy differences between the United States and Egypt, and the United States and Israel, we find radically divergent attitudes toward the two Middle Eastern states. Although the Suez crisis is often cited as a nadir of American-Israeli relations, the disagreements of late 1956 did not destroy or weaken the countries' ties. Indeed, as Cold War tensions seemed to be more relevant to Middle East politics at the end of the decade, Israel appeared—in the press and in policymaking—to be closer to the United States. In contrast, American images of Egypt and U.S.-Egyptian relations continued to deteriorate after Suez.

In this context, Israel was the central player in contradictory cultural narratives. On the one hand, both Israel and Egypt apparently violated the principles of international law and were punished for their infractions, through international censure as well as military action. On the other hand, Israel was the champion of Western interests in the Middle East and was threatened by Soviet expansion and arms deliveries in the region. Yet, both of these narratives were threads in a pervasive Cold War understanding of international affairs and were shaped by that perspective. Since their struggle for independence almost a decade before, Israelis had been increasingly described in popular and political culture as similar in values and characteristics to Americans, as natural allies in a Cold War world. Thus, as the United States became more active in the Middle East with the Suez crisis, and increasingly concerned about the Cold War tensions in the region, it is not surprising that the cultural images of Israel would be reflected in the political and popular discussions of contemporary international relations. The following chapter examines the contradictions of the cultural narratives surrounding Israel and the Arab states in the late 1950s, and how U.S. goals and relations with the Jewish state changed following the upheaval of the Suez crisis. It illustrates how these political events can be reread in light of the popular images of Israel and Jews that had become pervasive by the late 1950s.

FOREIGN POLICY DILEMMAS: BORDER RAIDS AND ARMS SUPPLIES

The Israeli involvement in the Suez crisis stemmed from two of the key foreign policy issues of the mid-1950s: border raids and arms supplies to the Middle East. American responses to these issues were complicated and inconsistent. The seriousness of border tensions was exemplified by the February 1955 large-scale Israeli reprisal for a *fedayeen* attack. The Israeli raid into the Gaza Strip was connected to the future Suez invasion, because it encouraged Nasser to train and equip *fedayeen* guerrillas and to seek a source of new arms; it also brought condemnation of Israel by the United States. Eisenhower urged Ben-Gurion not to strike back for border raids even "under extreme provocation."[2] Despite the views of the Eisenhower administration, most press coverage of the raid and the Israeli policy of reprisals remained sympathetic to the Jewish state. Israel was described as being in an impossible position against Arabs who continued to raid across the border and refused to negotiate a peace. Moreover, the Arab response to the Israelis came across as ill-considered if not irrational. Residents of Gaza were described as going "on a rampage," in which among other acts, they burned a UN depot with their own food supply. In addition, the press commented on "Communist agitators" instigating the riots.[3]

The question of arms supplies to the Middle East, specifically the large shipment of Czechoslovakian arms to Egypt in September 1955, had an even greater impact on the politics of the region and provoked a more complicated reaction than did the Gaza raid. Following the sale, Israelis urgently requested from the United States new arms to balance the Egyptian supplies. The American response was lukewarm, as officials worried that arms to Israel would endanger the free flow of oil from the region to Europe. Dulles made the same argument at an NSC meeting— and also revealed his contempt for some Arab leaders. If the United States sent arms to Israel, he said, the Arabs might retaliate with an oil blockade of Europe: "While such action would be suicidal for the Arabs, many of them were fanatics and were capable of such misguided action."[4]

Israeli pressure on the United States for arms shipments was steady through 1956, as diplomats tried to convince their American counterparts that their two countries were on the same side in the Cold War. Even if Americans did not accede to Israeli requests, they agreed with the premise of the argument. For example, at a meeting among diplomats in October 1955 regarding the impending arms shipments, Assistant Secretary of the Bureau of Near Eastern Affairs George Allen was particularly critical of the Egyptian press which criticized U.S. aid and praised the Soviet Union. American and Israeli representatives at the meeting shared information as confidants, and the Americans sympathized with Israeli fears of arms from the "Communist world." Dulles told Prime Minister Moshe Sharett how gravely the United States viewed the Czech sale, concluding that "This is [the] most serious situation to arise since World War II, more far-reaching in consequence than Korea." Outside of the company of Israelis, Americans expressed understanding that Israel was "frightened," and that the Israelis felt that they didn't have the same bargaining power as the heavily populated, oil-rich Arabs.[5]

Press opinion usually agreed with that of the Eisenhower administration and the Israelis that the Czechoslovakian shipments were a threat to the stability of the Middle East. At the same time, most in the press criticized the U.S. decision not to supply Israel with arms. In the spring of 1956, a number of sympathetic portraits appeared of the "beleaguered" Israel, threatened by the Communist arms. These articles continued the pattern of celebratory press stories common since the founding of Israel. For example, one lushly illustrated story in *Look* focused on the "tiny nation fighting for its very life," with a strong army, although "short of weapons." The article included the by-then iconographic portraits of Israeli soldiers engaged in military exercises, patrolling on the border, and smiling in relaxation after a successful mission. The pioneering Ben-Gurion was also in evidence, as were farmers on their fertile land in the previously barren Negev ("a wasteland through all the centuries of Arab occupation"), and a mother with two small children staring across barbed wire at "her hostile Jordanian neighbors."[6]

There were other tributes to the strength of Israel's "tough little army" in the face of Communist arms. Early in 1956, for example, the *Saturday Evening Post* published a profile of the army, with its multinational fighters who had fused into one force with an "inner strength and spirit." A few months later, the *Post* ran another story about Israel's resilience in the face of threats by the noted columnist Joseph Alsop. Alsop recounted that on his recent visit to Israel he had the most "deeply impressive" political experience of his life. He was awed by something he described as "almost intangible," "the moral climate of Israel." "Israel is still living in its own legendary age," a state that he contrasted with that of the rich, "elder" nations of the West. Many Israelis had either encountered heroism or had their own heroic tales to tell from Israel's struggle for survival. The greatest strength of the country was "the sense of purpose Israel gives its people."[7] Alsop and others in the press, thus, embedded in their stories the narrative of a heroic, masculine people defying the "softness" of postwar Western life.

In contrast, in late 1955 and early 1956, most in the press remained critical of Nasser in subtle and obvious ways, though not ready to write him off as an enemy. One article in *Time* cautioned that although Nasser was "playing off East against West," the United States should be careful not to drive him "into the arms of the Communists." Press stories were also critical of Nasser's attempts to become the preeminent leader of the Arab world. In addition, journalists often assumed that the Arabs were to blame for the lack of resolution to the Arab-Israeli conflict, since they refused to talk about peace with Israel.[8]

While Israelis cultivated the image that they were desperately threatened by the Czech shipments and many in the United States sympathized with their plight, others knew that the actual military situation was far different. As noted in chapter five, American officials concluded that Israel was militarily stronger. It was superior to Egypt in most categories of ground weapons, and had important advantages in air and naval strength as well; at the same time, Israeli personnel strength was also twice as great as was Egypt's. Thus, Dulles sought to prevent "exaggerat[ion]" of the danger to Israel, while assuring Sharett of American support: "there cannot be action against Israel without strong reaction from the United States."[9]

Despite Dulles's reassurances, he and other officials worried that the Soviet Union was a danger to the region. Thus, in the short run, Israel felt threatened by an American wait-and-see policy, but in the long run, the Jewish state benefited to the extent that the Soviet Union and her proxies appeared to be the greatest threat to the region. Israel's assertion of identification with the West was, thus, thrown into sharp relief with the image of a neutralist and even "pro-Communist" country such as Egypt. Nineteen fifty-five, then, was a turning point for American popular and political images of the region and the Arab-Israeli conflict, because the Soviet arms deal confirmed the growing perception of distance between Nasser and the West, and heightened American fears that the Soviet Union might, indeed, make inroads in the region.

RE-VIEWING SUEZ

Following the controversy over arms shipments to the Middle East, the Suez crisis dramatically illustrated the explosive nature of politics in the area and clarified, for many Americans, where their loyalties lay. A tremendous amount of scholarship has been produced on the Suez crisis, nevertheless, it's important to briefly review the events of 1956, and reconsider how we interpret them in light of pervasive cultural and political narratives. While the episode is usually viewed as evidence of a great distance between the interests of Washington and Jerusalem, Suez and its reception in the United States fits into a more nuanced American image of Israel.

The invasion of Egypt by Israel, Britain, and France on 29–30 October 1956 had a number of causes. The stage was set for the invasion the previous July when the United States and Britain cancelled proposed funding for Egypt's Aswan Dam project and Nasser nationalized the Suez Canal Company five days later to obtain revenue to build the dam. Britain and France, as principle shareholders in the company, were furious. Meanwhile, the ongoing dispute between Israel and Egypt was characterized by tensions over refugees and borders (including increasing raids between the Gaza Strip and Israel), a blockade against Israel in the Suez Canal and the Straits of Tiran (at the mouth of the Gulf of Aqaba, closing Israel's port of Eliat), and the Egyptian-Czech arms deal.

For its part, the United States publicly condemned Nasser's decision to take over the canal company. About a week after the nationalization, Eisenhower and Dulles appeared together on television to criticize the nationalization and discuss its implications. The secretary of state explained that many countries depended on the canal, and that Nasser had taken it over only for bald ambition, the desire to expand Egypt's regional influence, and to get more revenue from its operation. Furthermore, to Nasser's assertion that he was striking a blow against "Western imperialism," Dulles countered that the nationalization was "an angry act of retaliation against fancied grievances." Both he and the president affirmed that the seizure could not go unchallenged.[10]

At the same time, in the months following the seizure, American leaders worked hard to forestall military action by Britain and France against Nasser. Yet, Nasser refused to accept foreign infringement on Egyptian sovereignty, and the British and the French refused to acquiesce to Nasser's control of the canal. Meanwhile, the British, French, and Israelis secretly planned their attack on Egypt. As agreed to by the three allies, Israel launched an attack into the Sinai on 29 October. Within two days, the Israelis had sent the Egyptians into a retreat and were approaching the Suez Canal. By 5 November, when British and French forces intervened ostensibly to protect the canal, Israel was in control of the entire Sinai. While the Israelis had displayed considerable skill and careful preparation for battle, the British and French forces were disorganized and ineffective, and the excuse for their attack seemed flimsy at best since Israel and Egypt agreed to a cease-fire within two hours of the Europeans' entry.

With the eruption of fighting in the Sinai, the reaction of the Eisenhower administration was swift and public. Eisenhower argued that a principle was at stake: to support the United Nations and negotiated settlements to international disputes. On the day of the Israeli invasion, the White House released a statement saying that it was pledged to assist any victim of aggression (here, meaning Egypt) under the 1950 Tripartite Declaration and would do so.[11] When the coordination of military plans among Britain, France, and Israel became obvious, Eisenhower gave an address which drew a fine line between upholding principles and supporting allies.[12] The UN remained the soundest hope for peace, Eisenhower argued, because there could "be no peace without law." Later that week, Eisenhower reiterated this theme: "We cannot subscribe to one law for the weak, another for the strong; one law for those opposing us, another for those allied with us. There can only be one law—or there shall be no peace."[13]

In private, Eisenhower was committed to the success of international law and the United Nations, but he did not hide his disdain for Nasser. Before the outbreak of fighting, at one NSC meeting in August, the president asked, "How could Europe be expected to remain at the mercy of the whim of a dictator?"[14] Other policymakers shared his views. For example, Secretary of Defense Charles Wilson argued during a November NSC meeting that Arabs were irrational: "We must avoid thinking that we can deal with the Arabs as we would deal with businessmen. The Arabs are moved by emotion and not by the judgments of businessmen."[15] Meanwhile, Eisenhower, concerned about the strategic importance of the canal through which two-thirds of Europe's oil passed, hinted that he might have acquiesced to the British and French attack if it had been executed more effectively. He observed, "It's the damnedest business I ever saw supposedly intelligent governments get themselves into."[16] Yet, despite his sympathy for the Europeans, Eisenhower remained firm in his public position that their actions could not be allowed to succeed.

He was equally firm with regard to Israel. But, even though he condemned Israeli actions, Eisenhower's language indicated closer ties with Israel than with the Arab states. Although he said that the United States wanted to strengthen ties with both sides in the dispute, he reaffirmed on 31 October that it was a "basic matter of U.S. policy to support the new State of Israel." He charged that the "misguided" Egyptian policy of "rearmament with Communist weapons" aggravated the situation and fueled Israel's understandable anxiety for her safety. Moreover, although the United States had not been consulted and believed Israel, Britain, and France to be in error, he continued, "To say this . . . is in no way to minimize our friendship with these nations—nor our determination to maintain those friendships. We know that [Israel, Britain, and France] have been subjected to grave and repeated provocations." On 1 November, Dulles spoke before the UN General Assembly, emphasizing even more American friendship with the three allies, especially with Britain and France:

> I doubt that any representative ever spoke from this rostrum with as heavy a heart as I have brought here tonight. . . . The United States finds itself unable to agree with three nations with which it has deep ties of friendship, of admiration and of respect, and two of which constitute our oldest and most trusted and reliable allies.[17]

Dulles' and Eisenhower's repeated professions of friendship for Britain, France, and Israel made it clear to policymakers and ordinary citizen that this was really a "family quarrel" not a stand-off between enemies. In January 1957, Dulles told French Foreign Minister Pineau that their two countries had to "arrive at a common understanding on how *we deal with* the Egyptians when the Canal starts operating again." His tone was comradely toward France and dismissive toward Nasser.[18] Even if Britain and France were really the greatest objects of American sympathy, Israel was drawn into this friendly orbit. Eisenhower argued that it was very important that the United States not "single out and condemn ANY ONE NATION."[19] No U.S. official would have tried publicly to make much of a distinction in the relationships with Britain, France, and Israel. To do so would only have given the impression that the United States did not share a friendship with Israel. Thus, Israel was pulled along in the wave of affection and goodwill among the Europeans and Americans, and ended up appearing almost as close to the United States as were her NATO partners. Even when U.S. policymakers were pressuring the Israelis to comply with UN demands for withdrawal early in 1957, Dulles emphasized that they were being treated just as Britain and France had been.[20]

Many Americans ended up with the impression of an equally close relationship between the United States and all of the allies in the attack. Partisans of Israel, certainly, were quick to latch onto this image. For example, an occasional correspondent of Eisenhower's and a supporter of Israel, Eli Ginzburg, who was an administrator at Columbia University, praised the president's speech to the nation on 31 October, noting: "Your deep understanding of the fears and exasperation that had led to these actions and your promise to strengthen the bonds with friends who you considered to be in error was evidence of great leadership." Israeli diplomat Yaacov Herzog even concluded that Dulles was actually more sympathetic with Israeli actions during Suez than he was with European actions, because Dulles understood Israeli motivations, but not those of the British and the French.[21] Even if Herzog was overly optimistic about Dulles' sympathy with Israel in comparison with his feelings toward Britain and France, he was right in saying that the three countries acting in concert affected how their action was perceived by policymakers and the public alike. Israel, in this equation, unquestionably benefited from its association with America's closest allies.

The political crisis in the region ground on into 1957. Following strong UN resolutions, an American-threatened run on the British pound, and an oil squeeze on Europe, Britain and France had withdrawn from their positions in Egypt in November. But, Israel refused to withdraw fully until it received guarantees of free passage through the Straits of Tiran and UN control of the Gaza Strip. Meanwhile, Eisenhower and Dulles argued that guarantees for Israel could not be granted under threat of force, but at the same time wanted to forestall any UN sanctions against Israel. Throughout early 1957, American diplomats worked closely with Israelis, discussing and pressuring, trying to get them to withdraw before the United Nations imposed sanctions.[22]

Eisenhower took the issue back to the public, broadcasting a speech on 20 February 1957, to further press Israel into withdrawing immediately. The president noted that the United States and Israel shared strong bonds of values and principles, and was careful not to condemn the nation too strongly when he described the American-Israeli disagreement. He allowed that Israel faced grave and serious provocations from Egypt that led it to invade in the first place. Nevertheless, Eisenhower remained firm on the principle that disputes could not be solved through military force. He also took the occasion to condemn the Soviet Union and that country's flouting of international law in its November 1956 invasion of Hungary. But, he concluded that the Soviet actions had nothing to do with Israel complying with the UN resolution since more was expected of a free, moral nation such as Israel:

> It would indeed be a sad day if the United States ever felt that it had to subject Israel to the same type of moral pressure as is being applied to the Soviet Union. There can, of course, be no equating of a nation like Israel with that of the Soviet Union. The peoples of Israel, like those of the United States, are imbued with a religious faith and a sense of moral values. We are entitled to expect, and do expect, from such peoples of the free world a contribution to world order which unhappily we cannot expect from a nation controlled by atheistic despots.[23]

Thus, Eisenhower's statement in no way compromised the Jewish state's status as a friendly power and, in fact, firmly placed Israel in the camp of Western friends. His words drew upon and reinforced the cultural, political, and religious images of Israel that had become familiar in the public culture by the mid-1950s. Israel finally gave into the pressure, fully withdrawing on 8 March and, thus, averting UN sanctions. Following the withdrawal, there was a decade of calm on the borders with Egypt: Egyptian administration (though not soldiers) moved back into Gaza and passage through the Gulf of Aqaba remained open.

Outside of the White House and State Department, American reaction to the Suez crisis was complicated and not always consistent. In the early stages of Suez, there was sympathy with the Eisenhower administration's handling of the situation, though later on, Congress and the press had sharp disagreements with the administration's policies. The events in Suez received widespread coverage beginning in the summer of 1956. Soon after the canal company seizure, press sentiment, while unfriendly to Nasser, was less than sympathetic with the British and French who seemed to be motivated by old imperialist goals. Henry Luce, for example, argued that the West must take a "stand not for Imperialism but for Law and Economic Order in world affairs." *Time* executive and sometime Eisenhower consultant and speechwriter C. D. Jackson described the Egyptian leader as a manipulative dictator—though he cautioned that Nasser could not be paralleled with the "psychotic Hitler," as some had done. Others in the press were more outspoken in their criticism of Nasser. For example, NBC news commentator Bob Wilson declared in July 1956 that the "audacious conduct of Nasser is a threat to the welfare of Egypt, the Free World and the general peace" and the United States had to stop "the dangerous and false nationalism of this immature leader." (As discussed in chapter three, the word "immature" carried certain gendered connotations and cast doubt upon Nasser's masculinity.) By the fall, Nasser was usually referred to as a "dictator" and sympathy for Israel's position with respect to its other Arab neighbors increased.[24]

With the outbreak of hostilities on 29 October, many in the American press corps were too surprised to formulate a clear analysis of the situation. Yet, within a short period of time, the dominant trend in the press was to be strongly supportive of Israel. Examples of pro Israel editorials and columns following the invasion were found in the *Atlanta Constitution, Boston Herald, New York Post, Daily Mirror*, and David Lawrence's and the Alsop brothers' columns in the *New York Herald Tribune*. Common themes sounded were the unfair position in which the "beleaguered" Israelis found themselves, the failure of Western "appeasement" of Nasser, and that Israel was compelled to take action.[25] The use of the word "appeasement" was one way to make an indirect comparison between Nasser and Hitler, since the latter was the most infamous symbol of someone whom the West had mistakenly tried to "appease" in 1938. At the same time, the success of Israel's army, "a deadly machine full of disciplined power . . . swiftly mobilized from the *citizen soldier*," was widely praised and compared to Egypt's "ill trained army" that fought "mostly with windy communiqués."[26] Articles on the war quoted the Bible and recounted the history of Israel, "misshapen" by the Independence War and only about "the size of New Jersey."[27] Just as Eisenhower's words had echoed increasingly familiar cultural narratives about Israel, so too did the press call up the various images of Israel that had become widespread by 1956. Thus, images from other contexts helped to strengthen American identification with Israel at the height of this political disagreement between the United States and the Jewish state.

Many Jewish groups and private citizens were equally supportive of Israel. Jewish groups, except for the anti-Zionist American Council for Judaism, argued that Israel was forced to use military action for self-defense. A telegram from the leaders of the Union of Orthodox Rabbis of the United States and Canada argued that Arab threats to wipe Israel off the map evoked the specter of another genocide.[28] Others argued that the Communists were really to blame for the situation. Like many of his contemporaries, one rabbi made the common Cold War equation between Communism, neutralism, and nationalism:

> We now have the evil forces of the Communists, the Gran [sic] Mufti [of Jerusalem, a Palestinian leader] and the dictator Nasser, collaborating together for the sole purpose of enslaving and destroying the free world, the foundation of which they set into motion with the Bandung Conference [of nonaligned nations] in May of 1955.[29]

Meanwhile, other Jews were angered by Eisenhower's lack of explicit support for Israel. One irate, prominent Republican supporter, David Wolper, wired the president that he had lost his vote and his annual $10,000 contribution to the party, because of "your misguided stand on the Israel question."[30]

Other Jewish leaders, perhaps worried about the difficulty of justifying the Israeli invasion, chose the time of the Suez crisis to detail numerous abuses which the Arab states carried out against Jews in their own countries. In particular, Jewish leaders wrote to the White House complaining of unjustified internment, deportation, and seizure of property of Jews in Egypt and Syria during November and December 1956. American Jewish organizations and Israelis also worked in the immediate aftermath of the Suez fighting to encourage new fundraising efforts for Israel whose American economic aid had been put on hold since the invasion in late 1956 (this included $30 million in grants and a $75 million Export-Import Bank loan). Officials, such as Golda Meir, toured the United States in early 1957 on behalf of the Israel Bond Organization.[31]

Much of the correspondence to the White House carried similar messages as that from Jewish leaders. In the months following the seizure of the canal company and before the invasion of Egypt, the White House received numerous letters on the situation, the majority of which were hostile toward Nasser. For example, one letter reported that people were "afraid that with the aid of Russia, Egypt will wipe out the only democratic country in the Middle East [Israel], and we will lose a good friend."[32] Following the invasion, the public response remained supportive of the president and the United Nations, and held little sympathy for Egypt, except for limited correspondence from Arab groups.

It seems that one reason direct criticism of Eisenhower's Suez policy was muted was due to its ambiguity. The president's invocations of international law and his previous criticism of Nasser's actions, along with his sympathy for and implied support of the U.S. allies, allowed many to support *both* the president and Israel in the Suez crisis. Thus, the underlying message of the majority of letters and telegrams to the White House after November 1956 was similar to that in the public response to the 1955 arms deal: supportive of Eisenhower and Israel, *and* hostile toward Nasser.[33]

Once the fighting stopped, sympathy for Israel in the United States rose, possibly, because there no longer appeared to be any danger of U.S. involvement in the war. Moreover, according to its many supporters in the United States, Israel's demands were modest: freedom of navigation through the Gulf of Aqaba and secure borders with Gaza. Domestic lobbying helped to build American support for Israel's position, creating sympathy that had not existed in October. These views were reflected in press accounts that stressed Israel's willingness to negotiate, its dramatic military success, and the implication that although Eisenhower was trying to get Israel to withdraw, the two countries shared common interests. From this perspective, disagreement between the United States and Israel was only a "semantic battle."[34]

Press stories detailed the pressure on Israel to withdraw in early 1957. Many supported the U.S. government decision to push for Israeli withdrawal, while at the same time expressing great sympathy with Israel's security and economic interest in the occupied areas. Some articles were supportive of the Israeli desire that UN forces remain, as well as the proposal for American guarantees of free passage through the Gulf of Aqaba.[35] Stories were critical of the United Nations and the "double standard" imposed on Israel as well as Britain and France, while undemocratic, immoral governments [i.e., the Soviet Union and Egypt] violated the precepts of the international organization with impunity.[36] Correspondence to the White House also continued in February and March 1957 from Jewish groups, congressmen, other organizations—such as the Pennsylvania Federation of Labor—and from private individuals.[37] Most were concerned about Israel's security, that it was treated differently than were other countries, and stressed the commonalities between Israel and the United States. This last point was stated quite dramatically by a Republican Party activist and acquaintance of Eisenhower's, Leonard Finder, who asserted that Israelis were like American pioneers of yesteryear, threatened by hostile "Indians" eager to "exterminat[e]" them. The "pioneers," Finder concluded, shouldn't be made to return the "weapons of destruction" to their enemies.[38]

Former President Harry Truman added his voice to the fray. He decided in February 1957—while Israel was under great pressure from the United States and United Nations—to help reinaugurate the Israel bond drive in the United States. Speaking at a fundraising dinner in Miami, Truman criticized the Eisenhower administration and supported Israel's right to defend herself from "bandits and thugs" [i.e., the *fedayeen* and Nasser's government]. Other prominent supporters of Israel shared Truman's opinions and tried to diffuse the pressure on the country. Reinhold Niebuhr wrote in the *New Republic* in February about "Our Stake in the State of Israel." Israel, Niebuhr argued, was "the only sure strategic anchor for the democratic world." Not only did he support the right of Israel to hold on to Gaza and the Straits of Tiran, he condemned U.S. efforts to push for withdrawal as analogous to the policies of appeasement at Munich, and compared Nasser to Hitler. He concluded that the president was "co-operating with the pawns of Russia."[39]

Majority Leader Senator Lyndon B. Johnson was another vocal supporter of Israel. He argued that the United Nations "can't apply one rule for the strong and another for the weak; it cannot organize its economic weight against the little State when it has not previously made even a pretense of doing so against large States." Many other members of Congress also voiced their support for Israel and delegations lobbied both the White House and the State Department to reject the proposed UN sanctions; some were more public, appearing on such television shows as *Meet the Press*. They, too, criticized the UN's "double standard" against Israel.[40]

Overall, in the press, government, and among the majority of Americans who expressed opinions in the public culture, Israel's situation in late 1956 and early 1957 was viewed with sympathy. Even though Israel had initiated military hostilities and was criticized by the Eisenhower administration, it was often viewed as a victim of aggressive Egyptians, especially Nasser who was compared to Hitler in various direct and indirect allusions. Moreover, in the face of Soviet actions in Hungary (and elsewhere) and Egyptian raids and blockades against Israel, many Americans charged that Israel was being unfairly singled out. Favorable views of Israel were further heightened by the sale of east European arms to Egypt the year before and by the Jewish state's association with the closest American allies, Britain and France. Finally, the muted and ambiguous criticisms of Israel coming from Eisenhower and Dulles left many Americans the space to support their president and Israel. Thus, although the Sinai episode represented a time of disagreement between Washington and Jerusalem, this disagreement and hostility is often overstated. And, if the episode is viewed just through the public culture, it appears to have actually strengthened American ties and identification with Israel in the long run. Suez marked another turning point for American images of the Middle East. Following the crisis, the United States became more involved in the politics of the region as never before, while Americans redefined those politics within a Cold War framework.

THE EISENHOWER DOCTRINE AND ARAB NATIONALISM

Before Suez, Great Britain was the dominant Western power in the Middle East; but circumstances changed. Britain was severely weakened by its failed policy, and U.S. policymakers focused their attention on the growing Soviet presence in the Middle East as well as on Nasser's efforts to dominate regional politics. The inadequacies of the 1955 Baghdad Pact were revealed as an alliance that had both failed to prevent Soviet inroads in the region or spreading anti-Western sentiments. Dulles asserted: "We believe that the bad turn of events can be dated from the active intervention of the Soviet Union in the area."[41] He and others in the administration believed that the Soviet Union had to be the focus of American policy in the region. American diplomats also sensed an opportunity to build a strong American position, because of the popularity of American actions in standing up to Israel, Britain, and France. Many in the press agreed with the administration's assertion that East-West tensions were really the dominant political issue in the Middle East. *Time*, for example, dubbed the Arab-Israeli conflict "the liveliest front of the cold war."[42]

This shift in focus, then, took place at both a policy level and at a popular level—evident in the press coverage of the time. While the changing American approach to the Middle East may have been spurred on by the Suez crisis, it is interesting to note that it overlapped with pervasive cultural narratives about the Arab-Israeli conflict and those involved in it. At a popular and political level, American focus in the Middle East shifted to Cold War issues even while the framework through which Americans viewed the region was based on vivid images of the Arab-Israeli conflict and its protagonists.

Eisenhower and Dulles expressed their concern to congressional leaders and other U.S. officials that the United States had to move into the "vacuum" left by Britain and France lest the Soviets do so. Eisenhower believed that the United States should build the strength of "friendly" powers such as Saudi Arabia, Iraq, and Jordan, and thus weaken the influence of Egypt.[43] In meetings with congressional leaders at the end of December and the beginning of January, this appeared to be the top priority of the administration and, thus, the justification behind the urgency of what became known as the "Eisenhower Doctrine."[44] In his 5 January speech to Congress outlining the new policy, the president argued that the Soviets and "international Communism" posed a direct threat to the region.[45] Under the plan, Congress would authorize the president to use force in the Middle East to aid a country that was threatened by international Communism and requested aid to combat the threat. The plan also called for the United States to build up local security forces, but not to contribute to any arms race between the Arabs and Israelis. Finally, the proposal gave the president greater flexibility allocating financial aid to the area. The plan called for a budget of $200 million a year for unspecified economic and military needs in the Middle East.

The president's request for sweeping discretionary powers to act against Communist threats barely mentioned regional political issues. Thus, the disputes of Israel, Egypt, and the other Arabs states became subsumed under the American understanding of Cold War threats. Dulles explained to the Senate Foreign Relations and Armed Services Committees that the new policy was necessary, because "the stakes are so great" since "the leaders of International Communism" had already taken great risks to "win the Middle East." He only referred indirectly to the most recent clash in the region, Suez.[46] The Eisenhower Doctrine received support from many quarters. Congress overwhelmingly passed the policy in March 1957. Many in the press supported it, agreeing with the administration that the "inner mechanism of trouble" was the Soviet presence in Egypt.[47] Many in Israel remained dissatisfied that there wasn't a clearer security guarantee for Israel; many Arab states remained similarly unenthusiastic.[48]

In addition to the Eisenhower Doctrine, the second major theme of American Middle East policy in the post-Suez period was hostility toward Arab nationalism and Nasser. After Suez, American reports about Nasser did not inspire any confidence in the Egyptian leader. For example, Ambassador Hare wrote of Nasser to Washington in mid-1957: "He is both frank and secretive, straightforward and conspiratorial, bold and irresolute, generous and petty, . . . a veritable Doctor Jekyl and Mister Hyde." Just as before the crisis, American policymakers viewed the Egyptian leader with suspicion, and many, including congressional leaders, doubted whether Nasser could be trusted to negotiate and live up to any commitments to the international community. It seems that Nasser's independence, neutralism, and willingness to deal with the Soviets had forever tainted him. Dulles even went so far in private as to adopt the extreme comparisons of Guy Mollet and some of Israel's strongest supporters, likening Nasser to Hitler.[49]

The American press, also, made little attempt to hide its continuing hostility toward Nasser. For example, one *Time* article in January 1957 ridiculed Nasser's profession of neutralism. The plans of the "Dictator of the Nile" to "Egyptianize" banks and other foreign companies (turn over ownership and management to native born Egyptians) were described as a shortsighted power-grab.[50] A *Life* editorial that same month argued: "The U.S. . . . should lose no time in making it clear to Nasser that the dangerous Middle East situation will not be permitted simply to revert to the pre-invasion status quo." (Meanwhile, no mention was made of Israel and its occupation of portions of the Sinai.)[51]

In the late 1950s, with a series of crises in the Middle East, including the threat to King Hussein's throne in Jordan, the instability of the Lebanese government, the formation of the United Arab Republic (UAR) between Egypt and Syria, and the coup in Iraq, many Americans worried over what appeared to be a "tide of anti-Americanism" among Arabs. Nasser's position as "undisputed leader of the Arab world" created further anxiety since many observers had already decided that he was pro-Soviet and, therefore, anti-American. A few journalists urged a reconsideration of American policies and continued unquestioned support for Israel which they argued was alienating the Arabs. But these voices were in the minority. Many in the press, moreover, believed that Middle Eastern politics were not rational. Arabs were unpredictable and regional upheavals defied "any sober political analysis."[52]

Perhaps one of the most difficult issues for Americans to understand in the late 1950s was "Arab nationalism." This concept was unfamiliar to many, as witnessed by the reaction of Henry Luce who, on his travels to Egypt in 1956, reacted strongly to the assertion that the country was "part of the Arab nation." "What the hell does that mean?" the astonished publisher asked his companions. He learned of the concept of "OMMA" [ummah—the community of Muslims, political, social, and spiritual], "children of one mother" and was impressed that this was a constructive concept, not merely a xenophobic one as he believed "pan-Arabism" had been in the past.[53]

In the late 1950s, there were a number of press stories that sought to educate Americans about the concept of Arab nationalism. For example, one article in the *New York Times Magazine* recounted the history of Arabs in the Middle East, their expansion, height of power, and the cultural and religious concepts that underlay the idea of unity in the twentieth century. Although the author was hopeful that a "neutral," "progressive," and "mature" Arab commonwealth would be a force for good in the world, he argued that there were many obstacles to this ideal, including the Arabs' "unhappy traits" and "squabbling." Many journalists continued to be puzzled about the concept of Arab nationalism which was "difficult to define" and had "illogical peculiarities." If Arab nationalism seemed ill-defined to Western journalists, it led some to conclude that the Arabs needed a clear social creed and ideal, such as the respect for freedom that governed English-speaking peoples.[54] The supposed "squabbling" of Arabs was also described as a tendency to guile, deception, and "intrigue." Such characteristics, some journalists assumed, shaped the political structure of the modern Middle East. Feudalism was giving way to police states, "because the roots of intrigue and personal ambition and the age-old double cross are so deeply imbedded in Arab existence that the police state is able to function with peak efficiency." Nasser possessed all of these character traits, he was "the acknowledged master of intrigue on a grand scale."[55] Some stories were quite hostile to the concept of nationalism. For example, a story in *The Christian Century* argued that Arab nationalism was a symptom of

> The near-pathological Arab state of mind . . . [which] shows itself by a pathetic inability to face facts and enter into commitments. . . . It voices the age-old excuse of fatalism and lethargy. . . . The nub of the contrast between Israel and its Arab neighbors is that Israel possesses in such full measure the integrity they lack.[56]

When by the end of the decade, Arabs had not fulfilled their goals of unity and nationalism, some journalists repeated their harsh judgments not only about the political difficulty of achieving unity, but also about the defects of the Arab character and society. One journalist, for example, concluded that the Arabs "seem utterly incapable of unit[y], almost totally uncreative, riddled by differences of the most puerile kind, hamstrung by violence and political deceit. If Turkey was the sick man of Europe, the Arabs are the world's problem children." The political problems of the Arabs it seems could be traced from their "ferocious, fanatical, mob-mad, intolerant" traits, even if they were also known for their "kind[ness]." Characterizations of Arabs also emphasized—as they had earlier in the decade—their lack of political and economic progress in contrast with the modern, egalitarian Israelis.[57]

For many journalists, Nasser symbolized all that was wrong with Arab society. The American press acknowledged Nasser's role as a nationalist leader, but it questioned his legitimacy. For example, the press often noted that Arab societies were notoriously unequal, and that the legacies of this inequality as well as years of colonialism led many to view Nasser as an "idol." Despite Nasser's profession that he was working toward a more egalitarian society, many journalists did not trust that Arab citizens would be better off under his rule.[58] Even more than in the mid-1950s, late in the decade, especially after the 1958 formation of the United Arab Republic between Egypt and Syria and the military coup in Iraq, the press often labeled Nasser as a pro-Soviet, anti-Western leader. His announcements that the Arabs would "erase" Israel and that Egypt was stronger in the late 1950s than it was when it "beat the French, the British, and the Israelis" were seen as overly belligerent as well as unrealistic threats. One article noted that Israel had "humbled" the Arabs in the 1948 and 1956 wars. At the same time, some allowed that Nasser was a strong leader who should not be dismissed completely. *Life*, for example, solicited an article from the Egyptian leader in mid-1959, giving him an opportunity to put forward his views on nationalism and neutralism. Nasser took the opportunity to explain his record of opposition to regional Communists, and charged that the West was responsible for the growth of Communists in the Middle East, because of its support for unpopular leaders like Nuri es Said in Iraq (overthrown in the 1958 coup).[59]

Like those in the press, many American policymakers continued to harbor misconceptions about Arabs and Arab nationalism. For example, an NSC paper from early 1958 implied that Arab nationalism was motivated by the insubstantial goal of asserting an "Arab place in the sun." Moreover, Arabs (especially the "semi-educated urban element") seemed to be motivated more by the ill-defined "*mystique* of Arab unity." The report also concluded that Arabs were vulnerable to Communism not just because of their nationalist aspirations, but because their native "institutions and religions lack[ed] vigor." Arab masculinity, it seems, remained suspect in the minds of some American policymakers in 1958.[60] U.S. policymakers also had difficulty understanding Arab nationalism, because they frequently confused it with Communism. However they defined it, policymakers were alarmed at the growing strength of Arab nationalism. By 1958, Dulles, for example, believed that the United States could not "successfully oppose it [nationalism], but we can put up sand bags around positions we must protect—the first group being Israel and Lebanon and the second being the oil positions around the Persian Gulf." Arab nationalism, then, drew lines of loyalty that put Israel and the United States on the same side in the Middle East.[61]

It's worth noting that while the concept of Arab nationalism highlighted the unity of the Arabs, this was not only an idea that was confusing for Americans, but one that tended to lower Arab prestige in American eyes. In a culture that has always prized distinctiveness and independence (the politics of the Cold War alliances not withstanding), to describe a people as part of a collective group made them seem less developed politically. Thus, while from the Arab perspective, "Arab nationalism" was a sign of strength for all Arabs, for Americans, it's fair to say that it would have been seen as a sign of weakness. In addition to Arab nationalism, though, there is another reason that Americans saw Arabs as part of a collective: the very nature of the Arab-Israeli conflict. Thus, the situation is described as one against the many, and the very language is loaded with implications of strength, distinctiveness, and national integrity. This image of Arabs as part of a collective, then, is based upon the politics of the Arab-Israeli dispute, the assertion of Arab nationalism, and a general alienation from and ignorance about Arabs and their cultures. To a certain extent, such rhetoric is inevitable—it is used throughout this book—but we must still consider its impact.

LOOKING AT ISRAEL IN THE LATE 1950S

American attitudes toward Israel, at the popular and political level, went in the opposite direction of those toward Arabs. Despite American displeasure at Israeli actions during the Suez crisis, with their military victory over Nasser and their partnership with the British and the French, the Israelis had demonstrated their membership in an alliance of Western nations that opposed the danger and disorder of radical nationalism, revolution, and, by extension, the Soviet Union. In the late 1950s, Israelis appeared as more natural (and militarily adept) potential Cold War partners than did their Arab adversaries. Israeli leaders tried their best to take advantage of American anxiety over Soviet expansion to emphasize their value as strategic partners in the Middle East. Although the Jewish state continued to have some policy disagreements with the United States, Israeli leaders argued that the Cold War, not the Arab-Israeli conflict was the real reason for the Middle East crisis. The solution, said the Israelis, was a strengthening of the Eisenhower Doctrine, and a blending of the NATO and Eisenhower Doctrine countries since the Soviet Union was equally a threat to Europe and the Middle East.

The Israelis tried to demonstrate their loyalty, for example, by immediately reporting to U.S. officials about a meeting between Abba Eban and Soviet Foreign Minister Gromyko in the fall of 1957, and detailing Soviet threats to Israel if it continued to support U.S. policies. To demonstrate their country's value, after 1958, Israeli officials planned a "bulwark" in the Middle East against Soviet encroachments, consisting of Israel, Iran, the Sudan, Ethiopia, and Turkey. American diplomats supported the initiative and tried to foster closer ties between these countries and Israel. In addition, Americans responded to some of the Israeli arguments, treating the country's representatives as partners if not confidants. For example, in one meeting that Dulles had with Eban and other officials, the secretary noted that of course both he and Eban knew that the Soviet Union was the real danger in the region, while the Arabs had to be taught this. He spoke of the Arabs as if they were children who were "gradually becoming educated" to the danger. Moreover, Dulles disparaged the Arab desire for arms as frivolous: "the Arabs loved arms, just as once, crowns and diadems were treasured by kings and queens."[62]

Israel's proven fighting ability and military strength made it a country that many Americans respected as a strategic partner. Even if there was a growing arms imbalance between the Israelis and Arabs in the wake of the Soviet arms shipments, many policymakers, such as Donald Bergus from the Office of Near Eastern Affairs, continued to believe that Israel was militarily superior: "We see no early closing of the gap between the Arab states and their inability to mobilize on the one hand and the impressive organization of Israel defense on the other." There were other indications that U.S. policymakers were confident of Israel's fighting ability, especially in comparison with its neighbors. For example, the NSC reported in January 1958 that "Only Israel would be capable of effective delaying action against a major power; Iraq would be capable of some minor harassing action." Confidence in Israel following the Sinai War was also apparent on the popular level, especially among Jews. The Israeli government played on this sentiment, sending over military heroes to campaign for bonds soon after the war.[63]

Although American policymakers were aware that the continuing influx of Soviet arms into the Middle East might eventually change the balance of power, they remained unwilling to supply the Jewish state with the heavy weapons that it requested, preferring to allow Israel to get most of its arms from other countries, especially France. Israeli officials, for the most part, acquiesced to the situation by the late 1950s, limiting many of their requests to replacement parts, light arms, and ammunition. The Jewish state continued to receive sympathetic attention to this issue in the press, just as it had earlier in the decade. News stories often agreed with the complaints of Israeli officials that their country needed more arms. One article, for example, praised Israel's toughness and preparedness but worried that if the Russians continue to buildup Egypt, the Jewish state could be overwhelmed "by the sheer weight of military hardware."[64] The debate over American arms supplies to Israel was an old dispute, and just one of the policy disagreements between the two countries in the late 1950s.

Israeli officials were also eager to get more economic aid from the United States. Soon after the resolution of the Suez crisis, Israel requested additional economic aid, because of a short-term foreign exchange problem. But on this issue, as well, U.S. officials were reluctant to accede to Israeli requests. The Assistant Secretary of State for Near East, South Asian, and African Affairs William Rountree told the Israelis in mid-1957 that the financial problem was due to Israel's attack against Egypt and its continuing immigration—two policies that the United States didn't want to support. Moreover, Rountree argued that giving more aid to Israel at that time would seem to reward Israeli withdrawals which were to have been done unconditionally. In his meeting with Israeli diplomats a few days later, Dulles also put off requests for additional aid explaining that while the U.S. government had sympathy with Israel's situation, the funds were then limited and were really more for countries that couldn't yet borrow. He recommended that Israel turn to the Export-Import Bank instead. He added that it was "abnormal" for a country to base its policies on foreign aid and he further counseled against continuing immigration into Israel.[65]

The immigration situation was a third area of disagreement that continued after the Suez crisis. Some policymakers saw the post-Suez period as a time when the United States could use its increased influence to resolve outstanding disputes in the region. U.S. policymakers tried to make sure that American monies were not used to support further immigration to Israel (in early 1957, U.S. officials estimated that Israel would admit more than 100,000 new immigrants that year). Americans also made new efforts to link any increased aid to Israeli willingness to accept the "principle" of repatriation. After the Israelis took Dulles's advice in 1957 and went to the Export-Import Bank for a loan, the request was deferred in an effort to get Israel to repatriate refugees and lessen Jewish immigration. American pressure was not necessarily to force Israel to alter its "official" position on Jewish immigration—something Americans doubted would happen—but to force Israel to quietly control immigration as it had done at particular times in the past.[66]

The American position on Arab refugees, meanwhile, changed little from the early 1950s. In the period after Suez, American policymakers made explicit what they had believed all along: most Arab refugees could not go back to Israel, so Israel need only make a token gesture of repatriation. Thus, if Israelis accepted the "principle" of repatriation, this would break a diplomatic deadlock, while only a small number of Arabs would actually choose to go back to Israel and live as citizens of the Jewish state. The United States would help to steer Palestinians away from Israel by subsidizing a generous compensation program for those who resettled in Arab countries. Amid the efforts to prod Israelis to accept the formulation, there were also condemnations of "the intransigent attitude in some Arab quarters toward *any* settlement of the refugee problem." Officials expressed the belief that the *primary* reason for the failure to solve the refugee problem was Arab refusal to accept any alternative to repatriation and a narrowly defined plan of compensation set forth in a 1948 UN resolution.[67]

Disagreements between the United States and Israel continued past 1957, but the events of 1958 created in Washington's halls of power greater worries about the advances of nationalism and neutralism in the Middle East. Three key developments touched at least five countries: the formation of the United Arab Republic between Egypt and Syria, the military coup in Iraq overthrowing the monarchy, and the weakening of the

Lebanese and Jordanian governments (leading to the intervention of U.S. troops in Lebanon in 1958). Each of these events, which seemed to signal the contraction of traditional, pro-Western power, was interpreted as an advance for the Soviet Union. Such upheavals led policymakers to two different conclusions. First, that they had to be careful not to alienate the Arabs due to their policies toward Israel. But, second, that they needed Western allies in the Middle East, and the most eager aspirant to this position was Israel. Israel, for example, proved its value as a Western ally by allowing British overflights to Jordan to assist in supporting King Hussein's shaky throne in July 1958. Israel became, in the words of political scientist Abraham Ben-Zvi, "a de facto partner of the Western powers" in the effort to protect the Jordanian government.[68] Israel was rewarded with the delivery of one hundred 75mm antitank weapons from the United States and the assurance that the United States would similarly protect all nations so threatened, including Israel. For his part, Prime Minister Ben-Gurion proposed that Israel should be at the center of a ring of countries dedicated to stopping the expansion of influence from Nasser and the Soviet Union. Ben-Gurion offered Israel's services in helping to establish internal security and police services in other countries to protect against subversion.[69]

The impact of these political upheavals in 1958 and the reconsideration of how Israel fit into U.S. policy were reflected in two National Security Council papers outlining U.S. policy toward the region. NSC 5801/1 was written early in 1958, while NSC 5820/1 was written toward the end of the year.[70] In the former paper, the key objectives were to maintain Western access to the resources and passage rights in the Middle East, and to deny the Soviets control of the same. In addition, the authors wanted to encourage friendly governments to develop economically and to resist the threats posed by Communist infiltration, to resolve the Arab-Israeli conflict, and to prevent any growth in Soviet power and hopefully reduce the influence that it had already gained. The report further stated that the U.S. position in the region had suffered, because Arabs believed that Americans opposed Arab nationalism and unfairly supported Israel.

A few months later, the sense of alarm was heightened in NSC 5820/1. The priority among the main objectives was reordered and put in starker, more desperate language. The primary objectives were now the "denial of the area to Soviet domination" and the continued access to oil for western Europe. The secondary objectives then included the resolution of the Arab-Israeli conflict, the promotion of stable economic and political systems, the continued access to strategic positions and free passage in the region, the expansion of Free World influence, and reduction of Communist influence. While the report echoed the earlier one in its assessment that the current events in the region were "inimical to the U.S.," it more directly blamed the "emergence of the radical pan-Arab nationalist movement" as well as the USSR inroads for these trends. Over the year then, U.S. policymakers appeared to be more alarmed at the radical threat to American interests in the region, and even more willing to label the Soviets as the chief adversary in the Middle East.

Finally, the growing American focus on the Cold War as a way to explain Middle East politics and the deepening cultural familiarity and admiration for Israel came together in the reaction to Israel's tenth anniversary in 1958. While American officials were still cautious about how much they would embrace Israel in public, Israel was anxious for a great celebration which would garner recognition from abroad. Instead of sending a high-level representative, such as a head of state, as Israel desired, the secretary and president decided that the United States would be represented by its ambassador to Israel, Edward Lawson.[71] Nevertheless, American officials showed that they, indeed, were committed to the state's existence and gladly joined in celebrating the anniversary. Israeli diplomat Yaacov Herzog recalled that Dulles took the occasion of the anniversary to reiterate his friendly feelings toward the state. At a dinner at Abba Eban's home,

> [Dulles] spoke very warmly of the Judeo-Christian heritage, of what the Jewish people had given to the world, of Israel symbolizing this message down through the ages. You could clearly see that his attitude to Israel did derive . . . from a spiritual approach. . . . Despite the difficulties of the early years, his record on Israel . . . was a quite good one.[72]

Herzog recounted that Israeli diplomats had built a close relationship with the secretary who became more sympathetic to Israel's need to have a deterrence capacity, and Israel's need for arms and economic aid: "Generally in major issues he developed a very positive attitude and one of deep understanding." Other diplomats also thought that American-Israeli relations improved later in the Eisenhower administration, particularly after 1958. Abba Eban observed: "Nineteen fifty-eight was the year of the greatest assistance to Israel financially. And in August of that year, I received from Dulles a letter outlining his views of Nasserism as the subversive force." Eban recalled that "The United States was obviously coming to regard Israel not as a burden to be chivalrously sustained, but as an asset in the global and ideological balance."[73]

Outside of official Washington, American attitudes toward the Israeli anniversary were much less guarded, more openly celebratory—though this was nothing new. On each anniversary of Israel's formation, the American press had routinely published assessments of the "youngster," charting its growth and development. In the late 1950s, and especially on the occasion of the tenth anniversary, press stories often focused on familiar themes. For example, the young country was threatened by dangers all around, especially "Nasser's hostile Arab empire of 32 million [which] swirls ever closer to tiny 8,050-square mile Israel and its 2 million determined people." The country's survival to its tenth anniversary was described as a testament to the "proud little nation" that had "fought continuously for the right to exist." The press often concurred, especially after 1958, in the idea that the Cold War was central to Middle East politics. Israel continued to be referred to as "the Middle East's fastest-growing and toughest nation." And, attention continued to be paid to the multiethnic character of the immigrant nation, and the new *sabra* "superman" that it was building. Once again, the anniversary brought renewed attention to Ben-Gurion, dubbed by one journalist, "Mr. Israel": "Both [Israel and Ben-Gurion] are small, cocky, energetic, loaded with brains—and likable." Anniversary coverage included references to Israel's trade deficit, serious dependence on foreign aid, and military expenditures that ate up the government budget. Nevertheless, stories most often focused on all that had been accomplished by the capable Israelis.[74]

Along with the press stories, several nonfiction books—sounding similar themes—were published about the first ten years of Israel. One account emphasized that Israel's security was always threatened. A review of the book agreed in language long since familiar to American readers: "[Israel has] a constantly alerted citizen-army; she is surrounded by hostile enemies in border countries. Even the Arab citizens of Israel . . . are a security problem within the state." Other books and reviews echoed familiar themes too. An account of Israel's foreign affairs focused on the state as an innocent child. A review agreed, likening Israel to "a new kid in a rough neighborhood."[75] Thus, many Americans continued to use the images—of youthful, proud, tough, threatened Israelis—that had become familiar over the previous decade. Indeed, through these images, Israelis were embraced culturally as friends and allies.

CONCLUSION

Regarding Israel, American policymakers had more in common with journalists than they might have wanted to admit. Although diplomats were less likely to effuse over Israel's accomplishments and her pugnacious leader, they accepted and contributed to a political narrative that increasingly painted Israel as a Western country surrounded by pro-Nasser—and therefore anti-Western—Arabs. Policymakers worked to create strong relationships with "moderate" Arab countries (such as Jordan, Lebanon, and Saudi Arabia), and the press also differentiated between the minority of radical "Arab fire eaters," and the majority of the people. Yet, at a time when Arab nationalism and "unity" were at the forefront of many people's minds (and shaped the rhetoric of regional politics), distinctions were hard to make. As a result, hostility toward Arabs, overall, only grew after Suez, especially when Nasser had invited the Soviet Union into the region and seemed determined to thwart American strategic plans. Many Americans had adopted the Israeli point of view that the Arabs were not committed to a peaceful solution to the Arab-Israeli conflict. Many continued to agree with the sentiments voiced by John Foster Dulles three years earlier: "The basic fact of the matter is that the Arabs do not want peace and will not negotiate in any way for any sort of settlement."[76]

At the same time, by the late 1950s, following a decade of cultural images that highlighted the similarity between Americans and Israelis, the Jewish state could be more easily seen as a Western ally in the Cold War. Israeli foreign policies were interpreted in light of these cultural images. Israel's alliance with Britain and France, and her actions against the "pro-Soviet" "dictator" Nasser helped to rewrite American attitudes toward the nation, even while U.S. policymakers sharply condemned its actions over Suez. Other policy disagreements between the United States and Israel continued long after Suez was over, but they became routine and secondary. For example, although Israelis wanted to obtain an offensive weapons capability greater than all of the Arab states combined, the U.S. policymakers turned down the requests, pointed out that their country was already quite generous with Israel, and encouraged Europeans to supply Israel with enough weapons for her self-defense. Meanwhile, the Americans continued close diplomatic relations with and extensive economic aid to the Jewish state.[77]

Back in 1955, Dulles had warned Prime Minister Moshe Sharett not to make any military moves against Egypt in reaction to the Czech arms sale. He reasoned that aggression on Israel's part would trigger the Tripartite Declaration leading the United States to take sides against the Jewish state, and erode political and popular support for the country: "Israel has a tremendous asset of good will of all American people. What a people will do in assisting another country depends more on such things than on treaties."[78] Dulles was right on this point, more so than he realized. Israel did enjoy tremendous good will from Americans on the eve of Suez, good will that was strong enough to blunt American policymakers' criticism of the Israeli attack of Egypt and defiance of the United States and United Nations. The image of Israelis as insiders was not only not threatened, but reaffirmed in the Suez crisis and its aftermath.

Conclusion

In 1959, Leon Uris observed that "'since Sinai,' Israel has plunged ahead a decade each year . . . now that the tension has been eased and the question of survival has been settled." He concluded, "Israel to me is a symphony of progress." The author of the best-selling novel *Exodus* made his remarks in a *Look* article which previewed his new nonfiction book, *Exodus Revisited*. Along with photographer Dimitrios Harissiadis, he profiled the land of Israel, celebrating the country's development and growth by the end of the 1950s.[1] The photographs accompanying the *Look* article reprised all of the by then iconographic images of Israel, including a soldier standing guard on the frontier, children playing in the shadow of Arab guns, a nubile young *sabra* in shorts, scientists in a modern lab, and panoramic views of the landscape. His glowing portrait reflected his assessment of the situation in Israel at the end of the decade. In the years after the 1956 war, Israelis, he argued, had a new assurance and confidence in their survival, because of their convincing victory over Egyptian forces. Uris' profile also found Israeli strength in its position as a nation with a special mission for the whole world: ". . . Israel, who once gave a groping mankind its moral cornerstone, fulfills its ancient mission as a bridge from darkness to light." Uris was one of the foremost contributors to the narrative that stressed both Israel's uniqueness and its similarity with other nations, especially the United States. The clearest example of this message, as well as the most important ways in which images of Israel were transformed from the late 1940s to the late 1960s is found in Uris' influential *Exodus*.

Leon Uris' *Exodus*, a novel in 1958 and a Hollywood film in 1960, became an enduring cultural touchstone for a generation of Americans and American Jews, because it echoed many of the themes of the previous decade's cultural discourse and asserted them as unchallenged truths.[2] The story reprised familiar images, weaving them into a narrative about the meaning and creation of Israel, the Jewish character, and the relationship between Israel and the United States. Uris' broad brush takes in the history of European antisemitism, nineteenth- and early-twentieth-century Zionism, and the Holocaust. To anyone familiar with fiction about the Jews in World War II and the formation of Israel, *Exodus* fills the comfortable contours of an established genre, although it is unique in the way that the massive work addresses so many issues all at once. Moreover, *Exodus* achieved a distinct balance between the tensions of Israeli similarity to and difference from Americans by valorizing Israeli difference *using* the language of American cultural ideology. The fictional story centers on the romance between an Israeli soldier and pioneer, Ari Ben-Canaan, and a Christian, American nurse, Kitty Fremont. The triumph of Israeli survival becomes synonymous with the union of the fiercely passionate, although resolutely different characters.

The all-American, beautiful, blonde, and very feminine Kitty is hard working and reaches out to people in need, exemplifying the American self-image of a compassionate people eager to help underdogs. Inviting the identification of non-Jewish readers, Kitty has vague antisemitic notions based on ignorance rather than malice, for example, confessing that she doesn't usually think of Jews as fighters. Yet, she soon sheds her antisemitism and becomes converted to the Zionist cause because it "is not a case of politics but of humanity."[3] The courtship and sexual tension between the American and Israeli characters is a metaphor for the relationship between the two countries that they represent. In each, the parties are both similar and different, and inextricably drawn to each other by a great passion and sympathy. In addition, the character of Kitty is also attracted to Israel and Israelis as a compassionate mother would be. Her maternal relationship to the Jews symbolized what Harry Truman and other Americans described as their own parental role in the "birth" of the "infant" state. The Israeli Ari also embodies a stereotypical character. He is tough, masculine, and ingenious. A clever fighter, whose body is frequently described as "hard and powerful," Ari is braver than "ordinary human being[s]" and able to withstand great physical trials. He is world's away from the iconographic Jewish *schlemiel* of the pre-1948 period. *Exodus* is peopled by other strong Jews who survive the Holocaust and "tough and tender" *sabras* who fight the Arabs and the British for a homeland.

Like many of the characters from earlier fiction, the Israelis in *Exodus* are not only remarkable soldiers, but are also pragmatic pioneers and hardworking farmers. By the end of the 1950s, the narrative of pioneering Jews "making the desert bloom" was so widely accepted that it appeared in all sorts of fictional works, even those not set in the twentieth century. For example, in the 1959 biblical film *Solomon and Sheba*, the Jews are adept farmers. Solomon observes, "Can you believe that only a few years ago this was all a desert. . . . It is a joy to make the desert bloom."[4] Not only are the Israelis of *Exodus* pioneers, their communal farms are also romanticized. In an era when Americans were harking back to their own pioneer heritage, these sentiments could not but evoke nostalgia in Uris' audience (especially when parts of the Israeli landscape were compared to the United States). Uris' Israelis are also industrialists building bustling cities. "The sound of the hammer, the music of the drill, the concrete mixer, the welding torch never stopped in Israel!" effuses Uris.[5]

Uris' story asserts that the agricultural, industrial, and cultural institutions of the new state are firmly grounded in a Western culture and politics. For example, the religious heritage of the state is prized, but the characters are above all modern, not bound by "outmoded" religious rules. Ari's family and many of the *kibbutzim,* for instance, raise pigs. Uris also writes that the communal settlements were founded out of necessity, not because Israelis were Socialists. The novel's and film's characters are also committed to international law. They support the UN and, as in earlier fictional and press accounts, *Exodus* recreates the politicking and voting for the partition resolution in 1947. Importantly, the episode is depoliticized as a moral issue: "the six-thousand-year-old case of the Jewish people was placed before the conscience of man," writes Uris.[6]

Exodus reprises several other familiar themes in the popular and political narratives of Israel's formation. One was that the creation of the state was a David and Goliath story in which the Jews miraculously overcame great odds. Similarly, the story also uses the familiar birth metaphor to describe the formation of Israel. Uris also makes it clear that the creation of the Jewish state was inevitable because of the history of antisemitism, the legacy of the Holocaust, and the spiritual meaning of Jewish redemption.[7]

The spiritual meaning of "the people of the Book" finding their way home is constantly referred to in biblical quotations, spoken by both the narrator and all the major characters, and in allusions between biblical events and contemporary political ones. For example, when the British refuse to let a ship of refugee children sail for Palestine, the Zionist fighters respond with quotes from the biblical Exodus, "Let My People Go." In *Exodus*, the spiritual importance of Israel's creation is dramatized even more, making the Jewish state a divine mission with unquestioned legitimacy. For example, Kitty says of a group of Haganah soldiers, "This was no army of mortals. These were the ancient Hebrews . . . It was the army of Israel, and no force on earth could stop them for the power of God was with them!" The purpose of Israel was, above all, a divine one. The Christ-like figure of the young Jewish Karen who ends up giving her life for Israel sums up the message: "this . . . is the crossroads of the world. . . . where God wants His people to be . . . to . . . guard His laws which are the cornerstones of man's moral existence."[8]

Uris further appeals to his Christian readers by showing that Kitty comes to believe there is a strong bond between Jews and Christians, "I have learned that it is impossible to be a Christian without being a Jew in spirit." In this way, she exemplifies the Judeo-Christian ideal of the 1950s. A work contemporary to *Exodus* that emphasized Judeo-Christian unity was the very popular, award-winning biblical film epic of *Ben-Hur*. Similar in theme and iconography to other 1950s biblical films, the film blends the story of Jews and Christians in the ancient Middle East. The title character is an elite Jew fighting against wrongful imprisonment under the Romans. At the same time, the film tells of Jesus' life and martyrdom. The stories converge at the end: Judah Ben-Hur's political liberation is meaningless until he is saved by Jesus' love. Made the same year as *Ben-Hur, Solomon and Sheba* emphasizes Judeo-Christian unity by demonstrating the vast gulf between monotheism and sexually and morally corrupt paganism.[9]

Exodus also goes over familiar ground in its dichotomy of noble Israeli actions and evil Arab ones. The Arabs in the novel embody all of the negative stereotypes of the previous decade's popular culture. They are associated with Nazis, both as collaborators with the Germans and as people who adopt Nazi methods. They are pictured as hopelessly primitive in their economic, political, and justice systems. They have no understanding of democracy, and ordinary Arabs are merely manipulated by devious leaders. They are described as irrational and passionate, inept fighters, cowardly, dishonest, brutal, and—in the gendered tropes of the decade—lecherous, praying on innocent, fair young women.

The contrast between the Israelis and their darker neighbors is that much greater, because Israel is depicted as a Western country, dominated by Europeans. Israel's international and multicultural character is mentioned, but while this is given lip service, as in the earlier fiction, the Western heritage clearly dominates. Throughout the story, Uris emphasizes the closeness which the Israelis feel toward their fellow Westerners, Americans, and dismisses the Soviet support for the state in 1947 and 1948 as mere political maneuvering. The novel ends in the early 1950s, at which point Israel is described as self-reliant and strong, a fitting ally for the United States: the "mother," Kitty, is prepared to return to the United States, because her "baby" Israel has "grown up" and no longer needs her. Finally, the novel also looks at the relationship of American Jews to Zionism. Two American Jewish Zionists, one a captain of refugee ships and the other the head of the *Hadassah* health and social agency, both assert their loyalty to the United States as well as their determination to establish a Jewish state. They reassure readers that there is no conflict between loyalty to Israel and to the United States.

The impact of Uris' story was unparalleled, solidifying the image of Israel and the American relationship to that country for years to come. One review, for example, observed that although the book appeared to be a simple melodrama, "in these pages . . . we begin to share an epic vision of both man's capacity for evil, and of his faith and talent for the creative and the common good."[10] The most powerful reaction to the book came from American Jews. Like Uris' character Bill Fry, the American captain who ferries Jewish refugees to Palestine, American Jews felt a powerful identification with the warrior Jews. In the words of Arthur Hertzberg, American Jews wanted to have their own "Valley Forge" with the British and share in a "wild west story" complete with savage Indians. Hertzberg concludes that the book "became very nearly the 'Bible' of American Jews . . . [who] were hoping to imitate the Israelis. They wanted to be believable to themselves as 'cowboys' in America, as active wielders of power on American soil."[11]

Some contemporary critics spoke out against Uris' idealization of Israeli heroes. Sidney Hyman, for example, in *Harper's,* wrote that Israelis were ordinary human beings, not lofty stereotypes. Yet, in his critique of the images, Hyman reaffirmed the power that they held for American Jews and Christians alike. He noted that after years of antisemitic charges, American Jews [men] doubted their own worth: "The image of the new Israeli pioneer-fighter arms the American Jew with an answer to these doubts." For their part, Hyman wrote that Christians identified with the sense of purpose in Israel and envied the small nation in which the actions of every person could make a difference.[12] Thus, Hyman argued that although the Israel of the popular imagination did not represent the "real" country, it had a powerful impact, creating an emotional and cultural identification between Americans and Israelis.

The impact of *Exodus* was predicated, in part, on the transformation of the image of American Jews in the late 1940s and 1950s. As antisemitism declined and Jews became more accepted in the United States, readers and filmgoers could more easily identify with the Israeli characters in *Exodus*. From the late 1940s to the late 1950s, American Jews' assimilation and achievements were often documented in popular culture. Jewish success in various areas of American life was also celebrated in the press, such as in a 1955 *Reader's Digest* article which traced the history of Jews in the United States: "In every phase of American life in which they have participated, Jews have exhibited a wealth of talent and ability."[13] By the late 1950s, the story of Jewish assimilation included the assumption that Jews would continue to maintain their unique group identity, even as they "became" American in all other ways.[14] The universalist assumptions of the 1940s were, thus, replaced by the Cold War paradigm which stressed that diverse ethnic groups could have a common political ideology. This formulation, in turn, helped to quiet charges made by some that Jews had a "dual loyalty."[15]

In the cultural narrative that focused on the United States as a haven for persecuted immigrants, Jews were the quintessential success story, a group whose achievements seemed to confirm the value of the American experiment and the nobility of its ideals. From the point of view of many Americans, Israel also had a role in the cultural narrative of giving shelter to threatened immigrants. Thus, Jews were both the persecuted immigrants (in the United States) and the providers of refuge (in Israel), recreating the American success story. Press stories often made the parallels between the United States and Israel in this regard explicit. For example, a 1960 article in *Look* concluded that "the ingathering of the exiles in Israel bears a clos[e] resemblance to the filling up of the United States."[16]

By the end of the 1950s, at least in the public culture, signs of antisemitism were quickly condemned. The national press took note of a brief resurgence of antisemitism in the South in reaction to the push for integration in the 1950s and the Jewish involvement in that movement. Most prominently, in 1958, a Jewish community center in Nashville and temples in Miami and in Atlanta were bombed. The acts of violence were covered in the national news whose stories made it clear that the perpetrators were extremists with a message that was unacceptable to all Americans.[17] In a related assumption that would become more common in later years, criticism of Israel was also condemned in the press as coming dangerously close to antisemitism. For example, editors of *Commonweal* in 1956 criticized a column in a small Catholic magazine which spoke out against the existence of Israel. The editorial argued that such thinking was dangerous: the ghosts [of six million Jews] walk through history as a constant reproach to the Christian conscience and, in this context, as a necessary reminder of the way discussions of the Arab-Israeli dispute should not be carried out."[18]

If the decline of antisemitism helped to encourage the political acceptance of Israel, the U.S.-Israeli ties helped to hasten the end of prejudice against Jews. Similarly, the cultural narratives that swirled around Israel permeated popular as well as political culture, constructing a story of Israeli similarity to Americans. As Jews in the United States became more accepted, Israelis, too, became "Americanized." In addition, in the confusing and sometimes contradictory cultural narratives, Israelis and Jews became "Christianized" in the 1950s. Importantly, as Israelis came to resemble Americans in culture, and religious and political interests, Arabs seemed even more alien, not just because of their enmity with Israel, but because of the seemingly unbridgeable cultural divide with the United States.

As this study has argued, assertions of Israeli and American similarity were found in the political as well as popular culture, with policy-makers often invoking the same language and assumptions about ethnic characteristics as did best-selling potboilers or journalists. For example, former President Harry Truman highlighted American and Israeli similarity before the Zionist Organization of America in 1957:

> Here was a country founded on the love of human freedom, just as our own country was based on the ideal of freedom. / Here was a country designed to be a haven for the oppressed and persecuted of the earth, just as our own country had been. / Here in the land of Moses and the prophets was a rebirth of a nation dedicated, as of old, to the moral law and to belief in God. / . . . I believe it has a glorious future before it . . . as an embodiment of the great ideals of our civilization.[19]

The assumptions of American and Israeli similarity were further encouraged by the policy decisions coming out of Washington and the rhetoric used to describe those policies. Continuing U.S. aid, the decision to deemphasize many disagreements between the two nations (e.g., the dispute over the status of Jerusalem), and a budding strategic reliance on Israel, especially in the late 1950s, combined to signal to most Americans that the United States and Israel were at least "friends," if not "partners" in a Cold War world. Meanwhile, the increasingly divisive policy disagreements between Americans and Arabs, especially "radical" Arabs who insisted on challenging the Cold War paradigm, signaled a growing distance between Americans and Israel's antagonists.

The early Cold War, then, was a time of tremendous change in both Arab-American and Israeli-American relations. It is a period of the

Israeli-American relationship that has often been neglected by historians, except for the story of Israel's formation and the Suez War. But this period is essential for understanding the multifaceted U.S.-Israeli relationship in the 1970s and after. Although few U.S. weapons went to Israel and the economic aid of these years was but a fraction of what would follow, it was in the late 1940s and 1950s that Israelis were redrawn in popular culture to resemble Americans, and that they became "insiders" in American political culture.

This book began with the assertion that by the early 1960s many Americans viewed their country's relationship with the Jewish state as "special." This belief in a "special relationship" based on some kind of shared history and culture, and roughly akin to a pseudo-familial connection between the countries, was shaped by the preceding decade's evolving cultural images. In multiple, sometimes contradictory, popular and political narratives in the late 1940s and 1950s, Israelis and their American Jewish cousins were seen to have unique characteristics that made them both similar to Americans, and representatives of a distinct heritage. The image of Israelis and Jews changed over this decade, as Jews seemed to gain in strength, courage, and competence. Leaving behind the stereotype of a weak victim, a "new Jew" was discursively constructed who embodied the virtues and aspirations of the American past and present. In the images of Israelis, then, Americans constructed their own self-image at mid-century. Furthermore, these narratives cut across American culture, and were adopted by Washington policymakers as well as Hollywood filmmakers and ordinary Americans. They had a powerful resonance, because they invoked a Cold War ideology that simplified the messy contradictions of international and domestic life to celebrate a story of rebirth and redemption in a dangerous world. Thus, the Israel of the American imagination in the 1940s and 1950s embodied the hopes, ideals, and values of Cold War America.

Notes

PREFACE

1. For a sample of the historiographic discussion on this issue see, the roundtable debating the parameters of the special relationship, "Fifty Years of U.S.-Israeli Relations," *Diplomatic History* 22, no. 2 (Spring 1998): 231–283.

2. See Allon Gal, "Overview: Envisioning Israel—The American Jewish Tradition," and Jonathan Sarna "A Projection of America as it Ought to Be: Zion in the Mind's Eye of American Jews" (esp. 41, 57), in Gal, ed., *Envisioning Israel* (Jerusalem and Detroit, 1996).

Although this book focuses on the ways in which cultural and political images resonated for both Jews and non-Jews, I note that Jewish men—rising to literary prominence and holding important positions in Hollywood—fashioned many of these cultural and media images. Yet, their impact was not necessarily predictable. The main focus of this study remains the narratives of public culture—regardless of who created them. For discussion of the cultural influence of postwar American Jews as well as the way in which this has been distorted by antisemites, see Stephen Whitfield, *In Search of American Jewish Culture* (Hanover, NH, 1999) and Neal Gabler, *An Empire of Their Own* (New York, 1988).

3. While previous studies have focused on public opinion more narrowly defined (see for example, Eytan Gilboa, *American Public Opinion Toward Israel and the Arab-Israeli Conflict* (Lexington MA, 1987); and Bruce J. Evenson, *Truman, Palestine, and the Presidency* (New York, 1992)), this book traces multiple cultural narratives through fictional and nonfictional works, political memos, the press, and public opinion. It is informed by the work on cultural narratives found in Edward Said, *Orientalism* (New York, 1978) and *Culture and Imperialism* (New York, 1993), as well as by the work of historians who have recently been using a "discursive analysis." For examples, see Gail Bederman, *Manliness and Civilization* (Chicago, 1995); and Frank Costigliola, "The Nuclear Family," *Diplomatic History* 21, no. 2 (Spring 1997): 163–183. For a study which examines postwar narratives as they shape the memories of American Jews see Hasia Diner, *Lower East Side Memories* (Princeton, 2000).

CHAPTER ONE: IMAGES OF THE "NEW JEW" IN POSTWAR CULTURE

1. This paragraph draws on Leonard Dinnerstein, *Antisemitism in America* (New York, 1994), esp. 58–68 (quote is from 66). For further background see also Frederic Cople Jaher, *A Scapegoat in the New Wilderness* (Cambridge, 1994).

2. Patricia Erens, *The Jew in American Cinema* (Bloomington, IN, 1984), esp. 135–8, 143, also 125–164; and Lester Friedman, *Hollywood's Image of the Jew* (New York, 1982), 57–85.

3. This paragraph draws upon the analysis of Philip Gleason, "Americans All," *Review of Politics* 43 (1981): 483–518.

4. "They Got the Blame," originally circulated as a pamphlet directed at adults, and was then turned into a comic for children. Copy of comic, pamphlet, and letter M. R. Robinson to "Dear Friend," Papers of Philleo Nash, OWI file/ Alphabetical Domestic propaganda, box 8, Harry S. Truman Library.

5. Gunnar Myrdal, *An American Dilemma* (New York, 1944), 1004.

6. Address by Louis Nizer at presentation of award to Harry S. Truman, 18 February 1948, President's Secretary's Files (hereafter, PSF), General File (hereafter, GF), Appointments 14–31 March 1948, box 88, Truman Library.

7. For further discussion of trends in antisemitism see Charles Stember et al, *Jews in the Mind of America* (New York, 1966); and Leonard Dinnerstein, *Uneasy at Home* (New York, 1987).

8. The studies of American refugee policy during World War II are numerous. For two differing interpretations, see David S. Wyman, *The Abandonment of the Jews* (New York, 1984); and Richard Breitman and Alan Kraut, *American Refugee Policy and European Jewry, 1933–1945* (Bloomington IN, 1987). This paragraph also draws on Henry L. Feingold, *Bearing Witness* (Syracuse, 1995).

9. Dinnerstein, *Antisemitism in America*, 150; quote from *Look*, November 29, 1955, 34.

10. See Eric Goldstein "Race and the Construction of Jewish Identity in America, 1875–1945" (Ph.D. diss., University of Michigan, 2000), esp., 14–18, 420–424. Also, Whitfield, *In Search of American Jewish Culture*, 143–150.

11. *Crossfire*, (RKO, 1947). Film copy from the Motion Picture Collection of the Library of Congress (hereafter, MPC). Review of *Crossfire*, based on novel *The Brick Foxhole* by Richard Brooks, directed by Edward Dmytryk, *Variety*, June 25, 1947.

12. The contemporary sociological study by T. W. Adorno et. al, isolated a particular antisocial "personality" more conducive to such "irrational" beliefs. T. W. Adorno et. al., *The Authoritarian Personality* (New York, 1950).

13. Stember et al., *Jews in the Mind of America*, 54–56, 65; Gabler, *An Empire of Their* Own, 299.

14. The book remained on the *New York Times Book Review* (hereafter *NYTBR*) best seller list for ten months. See *NYTBR* 1947–1948. The film won Academy Awards for best picture, best director, best supporting actress, and

received nominations for best actor, actress, and supporting actor. It was the eighth top grossing picture of the year. See Terry Ramsaye, ed., *International Motion Picture Almanac 1948–1949* (New York, 1949); and Friedman, *Hollywood's Image of the Jew*; Laura Z. Hobson, *Gentleman's Agreement* (New York, 1947); film copy from Motion Picture Collection (hereafter, MPC) Library of Congress.

15. William DuBois, "Schuyler Green's Metamorphosis," *NYTBR*, March 2, 1947, 5.

16. Quoted in Dinnerstein, *Antisemitism in America*, 108.

17. Hobson, *Gentleman's Agreement*, 9, 154.

18. Ibid., 176.

19. Ibid., 188.

20. See Gabler, *An Empire of Their Own*, 356–357. Also see, Larry Ceplair and Steven Englund, *The Inquisition in Hollywood* (Berkeley, 1970, 1983).

21. Gabler, *An Empire of Their Own*, 279.

22. Friedman, *Hollywood's Image of the Jew*, 145, 162.

23. See Stember et al, *Jews in the Mind of* America, 56, 65.

24. The depiction of Samuels' "sensitivity" also seems to be a holdover from the novel on which the film is based, *The Brick Foxhole* by Richard Brooks, in which the character is murdered because he is gay not Jewish. Patricia Erens, "Between Two Worlds," in *The Kaleidoscope Lens*, ed. Randall Miller (New York, 1980), 126.

25. For example, I. Burton Kaufman and the Bureau of War Records of the National Jewish Welfare Board, *American Jews in WWII* (New York, 1947).

26. Bruce Bliven, series in *The New Republic*: "U.S. Anti-Semitism Today," November 3, 1947; "Salesmen of Hate," November 17, 1947; "Myths About the Jews," November 24, 1947; "For 'Nordics' Only," December 8, 1947; "The Cold Pogrom," December 15, 1947; and "What *is* Anti-Semitism," December 22, 1947.

27. Jean-Paul Sartre, *Anti-Semite and Jew*, trans. George J. Becker (New York, 1948), 10.

28. For examples, see Thomas Lask, "The Anatomy of Prejudice," *NYTBR*, February 2, 1947, 28, and Leo Shapiro, "Analyzing Racial and Cultural Antagonisms," *NYTBR*, February 16, 1947, 28.

29. Hobson, *Gentleman's* Agreement, 270.

30. Irwin Shaw, *The Young Lions* (New York, 1948); and Norman Mailer, *The Naked and the Dead* (New York, 1948). The novels remained on the best seller list for a long time: Mailer's novel from mid-1948 to mid-1949 and Shaw's from the fall of 1948 to mid-1949. See *NYTBR*, 1948–1949, *New York Herald Tribune Book Review* (hereafter, *NYHTBR*), October 3, 1948, and May 9, 1948, and *Saturday Review of Literature*, October 2, 1948, and May 8, 1948.

31. Shaw, *Young Lions*, 301.

32. Ibid., 301–303; Studs Terkel, "*The Good War*," (New York, 1984), 470.

33. Shaw, *Young Lions*, 19.

34. Mailer, *Naked and Dead*, 6, 111, 544.

35. Ibid., 52, 59, 169.

36. John Higham, *Send These to Me* (New York, 1975), 219.

37. "Orphans Clothed," *Life*, November 17, 1947, 57–60; Truman's address to the Combined Jewish Appeal, Boston, 6 October 1955, Papers of Harry S. Truman, Speech File, box 57, Truman Library.

38. Mailer, *Naked and Dead*, 44–45.

39. John Hersey, *The Wall* (New York, 1950), 7.

40. Quotes are from, Joseph Viertel, *The Last Temptation* (New York, 1955), 2, 13, 49.

41. Shaw, *Young Lions*, 330, 621.

42. Viertel, *Last Temptation*, 131.

43. The book remained a best seller for eight months (*NYTBR*, 1950); William Shirer, "John Hersey's Superb Novel," *NYHTBR*, February 26, 1950, 1+.

44. Anne Frank, *Anne Frank: The Diary of a Young Girl*, Introduction by Eleanor Roosevelt (New York, 1952), 154.

45. Meyer Levin, "The Child Behind the Secret Door: An Adolescent Girl's Own Story of How She Hid for Two Years During the Nazi Terror," *NYTBR*, June 15, 1952, 1. See best seller lists *NYTBR* 1952.

46. See Ludwig Lewisohn, "A Glory and a Doom," *Saturday Review of Literature*, July 19, 1952, 20, and Levin, "Child Behind the Secret Door," 1.

47. The following relies upon Deborah Lipstadt's analysis of the press coverage in *Beyond Belief* (New York, 1986), 2, 39, 42–45.

48. Ibid., 140, 141, 248, 250, 254, 255.

49. Gilbert Gordon, "Fascist Field Day in Chicago," *The Nation*, January 24, 1948, 98–100.

50. Tony Kushner, *The Holocaust and the Liberal Imagination* (Oxford, 1994), 207.

51. Dorothy Seidman Bilik, *Immigrant-Survivors* (Middletown CT, 1981), 29. Other citations, Kushner, *Holocaust*, 216, 228; emphasis in the original.

52. Kushner, *Holocaust*, 212, 213–14.

53. Ibid., 215; Bilik, *Immigrant-Survivors*, 15.

54. For discussion of Hollywood depictions of the Holocaust, see Annette Insdorf, *Indelible Shadows* (Cambridge, 1983), Judith E. Doneson, *The Holocaust in American Film* (Philadelphia, 1987), and Bilik, *Immigrant-Survivors*.

55. Shaw, *Young Lions*, 672.

56. Ibid., 677.

57. *The Search*, MGM/Praesens Film, 1948, film copy from MPC.

58. Bosley Crowther, *New York Times* (hereafter, *NYT*), March 24, 1948.

59. Mailer, *Naked and Dead*, 420, 584.

60. Ibid., 592–93, Shaw, *Young Lions*, 680.

61. Hersey, *The Wall*, 187–88.

62. R. M. MacIver, "Mosaic of a People's Enduring Spirit," *NYTBR*, February 19, 1950, 7; emphasis added.

63. Hersey, *The Wall*, 427.

64. Frank, *Anne Frank*, ix.

65. Hersey, *The Wall*, 549–550.

CHAPTER TWO: THE UNITED STATES AND THE FOUNDING
OF ISRAEL

1. Henry Wallace, "In Rome as in Palestine," *The New Republic*, November 17, 1947, 12–13.

2. See Friedman, *Hollywood's Image of the Jew*, 91.

3. Viertel, *Last Temptation*, 152; emphasis in the original.

4. *The Juggler*, Columbia, 1953, copy from Motion Picture Collection, Library of Congress, Washington, D.C.; and *The Sword in the Desert*, Universal, 1949; copy from Motion Picture Collection, Library of Congress, Washington, D.C.

5. Viertel, *Last Temptation*, 153.

6. Telegram Weizmann to Truman, 9 November 1948, Papers of Clark Clifford, Palestine Telegrams and Cables, 1 of 2, box 14; Letter Weizmann to Truman, 30 April 1951, PSF, Subject File, Israel, box 181, Truman Library.

7. Examples are taken from I. F. Stone, "Palestine, Britain and the UN," *The New Republic*, August 2, 1948, 10; "Palestine: The Test and the Weakness," *Newsweek*, May 31, 1948, 29; "Israel is Born in Travail and Hope," *Life*, May 31, 1948, 21; "Israel Faces Facts of Life," *Life*, May 14, 1951, 117.

8. For one of many examples, see Letter Leonard Vogel to Charles Ross, 12 August 1946, OF, file 204 Miscellaneous (August to September 1946), box 772, Truman Library.

9. See Peter Hahn, *The United States, Great Britain, and Egypt, 1945–1956* (Chapel Hill, 1991); and William Stivers, *America's Confrontation With Revolutionary Change in the Middle East, 1948–1983* (New York, 1986).

10. Viertel, *Last Temptation*, 136.

11. This and the following paragraph, Alfred Lilienthal, *What Price Israel* (Chicago, 1953), 3, 110, 147, 230, 173.

12. Eleanor Roosevelt, *The Autobiography of Eleanor Roosevelt* (New York, 1958), 310; Telegram Eleanor Roosevelt to Truman, 21 August 1947, PSF, Personal File, file Eleanor Roosevelt, box 321, Truman Library.

13. Michael J. Cohen, *Truman and Israel* (Berkeley, 1990), 69.

14. Letter Roosevelt to Marshall, 22 March 1948. Also see, Roosevelt to Truman, 29 January 1948, Roosevelt to Marshall, 13 March 1948, Roosevelt to Truman, 22 March and 26 March 1948, Roosevelt to Truman, 11 May 1948, Roosevelt to Marshall, 16 May 1948. All can be found in PSF, Personal, file Eleanor Roosevelt (2), box 322, Truman Library.

15. Memo of Conversation Secretary of State to Under Secretary of State Lovett, 24 May 1948, *The Foreign Relations of the United States* (hereafter, FRUS), 1948 V: 1036–37.

16. "Palestine: The Bear and the Time of Peril," *Newsweek*, May 24, 1948, 31, and "Palestine: The Test and the Weakness," *Newsweek*, May 31, 1948, 26; Nat Barrows, "U.S. Prestige Seen at New Low in U.N. in Holy Land Dispute," *Washington Star*, May 17, 1948.

17. Eleanor Roosevelt, "My Day: Will the Arabs Continue to Defy the United Nations?" 19 May 1948, Papers of George Elsey, box 60, Truman Library.

18. See Cohen, *Truman and Israel*, 16. For samples of his contemporary views of Jews, see 21 July 1947, Harry S. Truman 1947 Diary Book, 1947 Diary and Manual of the Real Estate Board of N.Y., Truman Library.

19. Robert H. Ferrell, ed., *Off the Record* (New York, 1980), 45. Also, 68, 214–215.

20. For example, by September 1952, Truman fired off a letter to Secretary of State Dean Acheson asking him to investigate the reason that Max Lowenthal was denied a passport; he assumed that this happened, "because he happens to be a Jew." Memo Truman to Acheson, 25 September 1952, and Letter Acheson to Truman, 2 October 1952, PSF, Subject File, Cabinet, Secretary of State miscellaneous file, box 159, Truman Library.

21. Seth Tillman, *The United States in the Middle East* (Bloomington IN, 1982), 12.

22. Melvin Urofsky, *We Are One! American Jewry and Israel* (Garden City, NY, 1978), 111.

23. The literature on the United States and the founding of Israel is vast. For a sample, see David Schoenbaum, *The United States and the State of Israel* (New York, 1993); Zvi Ganin, *Truman, American Jewry, and Israel, 1945–1948* (New York, 1979), and Bruce J. Evenson, *Truman, Palestine and the Presidency* (New York, 1992).

24. Tillman, *United States in Middle East*, 14; and David McCullough, *Truman* (New York, 1992), 604.

25. See Bruce J. Evenson, "A Story of 'Ineptness': The Truman Administration's Struggle to Shape Conventional Wisdom on Palestine at the Beginning of the Cold War," *Diplomatic History*, Summer 1991, 15:3, 345–346.

26. Harry S. Truman, *Years of Trial and Hope, 1946–1952* (New York, 1956), 158, 166–67, 172; Cohen, *Truman and Israel*, 51.

27. Clark Clifford with Richard Holbrooke, *Counsel to the President* (New York, 1991), 23–24; Letter from Rabbi Samuel Thurman to Truman, 17 May 1948, Post Presidential Files (hereafter, PPF) 1395, box 504, Truman Library; Merle Miller, *Plain Speaking* (New York, 1973,4), 218.

28. There were reports of at least two other times when Truman made the same parallel. Allen Weinstein and Moshe Ma'-oz, *Truman and American Commitment to Israel* (Jerusalem, 1981) 83–84.

29. Letter Truman to Emanuel Neumann, 29 June 1948, Papers of David Niles, Israel File, box 30, Truman Library.

30. Sixtieth Convention Zionist Organization, 14 September 1957, Papers of David Lloyd, Speech file, box 59, Truman Library.

31. Letter from Golda Meir to Truman, 8 May 1969, PPF, Israel File, box 42, Truman Library.

32. Ferrell, *Off the Record*, diary entries for March 20 and 21, 1948.

33. Memo Philleo Nash to Charles Feldelson, 14 February 1951, Philleo Nash Files, Correspondence "F" file #2, box 6, Truman Library.

34. See A. J. Granoff Oral History (hereafter, OH), Truman Library; and Frank J. Adler, *Roots Moving in a Stream* (Kansas City MO, 1972); also, Letter Jacobson to Weizmann, 29 November 1948, Relating to Relations Between the

United States and Palestine and Israel, Papers of Chaim Weizmann, copies at Truman Library.

35. The Jewish advisor David Niles had extensive links to Zionist organizations and leaders, including Israeli diplomats Eliahu Epstein and Teddy Kolleck. See correspondence in boxes 30, 31, 34, 35, arranged by Israel as subject and date, Niles Papers, Truman Library.

36. Clifford's memoirs celebrate the recognition episode and his own role in it. Clifford, *A Memoir*, 3–24. See also Letter Epstein to Clifford, 24 January 1949, Clifford Papers, Subject File, Palestine Correspondence, Miscellaneous File, 1 of 3, box 13, Truman Library.

37. Clifford, *Oral History*, 101, Truman Library; McCullough, *Truman*, 619; emphasis added.

38. Clifford, *Oral History*, 103, Truman Library.

39. See Letter Eliahu Epstein to Clifford, 9 August 1948, and Letter Samuel Rosenman to Clifford, 30 July 1948 (and attachment 29 July 1948); both are found in Clifford Papers, Subject File, Palestine Correspondence, Miscellaneous, 1 of 3, box 13, Truman Library.

40. McCullough, *Truman*, 596.

41. Steven L. Spiegel, *The Other Arab-Israeli Conflict* (Chicago, 1985), 18; also, Cohen, *Truman and Israel*, 179.

42. Letter from M. J. Slonim to Clifford, 16 June 1948 and response, 23 June 1948, Clifford Papers, Subject File, Palestine Correspondence, Miscellaneous, 1 of 3, box 13, Truman Library.

43. Letter Chester Bowles to Clifford, 23 September 1948, Clifford Papers, Subject File, Palestine Correspondence, Miscellaneous, 1 of 3, box 13, Truman Library.

44. Cohen, *Truman and Israel*, 60.

45. This particular lobbying group, as it turns out, had already secured the backing of many congressmen, having eighteen on its advisory board. Letter Korff to McGrath, 12 February 1948, file Palestine, DNC Chairman, Papers of J. Howard McGrath, box 63, Truman Library.

46. Examples are found in Official File, May 1947, 204, Miscellaneous, box 773, Truman Library.

47. The height of material was received between 1947 and 1949 and most of the volume was pro-Zionist: 841,903 postcards, 86,500 letters, 51,400 telegrams. Memos to Philleo Nash from Andie Knutson, 24 July 1951, and 6 August 1951, Reports on Unsolicited Telegrams and Mail on the Palestine Situation, Nash Files, box 11, Truman Library. Also see Memos to Niles from G. L. Clark, the mailroom, 16 June 1948, 1 February 1950, 3 March 1950, 3 May 1950, same files. The correspondence is stored in boxes 774–777 in Miscellaneous and Palestine Letter Files arranged by dates, Official File; boxes 42, 44, 45, 51, 1189, 1219, 1220, 1731, 2740, filed by Jewish organizations and Israel subjects, General File; boxes 30, 31, 34, 35, filed by date and Israel as subject, Niles Papers, Truman Library.

48. Press Conference, May 15, 1948, Papers of Charles Ross, box 10, Truman Library.

49. Some notable exceptions to the press support were: the Alsop brothers, James Reston in the *New York Times*, and *a few* of the articles in *Time*, *Newsweek*, and *Life*. See Ganin, *Truman, American Jewry*, 150, 153 and Grose, 226; Evenson, *Diplomatic History*, 346.

50. Morrell Heald and Lawrence S. Kaplan, *Culture and Diplomacy* (Westport CT, 1977), 246–247. Opponents in the administration included Under Secretary of State Robert Lovett, his predecessor Dean Acheson, Department Counsel Charles Bohlen, Head of the Policy Planning Staff George Kennan, Director of United Nations Affairs Dean Rusk, the Joint Chiefs of Staff, and, most importantly, Secretary of State George Marshall and Secretary of Defense James Forrestal.

51. McCullough, *Truman*, 605.

52. Cohen, *Truman and Israel*, 93–94.

53. Note on Mr. James Duce, Vice President in Charge of Operations of the American-Arabian Oil Company, Niles Papers, Israeli Affairs 1948, box 30, Truman Library.

54. Cohen, *Truman and Israel*, 95.

55. Daniel Yergin, *The Prize* (New York, 1991), 426; Joseph Satterthwaite, Ohio, 19, Truman Library.

56. Quotes from, Truman, *Memoirs*, 193, Miller, *Plain Speaking*, 215, McCullough, *Truman*, 597.

57. McCullough, *Truman*, 610; Evenson, *Truman, Palestine and Presidency*, 9.

58. Truman address to Combined Jewish Appeal of Greater Boston, 6 October 1955, Lloyd Papers, Speech File, box 57, Truman Library; emphasis added.

59. Telegram Benny Goodman to Truman, 26 April 1947, Official File, 204 Miscellaneous, box 773, Truman Library.

60. For example, in April 1948, The Nation Associates produced a pamphlet collecting recent articles about the situation entitled "Palestine: A Pattern of Betrayal: The Role of the United States, Great Britain, and the United Nations Since November 29," file—Palestine, DNC Chairman, McGrath Papers, box 63, Truman Library.

61. For example, "Palestine: The Bear and the Time of Peril," *Time*, May 24, 1948, 28–9, and "Palestine: The Test and the Weakness," *Time*, May 31, 1948, 29; also, I. F. Stone, "Palestine, Britain and the UN," *The New Republic*, August 2, 1948, 10; Henry Wallace, "Palestine: Civilization on Trial," *The New Republic*, February 16, 1948, 9; Freda Kirchwey, "Mr. Bevin Goes Too Far," *The Nation*, January 22, 1949, 88–90.

62. Said Aburish, *Children of Bethany* (Bloomington, IN, 1988), 50, 93, 94.

63. For further discussion see, Issam Suleiman Mousa, *The Arab Image and the U.S. Press in Political Culture* (New York, 1984).

64. See for example, Edward Whiting Fox, "Paradoxical Study of a Changing Palestine," *NYTBR*, May 18, 1947, 6.

65. For example Nelson Glueck, "Religions in Palestine," *NYTBR*, June 26, 1949, 25.

66. Crane Brinton, "Sumner Welles in Palestine," *NYTBR*, June 13, 1948, 1; emphasis in the original.

67. "The Record of Collaboration of King Farouk of Egypt with the Nazis and Their Ally, The Mufti," Clifford Papers, Palestine Miscellaneous Memos

(2 of 3), box 14, Truman Library; "In Abraham's Bosom," *Time*, November 1, 1948, 37; "Nazi Prisoners in Egypt's Army: A French Intelligence Report," *The Nation*, January 22, 1949, 89.

68. Letter Rabbi Nathan Taragin of Young Israel Synagogue of Claremont Parkway (Bronx) to McGrath, 1 June 1948, McGrath Papers, file Palestine, DNC chairman, box 63, Truman Library; "Explosions Kill Jews as Arabs Defy the U.S.," *Life*, March 8, 1948, 36–37; "Israel is Born in Travail and Hope," *Life*, May 31, 1948, 21.

69. Thomas Sugrue, "Two Neophytes in a Troubled World," *NYTBR*, August 26, 1951, 16.

70. Memo Mr. Humelsine, Department of State to Matthew Connelly, White House, quoting Etheridge telegram, 15 March 1949, folder 1, and Webb to Truman, 27 June 1949, folder Secretary of State miscellaneous, PSF, Subject File, Cabinet, Secretary of State, box 159, Truman Library; Minister in Lebanon (Pinkerton) (for Etheridge) to Secretary of State, 28 March 1949, FRUS 1949 VI, 877–8; Letter Etheridge to Truman, 11 April 1949, PSF, Subject File, Israel file, box 181, Truman Library; Walter Eytan, *The First Ten Years* (New York, 1958), 53.

71. Memo of Conversation by Secretary of State, 8 September 1948, FRUS 1948 V Pt. 2: 1381; Forrestal to Chairman of the House Committee on Foreign Affairs (Bloom), FRUS 1949, VI: 698.

72. Truman to Etheridge, 29 April 1949, FRUS 1949 VI: 957 and Memo of Conversation by Secretary of State, 28 April 1949, FRUS 1949 VI: 954; Acting Secretary of State Webb to Embassy in Israel (conveying note from Truman to Ben-Gurion), 28 May 1949, FRUS 1949, VI: 1073.

73. NSC 47/2 "Report on U.S. Policy Toward Israel and the Arab States," 17 October 1949, FRUS 1949, VI: 1437–78; Howard Morley Sachar, *A History of Israel* (New York, 1996), 440; Memo Ambassador-Designate to Israel (Davis) to Assistant Secretary of State for Near Eastern, South Asian, and African Affairs (McGhee), 26 January 1951, FRUS 1951, V: 564; Department of State Position Paper, 12 October 1951, FRUS 1951, V: 894.

74. Sachar, *History of Israel*, 395.

75. Minister of Foreign Affairs of the Provisional Government of Israel (Shertok) to Secretary of State Marshall, 8 June 1948, FRUS 1948, V Pt. 2: 1104–05; Letter Blaustein to Truman, 27 September 1950, PSF, General File, file Bi–Bl, box 113; Memo of Conversation, 20 October 1950, Acheson Papers, box 65, Truman Library.

76. Etheridge to Secretary of State, 13 April 1949, FRUS 1949, VI: 914.

77. November 1950, Survey 115, Elsey Papers, Subject File, file—Foreign Relations—Periodicals, box 60, Truman Library.

78. "Toward Atonement," *Time*, October 8, 1951, 32–33.

79. Memo of Conversation, 8 May 1951, Acheson Papers, box 66, Truman Library. Also, Memo of Conversation, 22 March 1951, Acheson Papers, box 66, Truman Library.

80. Acting Secretary of State to the Embassy in Lebanon, 22 October 1952, FRUS 1952–54 IX Pt. 1: 1037; Memo of Conversation, 5 May 1952, Acheson Papers, box 167, Truman Library

81. Schoenbaum, *United States and State of Israel*, 86.

CHAPTER THREE: VIEWS OF THE NEW JEWISH STATE

1. Irwin Shaw and Robert Capa, *Report on Israel*, (New York, 1949, 1950); quote is found on 38–39.

2. The pioneering ideal had been widespread among American Zionists earlier in the century. See Sarna, "A Projection of America as it Ought to Be," in Gal, ed., *Envisioning Israel*, 41.

3. Shaw and Capa, *Report on Israel*, 33, 34, 14.

4. Ibid., 38, 67, 120, 125, 140.

5. John Hersey, "Our Far-Flung Correspondents: The *Kibbutz*," *The New Yorker*, April 19, 1952, 97–111; Ibid., 38, 67, 120, 125, 140.

6. Gertrude Samuels, "Israel: Five Years of Change," *New York Times Magazine* (hereafter, *NYTM*), November 7, 1954, 14.

7. Hersey, "Our Far-Flung Correspondents," 110.

8. George Biddle, "Israel: Young Blood and Old," *The Atlantic*, October 1949, 23.

9. "Israel Faces the Facts of Life," *Life*, May 14, 1951, 116–26.

10. Samuels, "Israel," 14; Henry Wallace, "Palestine: Civilization on Trial," *The New Republic*, February 16, 1948, 9; John Hersey, "A Reporter at Large: The Ingathering of the Exiles," *The New Yorker*, November 24, 1951, 92 +.

11. "Report on Israel," CIO Publications Department, Clifford Papers, Releases and Clippings file, box 14, Truman Library.

12. Press Release, 19 January 1949, Clifford Papers, Releases and Clippings, box 14, and Speech at Jewish National Fund dinner, 26 May 1952, Papers of Eben Ayers, General File, Palestine Press Releases, box 9, Truman Library.

13. J. L. Teller, "Israel and America," *The New Republic*, October 3, 1949, 14. Hersey, "Ingathering." "Report on Israel," CIO Publications Department.

14. For a sample of discussion of gender identity and Cold War policies see, Emily Rosenberg, "'Foreign Affairs' After World War II," *Diplomatic History* 18, no. 1 (Winter 1994): 59–70; and Frank Costigliola, "The Nuclear Family," *Diplomatic History*.

15. Finder to Eisenhower, 7 February 1957, Name Series, Whitman File, box 14, Dwight David Eisenhower Library; David Riesman, *The Lonely Crowd* (New Haven, 1950); William Whyte, *The Organization Man* (New York, 1956); Barbara Ehrenreich, *The Hearts of Men* (New York, 1983), 34; Rupert Wilkinson, *American Tough* (New York, 1986), 67–68.

16. Ben-Gurion Speech to National Press Club, Washington, 8 May 1951, Subject File, Celebration of Ben-Gurion's 100th Year, David Ben-Gurion Archives, S'de Boker, Israel.

17. Samuels, "Israel," 14. "David Ben-Gurion Began His Career in Palestine as a Vineyard Laborer," *Washington Post*, May 14, 1948. Leon Uris, *Exodus* (New York, 1958), 306, 388. "The Watchman of Zion," *Time*, March 11, 1957; the cover story was Ben-Gurion's third in the magazine since 1948. "Prophet With a Gun," *Time*, January 16, 1956, 25–28 +.

18. John Hersey, *The Wall* (New York, 1950), 408, 268; Perry Miller, *Errand into the Wilderness* (Cambridge, MA, 1956), 12; *Variety*, May 6, 1953 and *New York Times*, May 6, 1953; Biddle, "Israel," 25; James Combs, "The Western Myth and American Politics," in Combs, ed., *Polpop* (Bowling Green OH, 1984).

19. Alexander Melamid, "When Oil Flows Out, Money Flows In," *NYTBR*, January 15, 1956, 12.

20. Quoted in Emily Rosenberg, *Spreading the American Dream: American Economic and Cultural Expansion, 1890–1945* (New York, 1982), 197.

21. Quotes below can be found in Clapp, "An Approach to Economic Development: A Summary of the Reports of the United Nations Economic Survey Mission for the Middle East," for the April 1950 issue of *International Conciliation*, Papers of Gordon Clapp, Summary of Economic Survey, box 3, Truman Library.

22. "The Palestine Refugee Progam," Relief and Works Agency for Palestinian Refugees in the Near East; also, Memo Mr. Hare, NEA to The Secretary, 28 December 1949 with attachments, Clapp Papers, Memoranda of Drafts and ESM Report, box 3, Truman Library.

23. Press and Radio Opinion on the UN Economic Survey Mission to the Middle East, Sept. 13–Oct. 4. 1949, General Records of the Department of State Record Group 59 (hereafter, RG 59), Office Files of Assistant Secretary of State George McGhee, Records of the Bureau of Near Eastern, South Asian, and African Affairs, Lot File No. 53 D 468, Palestine 1948 Memoranda, box 18, National Archives II, Washington DC; Press, Radio Opinion on the Clapp Report to the United Nations, 28 November 1949, Clapp Papers, Memoranda and Drafts of the ESM Report, box 3; and, Press and Radio Reaction to the Final Report of the UN Economic Survey Mission for the Middle East, 24 January 1950, Clapp Papers, State Department-Gardinier, box 3, Truman Library.

24. "Realistic Approach," *New York Times*, January 10, 1950; John Rogers, "The Underdeveloped Middle East," *New York Herald Tribune*, February 11, 1950; Press and Radio Reaction to the Final Report, Clapp Papers, Truman Library. Also, see "Eden Projects," *New York World Telegram*, January 13, 1950.

25. Letter Locke to Truman, 26 December 1951, and Letter Locke to Truman, 24 September 1952; Locke's Correspondence with the President (November 1951–January 1953); Papers of Edwin A. Locke Jr., box 5 and Locke Speech, "The Arab Economy: The Truth and the Challenge," Beirut, Lebanon, 5 December 1952, Mission to the Near East—Address of Locke, box 4, Truman Library.

26. "Two-Pronged Defense," *Cleveland Ohio Plain Dealer*, November 17, 1951. Other articles and editorials referred to here are from November 1951 in the *New York Times, Washington Post, Hartford Courant, Business Week, New York Herald Tribune, New York Post, Wall Street Journal, Baltimore Morning Sun*, and *St. Louis Post-Dispatch*.

27. "Israel Faces the Facts of Life," *Life*, May 14, 1951, 124–5; emphasis added.

28. Memo Andie Knutson to Phileo Nash, 24 July 1951, and 6 August 1951, Nash Files, Reports on Unsolicited Telegrams and Mail on the Palestine Situation, box 11, Truman Library. Letters are in General File, filed by Israel as a subject and Jewish organizations by name, both by year in boxes 1189 and 45, Truman Library.

29. Paul Breines, *Tough Jews* (New York, 1990).

30. Howard Fast, *My Glorious Brothers* (Boston, 1948); Hersey, *The Wall*; Joseph Viertel, *The Last Temptation*; *The Sword in the Desert* (Universal Pictures, 1949); *The Juggler* (Columbia Pictures, 1953).

31. Viertel, *Last Temptation*, 370.

32. For descriptions of the Israeli military see, for example, "Tough Little Army," *The Saturday Evening Post*, February 18, 1956, 26–27+; "The New Israel," *Life*, July 18, 1949, 71–77; "Israel After Three Years," *Time*, May 21, 1951, 30; and "First Stage," *Time*, March 11, 1957, 15. Also, "Israel is Born in Travail and Hope," *Life*, May 31, 1948, 21; I. F. Stone, "Palestine, Britain and the U.N.," *The New Republic*, August 2, 1948, 10; emphasis added.

33. Cable to the International News Service, New York, 13 April 1953, Correspondence, 4–7, 1953, Ben-Gurion Archives.

34. Dean Rusk, Memorandum of Conversation, 28 March 1950, Acheson Papers, box 65, Truman Library.

35. For example, American Federation of Labor President William Green wrote to Truman of tough, battle-tested Israelis. Green to Truman, 26 September 1949, Official File, 204–D, Jewish State 1948–1949, box 775, Truman Library. For examples of this theme see the following stories from *Time*: "The Trojan Horse," November 7, 1955, 34; "Dimensions of a Crisis," November 21, 1955, 19; "The Hard Life," January 30, 1956, 20; "Eye for an Eye," April 23, 1956, 33–34; and "A People in Arms," *U.S. News and World Report*, March 25, 1955, 115–117.

36. "Israel is Born," *Life*, May 31, 1948, 28; Biddle, "Israel," 25, 21; "Israel Faces the Facts of Life," *Life*, May 14, 1951, 116–126; Howard Morley Sachar, *The Course of Modern Jewish History* (New York, 1958, 1977), 534.

37. "The Arabs: Will They Unite?" *Newsweek*, May 24, 1948, 28; "Blitz in the Desert," *Time*, November 12, 1956, 32ff; emphasis added; Gertrude Samuels, "New Roots, Old Land," *NYTBR*, April 27, 1958, 3; "The Watchman," *Time*, August 16, 1948, 26; "Trouble in Gaza," *Time*, September 12, 1955, 34–5; "Israel is Born," *Life*, 28.

38. Biddle, "Israel," 21; "Israel is Born," *Life*, 21. *Life*, in particular, included graphic photos of Jews killed by Arab bombs; see 26–7 in this article and in "Explosions Kill Jews as Arabs Defy the U.S." *Life*, March 8, 1948. Anne O'Hare McCormick, "Recognizing the Realities in the New Palestine," *New York Times* (hereafter *NYT*) May 15, 1948. For other examples, see "The Arabs," *Newsweek*, May 24, 1948, 28+, and "In Abraham's Bosom," *Time*, November 1, 1948, 37.

39. Chargé in Israel (Russell) to Department of State, 18 March 1954, FRUS 1952–4 IX Pt. 1: 1489; emphasis added.

40. Memo Mattison NE to Merriam S/P, 15 March 1949, Near and Middle East 1949–1950, RG 59, Country and Area Files, Lot 64 D 563, Records of the Policy Planning Staff, box 30, National Archives.

41. "State of Israel," *The Washington Post*, May 16, 1948; "Report on Israel," CIO Publications Department. Viertel, *Last Temptation*, 281.

42. Viertel, *Last Temptation*, 270; see Stember et al., *Jews in the Mind of America*, 161–2, 164, 166–7.

43. Edmund Wilson. *Red, Black, Blond and Olive*, (New York, 1956), 461.

44. Henry Wallace, "Palestine: Civilization on Trial," *The New Republic*, February 16, 1948, 10; "The Watchman," *Time*, August 16, 1948, 26; "Swing to the Right," *Time*, January 5, 1953, 26.

45. ORE 55, 28 November 1947, PSF, Intelligence File, box 254, Truman Library. The Acting U.S. Representative at the UN (Jessup) to the Secretary of State, I July 1948, FRUS 1948 V Pt. 2: 1183. See also, NSC 27, 23 August 1948 and NSC 27/1 3 September 1948, with the Minutes of the nineteenth meeting of the NSC, 2 September 1948, PSF, National Security Council Meetings, box 204, Truman Library.

46. Eben Ayers to Charles, 17 September 1948. Also see, Memo Lovett to Truman and Clifford, 25 September 1948. Both citations are found in Clifford Papers, Palestine—State Department Miscellaneous Memos, box 14, Truman Library.

47. Address by Henry Morgenthau Jr., ZOA Convention, 4 July 1948, Pittsburgh PA, Clifford Papers, Palestine/Speeches misc. 48–9, box 14, Truman Library.

48. "Palestine, a New Spain?" *The Nation*, March 13, 1948, 292; see NSC 27, 23 August 1948, and NSC 27/1, 3 September 1948, with Minutes of the nineteenth meeting of the NSC, 2 September 1948, PSF, National Security Council Meetings, box 204, Truman Library. Four years later, the chief concern of the NSC with regard to its Arab-Israeli policy was preventing "instability" and "the extension of Soviet influence." NSC 129, 1 April 1952, with Minutes of the 115th meeting of the NSC, 23 April 1952, PSF, National Security Council Meetings, box 210, Truman Library.

49. Memorandums of Conversation, 15 February 1950 (2), Acheson Papers, box 65; and Letter Jacob Blaustein to Truman, 27 September 1950; see also, Blaustein to Truman, 7 October 1950, PSF, General File, File Bi–Bl, box 113, Truman Library.

50. English translation of "Abe Feinberg and the Elections in Israel," *Ha'aretz* 12 August 1950, enclosed with letter Feinberg to Niles, 22 December 1950, Feinberg file, Niles Papers, box 33, Truman Library.

51. Memo of Conversation, 22 March 1949, Acheson Papers, box 64; Letter Weizmann to Truman, 30 April 1951, and Letter Ben-Gurion to Truman, 31 May 1951, PSF, Subject File, Israel, box 181, Truman Library. Also, Cable to International News Service, 13 April 1953, Correspondence, 4–7 1953, Ben-Gurion Archives.

52. Memo of Conversation, 5 January 1953, Acheson Papers, box 67a, Truman Library.

53. Memo of Conversation, 28 March 1950, Acheson Papers, box 65, Truman Library; Letter Congressman James J. Murphy to Secretary of State, 15 May 1950, RG 59, LM 60 Palestine and Israel Foreign Relations, roll 6, Confidential U.S. State Department Central Files, Palestine-Israel Foreign Affairs, National Archives.

54. Memo McGhee to Webb (n.d.) with attachment, "Summary of Current Arab Attitudes Toward the United States," RG 59, Office Files of George McGhee, Records of the Bureau of NE, SA and AA, Palestine 1948 [*sic*] Memoranda, Lot File No. 53 D 468, box 18, National Archives. Edwin Wright Oral History, 48–50, Truman Library. Also see, Letter Ben-Gurion to Barkley, 29 May 1951, Subject File, Ben-Gurion on the United States, Ben-Gurion Archives.

55. Acting U.S. Representative at the UN (Jessup) to the Secretary of State, 1 July 1948, FRUS 1948 V Pt. 2: 1183; NSC 47, Study of the United States Strategic Objectives in Israel, May 1949, FRUS 1949 VI: 1009–1012; Telegram Sharett to Elath, 22 January 1950, Correspondence, 1–5 1950, Ben-Gurion Archives.

56. Letter Jacob Blaustein to Truman, 27 September 1950, General File, PSF, file Bi–Bl, box 113, Truman Library. Memo of Conversation, 15 December 1950, Acheson Papers, box 65, Truman Library.

57. The Secretary of State to the Embassy in Israel, 29 December 1950, FRUS 1950 V: 1086. Ambassador in Israel (Davis) to Department of State 23 January 1953, FRUS 1952–4 IX pt. 1: 1102–1103. In the years before 1955, some press accounts emphasized Israeli aggressiveness. See "Bloody Frontier," *Time*, March 2, 1953, 24 and "Massacre at Kibya," *Time*, March 26, 1953, 34.

58. "The Watchman," *Time*, August 16, 1948, 25–28; "Strange Friendship," *Time*, January 10, 1955, 24; Alexander Ramati, "A Literary Letter From Israel," *NYTBR*, May 27, 1951, 15; Letter Jacob Blaustein to Truman, 27 September 1950, General File, PSF, file Bi–Bl, box 113, Truman Library.

59. "State of Israel," *The Washington Post*, May 16, 1948; see also Anne O'Hare McCormick, "Recognizing the New Realities in Palestine," *NYT*, May 15, 1948, and "Israel Faces the Facts of Life," *Life*, May 14, 1951, 116–26. Also, Memo by the Deputy U.S. Representative (Jessup) on the Security Council to the U.S. Representative at the UN (Austin), 2 June 1948, FRUS 1948 V Pt. 2: 1088.

60. Ambassador in Israel (Davis) to Department of State, 20 September 1951, FRUS 1951 V: 871; Acting Secretary of State (Bruce) to Embassy in Israel, 18 November 1952, FRUS 1952–4 IX Pt 1: 1065.

61. "The Arab Answer," *NYT*, May 27, 1948; J. L. Teller, "Israel and America," *The New Republic*, October 3, 1949, 13.

62. NSC 47/2, 17 October 1949, FRUS 1949 VI: 1434–1435; Memo of Conversation, 5 April 1950, Acheson Papers, box 65; and ORE 55, 28 November 1947, PSF Intelligence File, box 254, Truman Library.

63. Memo McClintock to Director of the Office of UNA (Rusk), 1 July 1948, FRUS 1948 V Pt. 2: 1173.

64. The Acting U.S. Representative at the UN (Jessup) to the Secretary of State, 1 July 1948, FRUS 1948 V Pt. 2: 1183.

65. Memo of Conversation, by Secretary of State, 8 September 1948, FRUS 1948 V Pt. 2: 1381.

66. Ehrenreich, *Hearts of Men*, 17; The Acting U.S. Representative at the UN (Jessup) to the Secretary of State, 1 July 1948, FRUS 1948 V Pt. 2: 1184; Comments from Bob Wilson, 28 July 1956, WHCF, General File, 122 BB Middle East Suez Situation (1), box 881, Eisenhower Library.

67. Hal Lehrman, "Pie in the Arab Sky," *NYTBR*, August 12, 1956, 3. The congressional quote is found in memorandum of conversation, 10 March 1950, Acheson Papers, box 65, Truman Library. Examples of descriptions of Arabs: "Uneasy Borders," *Time*, September 3, 1956, 20; "Independence War," *Time*, May 24, 1948, 32–34; "Blitz in the Desert," *Time*; and "Can Israel Solve Its Problems?" *Saturday Evening Post*, August 20, 1949, 30+.

68. Biddle, "Israel," 24; "State of Israel," *Washington Post*, May 16, 1948; Annex to NSC 129, 7 April 1952, with Meeting #115, 23 April 1952, PSF, National Security Council Meetings, box 216, Truman Library.

69. Report on the Near East, Address Dulles, 1 June 1953, Israel Relations (6), Dulles Papers, Subject Series, box 10, Eisenhower Library; and see, NSC Meeting #147, box 4, Truman Library.

70. See Memo Walter Bedell Smith to Eisenhower, 21 October 1953, Israel (6), Whitman File, International Series, box 29, Eisenhower Library. Also, Press Releases, 23 October 1953, Israelis Relations (7), and 28 October 1953 Israeli Relations (5), Dulles Papers, Subject Series, box 10, Eisenhower Library.

71. See for example letters in Israel 122 BB (1), and (5), WHCF, General File, box 817; Memo of Conversation, 26 October 1953, Israel Relations (6), Dulles Papers, Subject Series, box 10; see both releases, 26 October 1953, Subject Series, Israeli Relations (6), Dulles Papers, box 10; Press and Radio News Conference, 27 October 1953, WHCF, General File, Israel Relations (5) box 817, Eisenhower Library.

72. Memo Dulles to Eisenhower, 7 May 1954, Dulles-Herter Series, box 3, Eisenhower Library.

73. For example, see exchange of letters on the second round of negotiations, Letter Sharett to Johnston, 12 July 1954, and reply 7 August 1954, Proceedings on the Second Mission, Records Relating to the Eric Johnston Mission and the Jordan River Waters, RG 59, Lot 70 D 254, box 2, National Archives.

74. Memo IBS/PMN-GFP Dooher to NEA/P Richard Sanger, 4 December 1953, RG 59, Records Relating to the Eric Johnston Mission and the Jordan River Waters, Press Reaction, Lot 70 D 254, RG 59, box 1, National Archives.

75. Memo of Conversation, 21 October 1955, Dulles Papers, Subject Series, Israel Relations (4), box 10; NSC Meeting #262, 20 October 1955, Whitman File, NSC Series, box 7; NSC Meeting #297, 22 July 1954, Whitman File, NSC Series, box 5; Address Dulles before Council on Foreign Relations, 26 August 1955, Papers of Carl McCardle, box 7, Eisenhower Library.

76. ORE 48–48, 5 August 1948, PSF Intelligence File, box 255, Truman Library.

77. Memos of Conversation, 28 March 1950, 10 March 1950, 15 February 1950, Acheson Papers, box 66, Truman Library; Secretary of State to Representative Jacob K. Javits, 12 January 1950, FRUS 1950 V: 684.

78. "The Arab Answer," *NYT*, May 27, 1948; "Two-Pronged Defense," *Cleveland Ohio Plain Dealer*, November 17, 1951.

79. Newbold Noyes Jr., "Our Middle East Arms Embargo, *Washington Star,* May 21, 1948; "Israel is Born," editorial, *Life*, 28; "Jews in the Holocaust," *Saturday Review of Literature*, July 23, 1955, 27.

80. Viertel, *Last Temptation*, 213.

81. McGrath speech, 19 October 1948, Clifford Papers, Palestine Speeches—Misc. 48–49, box 14, Truman Library.

82. Letter Truman to Blaustein, 12 February 1949, General File, file Bi–Bl, box 113, Truman Library.

83. Statement of U.S. Objectives and Policies With Respect to the Area of the Arab State and Israel During the Period of the Cold War, 24 March 1952, Department of State, Psychological Strategy Board Files, Staff Members Office Files, box 7, Truman Library.

84. Memo for the President, NSC Meeting #19, 3 September 1948, PSF, box 220, Truman Library.

CHAPTER FOUR: THE 1950S RELIGIOUS REVIVAL AND "CHRISTIANIZING" THE IMAGE OF ISRAEL AND JEWS

1. Paul Carter, *Another Part of the Fifties* (New York, 1983), 114–116; Martin E. Marty, *Modern American Religion, Volume 3* (Chicago, 1996), 289, 301; Stephen Whitfield, *The Culture of the Cold War* (Baltimore, 1991), 89.

2. Whitfield, *Culture of Cold War*, 83; Marty, *Modern American Religion*, 278–279.

3. In addition, many other versions of the Bible flooded the bookstores in these years. "Sixty Years of Bestsellers" from lists by Alice Hackett, *NYTBR*, October 7, 1956, 6+. Observations in this chapter about religious publications are made from a survey of all *NYTBR* from 1947–1958, and a selected survey of *NYHTBR* and *Saturday Review of Literature*.

4. Quoted here from Patrick Henry, "'And I Don't Care What It Is': The Tradition-History of a Civil Religion Proof-Text," *Journal of the American Academy of Religion* 49, no. 1 (1981): 38, also, 35–47.

5. Reinhold Niebuhr, "America's Three Melting Pots," *NYTBR*, September 25, 1955, 6.

6. See Robert S. Ellwood, *1950: Crossroads of American Religious Life* (Louisville KY, 2000), 60–1, 3.

7. Naomi Cohen, *Jews in Christian America* (New York, 1992), 111; Marty, *Modern American Religion*, 54; Myrdal, *An American Dilemma*, 9–11.

8. Eleanor Roosevelt to Truman, 29 January 1952, Personal, Eleanor Roosevelt (2), PSF, box 322, Truman Library.

9. Memo of Conversation, by Stuart Rockwell, April 19, 1950, FRUS 1950 V: 863.

10. Whitfield, *Culture of Cold War*, 83.

11. Marty, *Modern American Religion*, 249.

12. See Richard H. Immerman, *John Foster Dulles* (Wilmington, Delaware, 1999), esp. 1–3, 14–15, 20–21. See Marty, *Modern American Religion*, 97, 125–26, and Ellwood, *1950: Crossroads*, 159.

13. Marty, *Modern American Religion*, 146 (quoting Charles Clayton Morrison), 99, 125, 133, 135; emphasis added; Dulles Speech, 11 October 1953, McCardle Papers, box 6, Eisenhower Library.

14. David A. Hollinger, *Science, Jews, and Secular Culture* (Princeton, 1996), esp. "Jewish Intellectuals and the De-Christianization of American Public Culture in the Twentieth Century."

15. Whitfield, *Culture of Cold War*, 85, 87.

16. McCarthy quote is from Ellwood; phrase "biblical tone" is Ellwood's, *1950: Crossroads*, 83–4.

17. Whitfield, *Culture of Cold War*, 81; also, Ellwood, *1950: Crossroads*, 160.

18. Speech at the American Jewish Tercentenary Dinner, 20 October 1954, Speech File, Dwight David Eisenhower Papers as President 1953–1961 (Ann Whitman File) [hereafter, Whitman File], box 10, Eisenhower Library.

19. Will Herberg, *Protestant-Catholic-Jew* (Garden City, NY, 1955, 1960), 87.

20. Niebuhr, "America's Melting Pot," 6.

21. Michael T. Benson, *Harry S. Truman and the Founding of Israel* (Westport CT, 1997), 34; Willard Johnson, "Religion and Minority Peoples," in *One America: The History, Contributions, and Present Problems of Our Racial and National Minorities*, eds. Francis J. Brown and Joseph S. Roucek (New York, 1952), 524.

22. Mark Silk, "Notes on the Judeo-Christian Tradition in America," *American Quarterly* 36 (Spring 1984): 65–85.

23. See Deborah Dash Moore, "Jewish G.I.s and the Creation of the Judeo-Christian Tradition," *Religion and American Culture* 8, no. 1: 31–53. quote from 34.

24. Ellwood, *1950: Crossroads*, 192, 185.

25. See Andrew Heinze, "*Peace of Mind* (1946): Judaism and the Therapeutic Polemics of Postwar America," *Religion and American Culture* 12, no. 1 (Winter 2002): 31–58.

26. The following discussion relies on Said, *Orientalism*.

27. See Fuad Sha'ban, *Islam and Arabs in Early American Thought* (Durham NC, 1991), 125, 133; Michael W. Suleiman, *The Arabs in the Mind of America* (Brattleboro VT, 1988), 9.

28. Edward Said, *Covering Islam* (New York, 1981), 10.

29. Eleanor Roosevelt to Truman, 15 May 1951, Eleanor Roosevelt and the United Nations Organization, Personal, PSF, box 322, Truman Library.

30. Mary Dick, "Arabic Made Easy," *NYTM*, February 5, 1950, 42; A. Ross, "Vast and Restless Arab World," *NYTM*, October 28, 1951, 25.

31. "Anti-Israel Arab Front Cracking," *Business Week*, April 8, 1950, 116–117; Department of State Position Paper: Lebanon, 5 May 1953, FRUS 1952–1954 IX: 1212.

32. "Palestine: The Oil Beneath the Tumult," *Newsweek*, December 15, 1947, 28; "Palestine: Divided They Stand" *Newsweek*, December 8, 1947, 40.

33. See the following articles for examples: Ross, *New York Times Magazine*, 7; "Seething Moslem World," *Newsweek*, October 29,1951, 36; "The Mysterious Arab World," *New York Times Magazine*, July 29, 1951, 8–9; "Strange World of Arabia," *New York Times Magazine*, August 18, 1957, 8; Seymour Freidin and William Richardson, "The Moslem Crescent," *Colliers*, July 26, 1952, 15; Osgood Caruthers, "The Enigma That Is the Arab," *NYTM*, October 20, 1957, 18; Osgood Caruthers, "Life by Intrigue: The Mideast," *NYTM*, August 17, 1958, 14.

34. Caruthers, "Enigma That Is the Arab," 18.

35. Department of State Position Paper: Arab-Israeli Relations, 7 May 1953, FRUS 1952–1954 IX: 1216.

36. Department of State Position Paper: Lebanon, 5 May 1953, FRUS 1952–1954 IX: 1211.

37. Biddle, "Israel," 19–25, esp. 23, 20.

38. Ninth of June 1956, Secretary's Speeches 1956 (1), McCardle Papers, box 7, Eisenhower Library.

39. See for example, Huston Smith, *The Religions of Man* (New York, 1958); and Bernard Lewis, *The Arabs in History* (New York, 1950, 1960).

40. R. M. MacIver, "Mosaic of a People's Enduring Spirit," *NYTBR*, February 19, 1950, 7; Louis Finkestein, "Saadia Gaon and Maimonides, Forgotten Men," *NYTBR*, February 19, 1950, 7.

41. Wilson, *Red, Black, Blond and Olive*, 396–397.

42. See "I am the Lord . . . ," *Time*, August 30, 1948, 26; "Israel Faces the Facts of Life," *Life*, May 14, 1951, 116–126; Biddle, "Israel," 19–25, esp. 22–23.

43. Dulles speech, 1 June 1953, Israel Relations (6), Subject Series, Dulles Papers, box 10, Eisenhower Library; Adlai Stevenson, "No Peace for Israel," *Look*, August 11, 1953, 43; T. A. Gill, "Sometime Holy Land," *Christian Century*, October 10, 1956, 1157.

44. Stevenson, "No Peace for Israel," 43.

45. Examples from *Time* include: "In Abraham's Bosom," November 1, 1948, 37; "5710," October 3, 1949, 47; "Till the End of Time?" December 26, 1949, 15; and "The Battle of El Anja," November 14, 1955, 37; and "Israel is Born in Travail and Hope" *Life*, May 31, 1948, 21. Murrow's portrait of Jerusalem is found in *See It Now: Murrow at Wake Island*, (1953) at the Museum of Television and Radio, New York.

46. Examples are from John Cogley "If I Forget Thee, O Jerusalem . . ." *The Commonweal*, January 8, 1954, 350–352, and "If I Forget Thee," *Time*, April 25, 1949, 30–31.

47. See Dana Adams Schmidt. "Israel's Little War of the Borders," *NYTM*, June 14, 1953, 14+, and Seth S. King, "Two Jerusalems, Two Worlds," *NYTM*, May 12, 1957, 12–13+.

48. Stevenson, "No Peace for Israel," 43; King, "Two Jerusalems," 12, and "Atlantic Report: Jerusalem Issue," *Atlantic Monthly*, May 1950, 10; William Green to Truman, 26 September 1949, Official File 204–D, Jewish State 1948–9, box 775, Truman Library.

49. Acting Secretary of State David Bruce to American Embassy in Israel, 18 November 1952, FRUS 1952–1954 IX: 1067.

50. See for example, *Scholastic*, November 29, 1956, 32.

51. Memos Andie Knutson to Philleo Nash, 24 July 1951, and 6 August 1951. Examples of letters are filed by Israel as a subject and Jewish organizations by name, and filed by years in boxes 1189 and 45, General File, Truman Library.

52. Hertzel Fishman, *American Protestantism and a Jewish State* (Detroit, 1973), 120–121.

53. For example, Chad Walsh, "Deborah and Barak," *NYTBR*, January 2, 1955, 20. From 1948–1960, there were six Hollywood features based on the Old Testament and eight on the New Testament. Richard Campbell and Michael Pitts, *The Bible on Film* (Metuchen NJ, 1981).

54. Michael Kammen, *Mystic Chords of Memory* (New York, 1991), 532–4, 537.

55. *NYHTBR*, October 10, 1948, 5; unlike the other novels discussed here, Fast's novel was not a best seller.

56. For further discussion of this aspect of the film, see Larry Kreitzer, *The Old Testament in Fiction and Film* (Sheffield, England, 1994), 22–27.

57. P. J. Searles, "A Novel About Isaiah," *NYHTBR*, November 6, 1955, 2.

58. Bradford Smith, "Life of Isaiah II," *Saturday Review of Literature*, November 5, 1955, 18.

59. Asch, *Moses*, 98.

60. J. Hutchens, "Mr. Asch at 75: Prophet with Honor," *NYHTBR*, November 6, 1955, 2; Lewis Nichols, "A Talk With Sholem Asch," *NYTBR*, November 6, 1955, 26; Searles, "Isaiah," 2.

61. Asch, *Moses*, 51, 118; Slaughter, *Song of Ruth*, 159. Examples of other super masculine characters are found in the films *David and Bathsheba* (Twentieth Century Fox, 1952), *The Prodigal* (Metro-Goldwyn-Mayer, 1955), *The Ten Commandments* (Paramount/Cecil B. de Mille, 1956), *Solomon and Sheba* (United Artists/Edward Small, 1959), and *Ben Hur* (MGM, 1959), and in the novel by Howard Fast, *My Glorious Brothers* (Boston, 1948).

62. Slaughter, *Song of Ruth*, 236.

63. Asch, *Moses*, 207, 397.

64. Quoted in Benny Morris, *Israel's Border Wars, 1949–1956* (New York, 1993), 156.

65. Robert Coughlan, "Modern Prophet of Israel," *Life*, November 18, 1957, 156, 154; "Moses and Ben-Gurion," *Time*, May 30, 1960, 43. Speech of Ben-Gurion to National Press Club in Washington, May 8, 1951, Celebration Ben-Gurion's 100th Year, Subject File, Ben-Gurion Archives.

66. Alfred Werner, "Palestine: The Great Metamorphosis," *NYTBR*, August 10, 1947, 27. Slaughter, *Song of Ruth*, 258.

67. Slaughter, *Song of Ruth*, 257.

68. Truman, *Years of Trial and Hope*, 214; Cohen, *Truman and Israel*, 6; Benson, *Truman and Founding of Israel*, 32–34.

69. Speech at National Conference of Christians and Jews, 11 November 1949, Palestine Public Relations, General File, Ayers Papers, box 9, Truman Library.

70. Clifford, *Counsel to the President*, 7–8; Benson, *Truman and Founding of Israel*, 54.

71. Whitfield, *Culture of Cold War*, 86–88, 90.

72. Ibid., 88.

73. Remarks of Eisenhower at the dedication of the Washington Hebrew Congregation Temple, 6 May 1955, Whitman File, Speech Series, box 12; and Eisenhower to Monsignor Nott, 12 August 1958, Whitman File, DDE Diary, box 35, Eisenhower Library.

74. Eisenhower speaking on trip to the Middle East, 27 November 1959, Whitman File, Cabinet Series, box 14; Address Eisenhower at the American Jewish Tercentenary Dinner, 20 October 1954, Speech File, Whitman File, box 10; Address by Eisenhower, 20 February 1957, Speech File, Whitman File, box 20, Eisenhower Library.

75. Eisenhower at the opening of Islamic Center, 28 June 1957, Whitman File, Speech Series, box 26, Eisenhower Library.

76. Quoted in Keith Kyle, *Suez* (New York, 1991), 45–46.

77. Memo Arthur Dean to Dulles, 9 December 1955, file Mr. Herbert Hoover Jr. (1), Subject Series, Dulles Papers, box 5, Eisenhower Library.

78. Address of John Foster Dulles at the First Presbyterian Church, Watertown NY, 11 October 1953, and Dulles Speech at the New York Herald Tribune Forum, 20 October 1953, Dulles Speeches 1953, McCardle Papers, box 6, Eisenhower Library.

79. Dulles at Iowa State College Commencement, 9 June 1956, Secretary's Speeches 1956 (1), McCardle Papers, box 7, Eisenhower Library.

80. Memo of Conversation, 26 October 1953, Israel Relations (6), Subject File, Dulles Papers, box 10, Eisenhower Library.

81. Memo of Telephone Conversation Secretary of State and Assistant Secretary of State for Policy Planning (Bowie), 12 January 1957, General Telephone Conversations, Dulles Papers, Eisenhower Library.

82. Dulles speech about his trip to the Middle East, 1 June 1953, LM 060 National Archives.

83. Abba Eban, *Abba Eban: An Autobiography* (New York, 1977), 134.

84. Sidney Hook, "Prophet of Man's Glory and Tragedy," *NYTBR*, January 29, 1956, 6–7+.

85. Egal Feldman, *Dual Destinies* (Urbana, 1990), 224–227 (quote is on 227); Fishman, *American Protestantism*, 69, 73–74.

86. Carter, *Another Part of the Fifties*, 150.

CHAPTER FIVE: ACCEPTANCE AND ASSIMILATION

1. National Security Council Meeting #352, 22 January 1958, National Security Series, Whitman File, box 9, Eisenhower Library.

2. Philip Roth, *Goodbye, Columbus and Five Short Stories* (New York, 1959).

3. Nathan Glazer, "The American Jew and the Attainment of Middle-Class Rank: Some Trends and Explanations," in *The Jews: Social Patterns of an American Group*, ed. Marshall Sklare (Glencoe, IL, 1958), esp. 138–139, 140–141.

4. Sholem Asch, *A Passage in the Night* (New York, 1953), 29.

5. Herman Wouk, *Marjorie Morningstar* (New York, 1955), 78. Gerald Green, *The Last Angry Man* (New York, 1956), 119. Saul Bellow, *The Adventures of Augie March* (New York, 1953).

6. John Brooks, "The Education of George Hurst," *NYTBR*, June 15, 1958, 5. Asch, *Passage*, 87–88. Asch's book was a best seller from December 1953–January 1954. (This and other best seller information is from *NYTBR* best seller lists.) Jerome Weidman, *The Enemy Camp* (New York, 1958). This was a bestseller from July 1958–December 1958.

7. Outside of the pages of novels, the elevation of the Lower East Side as the starting point of the American success story was widespread in American Jewish memory in the postwar period. For discussion see Hasia Diner, *Lower East Side Memories* (Princeton, 2000), 14, 15, 33, 59, 60, 69.

8. See *NYTBR* best seller lists, also, "60 Years of Best Sellers," *NYTBR*, October 7, 1956.

9. For more on the impact of the book see Edward Shapiro, *A Time for Healing* (Baltimore, 1992), 10, 157–158.

10. Meyer Levin, "Central Park Revisited," *Saturday Review of Literature*, September 3, 1955, 9–10; also, Florence Hexton Bullock, "Herman Wouk Spins a Tale in the Great Tradition," *NYHTBR*, September 4, 1955, 1.

11. Ads found in *NYTBR*, February 5, 1956, 12–13; emphasis in the original; *NYTBR*, March 25, 1956.

12. Myron Kaufmann, *Remember Me to God* (Philadelphia, 1957), 83.

13. Asch, *Passage*, 94.

14. Kaufmann, *Remember Me*, 257, 362.

15. For more on denominational changes see, Albert I. Gordon, *Jews in Suburbia* (Boston, 1959), esp. 97, and "The Synagogue." Rabbi Philip Bernstein, "What Jews Believe," *Life*, September 11, 1950, 162, and Virginia Schroeder, "Food Signifies Faith," *American Home*, September 1956, 104.

16. See Paul Ramsey, "Approaches to a Faith," *NYTBR*, September 1, 1957, 7.

17. Gordon, *Jews in Suburbia*, 126–127.

18. Caroline Turnstall, "Moving Saga of a Family," *NYHTBR*, September 8, 1957, 6.

19. Wouk, *Marjorie Morningstar*, 172, 174.

20. Weidman, *Enemy Camp*, 85; Kaufmann, *Remember Me*, 458.

21. See for example the collection Harold U. Ribalow, ed., *Mid-Century* (New York, 1955). *Commentary* was also a forum where these issues were discussed.

22. Bellow, *Augie March* was a best seller from October–December 1953; *Last Angry Man* was one from February–September 1957.

23. Marcus Klein, *After Alienation* (Cleveland OH, 1962), 34, 38.

24. Green, *Last Angry Man*, 56; Kaufman, *Remember Me*, 402.

25. See for example reviews of *The Young Lions* and *Three Brave Men*, *Variety*, March 19, 1958 and *NYT*, March 16, 1957.

26. *Home Before Dark* (Warner, 1958), and *Marjorie Morningstar* (Warner/United States Pictures, 1958). Film copies from MPC. *Marjorie* was also one of the top grossing films of 1958. Aaronson, ed., *The International Motion Picture Almanac 1960*, 737.

27. *Three Brave Men* (Twentieth Century Fox, 1957). Film copy from MPC. *NYT*, March 16, 1957.

28. See Stember, *Jews in the Mind of America*, 160–167.

29. *I Accuse!* (MGM, 1958). Film copy from MPC.

30. *The Naked and the Dead* (RKO Teleradio, 1958), and *The Young Lions* (Twentieth Century Fox, 1958). Film copies from MPC. *The Young Lions* was one of the top grossing pictures of 1958. Aaronson, *Almanac*, 737.

31. *Good Morning Miss Dove* (Twentieth Century Fox, 1955). Film copy from MPC.

32. See Susanne Klingenstein, *Jews in the American Academy 1900–1940* (New Haven, 1991), 41.

33. Arthur Hertzberg, *The Jews in America* (New York, 1989), 318, 342. For more on Jewish political power and Israel see, J. J. Goldberg, *Jewish Power* (Reading MA, 1996).

34. Howard M. Sachar, *A History of Israel* (New York, 1996), 118.

35. Sarna, "A Projection of America as it Ought to Be," 57.

36. Sklare, *America's Jews*, 213.

37. Richard Sullivan, "Always in Exile," *NYTBR*, September 5, 1954, and Salo W. Berson, "Three Centuries of Jewish Experience in America," *NYTBR*, September 12, 1954.

38. Kaufmann, *Remember Me*, 536.

39. Klingenstein, *Jews in American Academy*, 34–35.

40. Address Adlai Stevenson American Jewish Tercentenary, 1 June 1955, folder 5, Series 2 Speeches, Papers of Adlai E. Stevenson, box 151, Seeley G. Mudd Library, Princeton University.

41. Bernstein, "What Jews Believe," *Life*, September 11, 1950, 160–162+.

42. Weidman, *Enemy Camp*, 524.

43. Robert Fitch, "The Bond Between Christian and Jew," *Commentary*, May 1954, 444, 439–45; "Common Ignorance," *Time*, February 19, 1951, 59–60.

44. Jacob Taubes. "The Issue Between Judaism and Christianity." *Commentary*, December 1953.

45. See, for example, "Almost a Lutheran," *Time*, April 5, 1954, 66, 68.

46. See, for example, Herbert Mitgang, "A Lox is a Lox," *NYTBR*, March 8, 1953, 24.

47. Harry Gersh and Sam Miller, "Satmar in Brooklyn," *Commentary*, November 1959, 389, 397.

48. See Klingenstein, *Jews in American Academy*, 41.

49. Stember, *Jews in Mind of America*, 121–124; also, cited in Goldberg, *Jewish Power*, 117.

50. NSC Meeting #207, 22 July 1954, NSC Series, Whitman File, box 5, Eisenhower Library.

51. Memo of Conversation, 27 January 1955, FRUS 1955–1957 XIV, *Arab-Israeli Conflict, 1955*: 30.

52. NSC Meeting #207, 22 July 1954, NSC Series, Whitman File, box 5, Eisenhower Library.

53. Quoted in Schoenbaum, *United States and State of Israel*, 79.

54. Memos of Conversation, 27 January 1955, 8 June 1955, 14 February 1955, 11 July 1955, 18 October 1955, FRUS 1955–1957 XIV: 31, 232, 54, 285, 612. Also, Harry M. Fisher to Adlai Stevenson, folder 2, Series 1 Correspondence, Stevenson Papers, box 31, Mudd Library. Memo Dulles to Byroade 9 August 1954, Chronological Series, Dulles Papers, box 9, Eisenhower Library.

55. Memo w/attachments, Bureau of Near Eastern, South Asian, and African Affairs, 14 January 1955, FRUS 1955–1957 XIV: 14.

56. See, for example, Address of Governor Averell Harriman at the United Jewish Appeal, 21 March 1957, file Middle East Data, Lloyd Papers, box 34, Truman Library.

57. See for example, Memo of Conversation, 17 July 1951, file July 1951, Acheson Papers, box 67, Truman Library.

58. See for examples Jacob Weinstein to William McCormick Blair, 8 November 1955 and Material mailed 22 December 1955 to Rabbi Weinstein, Judge

Fisher, and Philip Klutznik, folder 1 Weinstein, Jacob, box 89; Address Adlai Stevenson before American Committee for the Weizmann Institute of Science, 2 December 1954, folder 6, Series 2 Speeches, box 150; John Foster Dulles to Stevenson, 24 August 1955, folder 17, box 25; Stevenson to Irving Engel, 23 January 1956, box 374; Jacob Weinstein to Alvin Fine, 26 January 1956, box 374; Stevenson speech to Israel Bond Drive, 11 September 1956, folder 3, Series 2 Speeches, box 158; Stevenson to Israel Bond Rally, 12 November 1955, folder 6, Series 2 Speeches, box 152; Henry Burman to Stevenson, 25 August 1953, box 31, Stevenson Papers, Mudd Library.

59. For examples, see Silver to Dulles 3 June 1954, 21 June 1954 with enclosures, 25 June 1954, file Silver, Abba Hillel 1954, box 87; Silver to Dulles, 2 September 1955, box 97, Dulles Papers, Mudd Library.

60. See, for example, C. D. Jackson to Dulles, 10 November 1953, and Memo Roderic O'Connor to C. D. Jackson, 16 November 1953, Israel Relations (5), Subject Series, Dulles Papers, box 10, Eisenhower Library.

61. Memo Otto Schirn, 7 August 1952, and Memo Murray Chotiner to Sherman Adams, 26 August 1952, Israel Relations (1), General File, WHCF, box 817, Eisenhower Library.

62. See Memo from Thomas Dewey to Dulles, 19 February 1953, and accompanying Memo by Nat Goldstein, Strictly Confidential Miscellaneous Reports, General Correspondence, Dulles Papers, box 4, Eisenhower Library.

63. Henry Stupell to Eisenhower, 6 September 1956, and Rabb to Stupell, 26 October 1956, Israel 118B, General File, WHCF, box 683; see correspondence with Eustace Seligman (who defended Dulles) and Dulles, and Emanuel Celler, 7 November 1958, 22 December 1958, 3 January 1959, General Correspondence, Dulles Papers, box 3, Eisenhower Library.

64. Stephen E. Ambrose, *Eisenhower, Vol. II* (New York, 1984), 387.

65. See letters, 118–B Jewish Matters 1952–53 (1,2), box 682 and Rabb to Henry Stupell, 26 October 1956, Israel 188–B (3), box 683, General File, WHCF, Eisenhower Library.

66. Max Rabb, OH, Eisenhower Library, 2, 6; Rabb to George Levinson 27 February 1957, Israel Relations (4), box 817; Rabb to Rabbi E. L. Silver, 20 November 1956, Telegram Silver and Meyer Cohen for the Union of Orthodox Rabbis to Eisenhower, 14 November 1956; Memo Rabb to Fisher Howe, Department of State, 20 November 1956; and Memo Rabb to Dulles, 31 December 1956, Israel 122BB (3), box 881; Memo Rabb to Bernard Shanley, 4 June 1956; Rabbi Blumenthal to Eisenhower, 23 May 1956, Shanley to Blumenthal, 6 June 1956, Israel 122 (4), box 817; Rabb to Bernard Katzen, 3 March 1956, Israel (2), box 817; Rabb to George Cassidy, 14 October 1957, and Rabb to Katzen, 15 October 1957, Israel (6), box 817, General File, WHCF, Eisenhower Library.

67. For examples of Katzen's defense of administration policy see, Memo Bernard Katzen to John Foster Dulles, 29 June 1953, General Correspondence and Memos, Dulles Papers, box 2, Eisenhower Library. *The Jewish Day Journal* clippings, July 11, 1954, and 12 July 1954; Katzen to Hagerty, July 15, 1954, and response from Hagerty to Katzen, 22 July 1954, Israel 122 (5), General File, WHCF, box 817, Eisenhower Library.

68. Maxwell Abbell to Rabb, 8 June 1956, Israel 122 (4), General File, WHCF, box 817, Eisenhower Library.

69. Javits recalled that out of his own political convictions, he supported the administration through the Suez crisis although his stand was unpopular. Jacob Javits OH, Eisenhower Library.

70. Memo Dulles to Eisenhower, 22 May 1956, Dulles-Herter Series, Whitman File, box 5; and Memo of Conversation Dulles and Javits, 23 May 1956, General Correspondence and Memos, Dulles Papers, box 1, Eisenhower Library.

71. Memo of Conversation, 18 March 1955, with Blaustein, Allen, and Bergus, COO48, roll 17, National Archives.

72. Telegram Dulles to American Embassy in London, 21 January 1955, file B'nai B'rith 1955, Dulles Papers, box 90, Mudd Library.

73. For example, regarding reactions to the Kibya incident see Klutznick to Dulles, 29 November 1953; Dulles to Klutznick, 3 December 1953, file B'nai B'rith 1953, Dulles Papers, box 67, Mudd Library.

74. Schoenbaum, *United States and Israel*, 64.

75. For discussion of this "ingathering," see Sachar, *History of Israel*, chap. 15.

76. Dulles' and Allen's views are discussed in Schoenbaum, *United States and Israel*, 121–122.

77. Sachar, *History of Israel*, 425.

78. For examples of the vocabulary adopted by Israel's supporters, see Letter Morris Seldin to Truman, 29 August 1949, State of Israel File 1949, General File, box 1189, Truman Library; Gertrude Samuels, "New Roots, Old Land," *NYTBR*, April 27, 1958, 3; OH Ogden R. Reid, Eisenhower Library.

79. See, for example, Telegram to Embassy in Israel, 24 August 1955, FRUS 1955–1957 XIV: 385.

80. "Homeless in Gaza," *Life*, November 21, 1955, 46.

81. "Israel Faces Facts," *Life*, 1951; Allan Nevins, "Israel Observed, Mind and Soul," *NYTBR*, June 30, 1957, 1+.

82. Address of Harry Truman (to be read by Asst. Sec. of State for Public Affairs) at the Mobilization Conference at the National Jewish Welfare Board, 17 October 1952, file—Jews, President Truman's Statement re, White House Files, Lloyd Papers, box 9, Truman Library.

83. "Prophet With a Gun," *Time*, January 16, 1956, 25–28+; Biddle, "Israel," *The Atlantic*, October 1949, 19, 22, 23.

84. For discussion see Morris, *Israel's Border Wars, 1949–1956*, 156, 177, 207, 215, 220, 225. The following overview relies on Morris' account.

85. See for example, Telegrams Dept. of State to Embassy in Israel, 24 and 27, August 1955, FRUS 1955–1957 XIV: 385–386, 406. See also quote from Morris, *Israel's Border Wars*, 207.

86. For example of American acknowledgment of the split among Israeli politicians, see Telegram from Embassy in Israel, 5 April 1955, FRUS 1955–1957 XIV: 139; quote from Morris, *Israel's Border Wars*, 303.

87. See, NSC Meeting #262, 20 October 1955, NSC Series, Whitman File, box 7, Eisenhower Library.

88. Memo Dulles to Byroade, 9 August 1954, Chronological Series, Dulles Papers, Eisenhower Library.

89. Memo of Conversation, 20 Novembeer 1955, FRUS, 1955–1957 XIV: 790.

90. Memo of Conversation, 18 March 1955, COO48, roll 17, National Archives; Memo Dulles to Eisenhower, 22 May 1956, Dulles-Herter Series, Whitman File, box 5, Eisenhower Library; Hahn, *Caught in the Middle East*, 189–190, 197.

91. Robert H. Ferrell, ed., *The Eisenhower Diaries* (New York, 1981), 308, 319; Press Conference, 4 October 1955, Israel Relations (1), General File, WHCF, box 817, Eisenhower Library.

92. Peter Hahn, "The View From Jerusalem: Revelations About U.S. Diplomacy From the Archives of Israel," *Diplomatic History* 22, no. 4 (Fall 1998): 509–532, esp. re *hasbara* (information) campaign in the United States.

93. See "The Trojan Horse," *Time*, November 7, 1955, 34; "The Battle of Anja," *Time*, November 14, 1955, 37; "Dimensions of a Crisis," *Time*, November 21, 1955, 19.

94. "Eye for an Eye" *Time*, April 23, 1956, 33–34; also, "The Hard Life," *Time*, January 30, 1956, 20; "Miserable Peace," *Time*, April 2, 1956, 30; "Divided Partners," *Time*, April 16, 1956, 26–27.

95. Blaustein to Dulles, *Time*, 29 February 1956, file Blaustein, Jacob 1956, box 100, Dulles Papers, Mudd Library.

96. See for example, Sachar, *History of Israel*, chapter 17, and Schoenbaum, *United States and Israel*, chapter 4.

97. Hahn, "View From Jerusalem," 525.

98. Lawrence W. Levine, *The Opening of the American Mind: Canons, Culture, and History* (Boston, 1996), 118.

99. R. Laurence Moore, *Religious Outsiders and the Making of Americans* (New York, 1986), xi.

100. *Toast of the Town: The Israel Anniversary Show* (1951), Museum of Television and Radio, New York.

101. Gordon, *Jews in Suburbia*, 102.

CHAPTER SIX: THE COLD WAR, SUEZ, AND BEYOND

1. Address by Dulles, 3 August 1956, Secretary's speeches 1956 (2), McCardle Papers, box 7; Address by Eisenhower, 20 February 1957, Speech Series, Whitman File, box 20, Eisenhower Library.

2. Telegram Eisenhower to Ben-Gurion, 9 April 1956, file Israel (5), International Series, Whitman File, box 32, Eisenhower Library.

3. See for example, Moshe Brilliant, "Israel's Policy of Reprisals," *Harper's* March 1955, 68–72; "Gaza Ambush, Rx for War," *Life*, March 14, 1955, 41–42+; "Gaza: A Bloody Testing Ground," *Newsweek*, March 14, 1955, 40; and "Clear and Present Danger on the Israel-Egypt Gaza Strip," *Life*, March 26, 1956, 28–29.

4. Memo William Rountree to John Foster Dulles, 8 June 1956, and Memo of Conversation, April 23, 1956, RG 59, C0048, National Archives; NSC meeting #262, 20 October 1955, NSC Series, Whitman File, box 7, Eisenhower Library.

5. Memo of Conversation, Department of State, 11 October 1955, 570–571; Memo of Conversation, 26 September 1955, 518; Telegram from Delegation at Foreign Ministers' meeting to the Department of State, 26 October 1955, FRUS 1955–1957 XIV: 657–658.

6. Chester Morrison, "Israel in Crisis," *Look*, May 29, 1956, 24–27.

7. Don Cook, "Tough Little Army," *Saturday Evening Post*, February 18, 1956, 26–27+; Joseph Alsop, "Why Israel Will Survive," *Saturday Evening Post*, September 8, 1956, 38–39+.

8. "Divided Partners," *Time*, April 16, 1956, 26–27; "Nasser's Frank and Startling Views," *Life*, April 16, 1956, 34–35; Henry Luce to C. D. Jackson, 21 April 1956 (with enclosure), Luce 56 (4), Papers of C. D. Jackson, box 71, Eisenhower Library.

9. National Intelligence Estimate (NIE), 15 November 1955, 771–772; Memo of Conversation, Department of State, 11 October 1955, 570; Telegram from delegation at the Foreign Ministers' meeting to the Department of State, 26 October 1955, FRUS 1955–1957 XIV: 658.

10. Television report to the nation by John Foster Dulles, 3 August 1956, Secretary's Speeches (2), McCardle Papers, box 7, Eisenhower Library.

11. Hagerty press release 29 October 1956, Middle East October 1956 file, Miscellaneous, Papers of James Hagerty, box 7, Eisenhower Library.

12. Press report on eastern Europe and the Middle East, 31 October 1956, file Middle East October 1956, Miscellaneous, Hagerty Papers, box 7, Eisenhower Library. Also see tape of Eisenhower's address, Museum of Television and Radio.

13. See Ambrose, *Eisenhower, Vol. II*, 429.

14. See Kyle, *Suez*, 181.

15. NSC meeting #303, 8 November 1956, NSC Series, Whitman File, box 8, Eisenhower Library.

16. Yergin, *The Prize*, 480; quote in Robert A. Divine, *Eisenhower and the Cold War*, (Oxford, 1981), 86.

17. Kyle, *Suez*, 403.

18. Memo of Conversation Department of State, 11 January 1957, FRUS 1955–1957 XVII, Arab-Israeli Dispute 1957: 22; emphasis added.

19. Note Eisenhower to Dulles, 1 November 1956, file Dulles, John Foster Nov 56 (1), Dulles-Herter Series, Whitman File, box 8, Eisenhower Library; emphasis in the original.

20. Memo of Conversation, 16 February 1957, FRUS 1955–1957 XVII: 185.

21. Eli Ginzburg to Eisenhower, 2 November 1956, file Ginzburg, Eli, Name Series, Whitman File, box 15, Eisenhower Library; Yaacov Herzog, OH, (1964), 19, Mudd Library.

22. See for example following exchange: Telegram Lawson to Dulles, 3 February 1957, Telegram Eisenhower to Ben-Gurion, 3 February 1957, Ben-

Gurion to Eisenhower, 8 February 1957, Israel (3), International Series, Whitman File, box 32, Eisenhower Library.

23. Eisenhower address to the nation, 20 February 1957, Speech Series, Whitman File, box 20, Eisenhower Library.

24. Memo Luce to editorial staff, 3 August 1956; Telegram Jackson to Luce, 18 August 1956, and Letter Luce to Jackson, 22 August 1956, Luce 1956 (2), Jackson Papers, box 71; Comments Bob Wilson 28 July 1956, 122BB Middle East Suez Situation (1), General File, WHCF, box 817, Eisenhower Library. For sample press stories, "Uneasy Borders," *Time*, September 3, 1956, 20, "Back to Reprisals," *Time*, September 24, 1956, 27, "Five Eyes for an Eye," *Time*, October 1956, 30.

25. See file 122 BB (2), General File, WHCF, box 881, Eisenhower Library. Also, Suleiman, *Arabs in the Mind of America*, 18–32.

26. "Blitz in the Desert," *Time*, November 12, 1956, 32+; emphasis added.

27. For example, "Israel: The Preventative War," *Time*, November 12, 1956, 39–40; "The Ashes of Victory," *Time*, November 19, 1956, 32–33.

28. Telegram E. L. Silver and Rabbi Meyer Cohen Menahel to Eisenhower, 14 November 1956, Israel 122BB (3), General File, WHCF, box 881, Eisenhower Library.

29. Kalmanowitz to Eisenhower, 23 November 1956, 122BB, General File, WHCF, box 881, Eisenhower Library.

30. Telegram Wolper to Eisenhower, 2 November 1956, 122BB (2), General File, WHCF, box 881, Eisenhower Library.

31. Telegram Rabbi S. Bernstein, American Zionist Committee for Public Affairs et al to Eisenhower, 27 November 1956, 122BB, General File, WHCF, box 881, Eisenhower Library. See assorted correspondence on the same subject in the same files, arranged in rough chronological order. Also, in *Time*, "Dollars for Israel," January 21, 1957, 16, and "Victor Without Spoils," January 28, 1957, 34.

32. Telegram to Eisenhower, 10 September 1956, and Letter to Eisenhower, 17 October 1956, 122 BB Middle East Suez Situation (1), General File, WHCF, box 881, Eisenhower Library. For other examples and correspondence August to October 1956 see same file and 122 BB (2). For correspondence November 1956 to March 1957, see 122 BB Middle East Suez Situation (2–9), boxes 881 and 882, and Israel (4), box 817. Many of the letters and telegrams seemed to be from Jews.

33. The sympathy for Israel was reflected in opinion polls. See Stember, *Israel in the Mind of America*, 181–189; George Gallup, *The Gallup Poll, Public Opinion Vol. II 1949–1958* (New York, 1972), 1454–57, 1465, 1472.

34. Spiegel, *Other Arab-Israeli Conflict*, 78; "First Stage," *Time*, March 11, 1957, 15. Also see "The Heat on Israel," *Time*, February 25, 1957, 26–7, and "Pressures," *Time*, March 4, 1957, 26.

35. See for example, "Victor Without Spoils," *Time*, January 28, 1957, 34, "Israel: Stubborn Nation on the Spot," *Newsweek*, February 18, 1957, 39, and "The Heat on Israel," *Time*, February 25, 1957, 26.

36. See for example, "The Crowd Looking On," *Time*, February 25, 1957, 26.

37. For example, Jim Novy to Eisenhower, 11 February 1957, Israel (4), General File, WHCF, box 817, Eisenhower Library. For other examples, see files 122 BB (7–9), General File, WHCF, box 882, Eisenhower Library.

38. Finder to Eisenhower, 7 February 1957, Name Series, Whitman File, box 14, Eisenhower Library.

39. Truman to National Israel Bonds Dinner, 16 February 1957, file 1957 February 15; also, Truman to Greater Miami Combined Jewish Appeal, 12 February 1957, file 1957 February 12, Lloyd Papers, box 59, Truman Library; Reinhold Niebuhr, "Our Stake in the State of Israel," *New Republic*, February 4, 1957, 9–12.

40. Johnson to Dulles, 11 February 1957, February 1957 (2), Dulles-Herter series, Whitman File, box 8, Eisenhower Library; "Three Views on Israel," *Foreign Policy Bulletin*, 15 March 1957, 102–103, and "Israel: Stubborn Nation on the Spot," *Newsweek*, February 18, 1957, 39. Senator Mike Mansfield appeared on the television program, *Meet the Press*, February 24, 1957.

41. Dulles memo to ambassador in Cairo, 20 December 1956, file Dulles, John Foster December 1956, Dulles-Herter Series, Whitman File, box 8, Eisenhower Library.

42. "Prophet With a Gun," *Time*, January 16, 1956, 25.

43. Eisenhower to Dulles, 19 December 1956, file Dulles, John Foster December 1956; also, Telegram Dulles to Eisenhower, 14 December 1956, file December 1956, Dulles-Herter Series, Whitman File, box 8, Eisenhower Library.

44. See for example, Notes on legislative leadership meeting, 31 December 1956, December 1956 Miscellaneous (1), box 20, and Notes on Presidential-Bipartisan Congressional Leadership meeting, 1 January 1957, January 1957 Miscellaneous (4), box 21, Eisenhower Diary, Whitman File, Eisenhower Library.

45. See address Eisenhower, 5 January 1957 and H. J. Resolution 117, McCardle Papers, box 8, Eisenhower Library.

46. Eisenhower Speech to Congress, 5 January 1957 with H. J. Resolution 117/Joint Resolution, McCardle Papers, box 8, and Dulles speech, 14 January 1957, Dulles, J. F. January 1957, Dulles-Herter Series, Whitman File, box 8, Eisenhower Library.

47. For example, see "The Crowd Looking On," *Time*, February 25, 1957, 26.

48. See, Telegram President's Special Assistant to Department of State, 4 May 1957, FRUS 1955–1957 XVII: 597–601; NSC 5801/1, 24 January 1958, file 1, NSC Policy Paper Subseries, White House Office of Special Assistant for National Security Affairs, box 23, Eisenhower Library.

49. Telegram from the Embassy in Egypt to the Department of State, 24 August 1957, FRUS 1955–1957 XVII: 714; Notes on Presidential-Bipartisan Congressional Leadership meeting, 1 January 1957, January 1957 Miscellaneous (4), Eisenhower Diary, Whitman File, box 21; and Memo of conference with the president, 23 July 1958, Staff Memos July 1958 (1), Eisenhower Diary, Whitman File, box 35, Eisenhower Library.

50. "A Turning Point," *Time*, January 28, 1957, 34.

51. "Double Task in the Middle East," *Life*, January 7, 1957.

52. See George Mardikian, "What We Americans Forget About the Arab World," *Reader's Digest*, November 1958, 62–66; James Morris, "Four Clues to the Middle East," *NYTM*, December 8, 1957, 9.

53. Luce to Jackson, 12 May 1956, Luce 56 (3), Jackson Papers, box 71, Eisenhower Library.

54. All from *NYTM*: James Morris, "What it Means to be Arab," November 16, 1958, 84, 22+; Osgood Caruthers, "The Enigma That is the Arab," 20 October 1957, 80, 18+; and James Morris, "Why the Arabs Do Not Unite," 6 December 1959, 120. 28–29+.

55. Osgood Caruthers, "Life by Intrigue: The Mideast," *NYTM*, August 17, 1958, 14, 84.

56. J. Coert Rylaarsdam, "The Arab State of Mind." *Christian Century*, May 16, 1956.

57. James Morris, "Four Clues," 9; James Morris, "Why the Arabs," 28–29+.

58. James Morris, "Two Arab Worlds: Pashas and People," *NYTM*, March 2, 1958, 9+.

59. For examples, see "Arab Logic," *Newsweek*, February 2, 1959, 34; "A Nervous Nasser," *Newsweek*, May 27, 1957, 55; "Nasser's Next Move—Closing the Ring Around Israel?" *U.S. News and World Report*, November 7, 1958, 67; Gamal Abdel Nasser, "Where I Stand and Why," *Life*, July 20, 1959, 96–97+.

60. NSC 5801/1, 24 January 1958, file 1, NSC Policy Paper Subseries, White House Office of Special Assistant for National Security Affairs, box 23, Eisenhower Library; emphasis in the original.

61. Memo of conference with president, 23 July 1958, Staff Memos July 1958 (1), Eisenhower Diary, Whitman File, box 35, Eisenhower Library.

62. Memo of Conversation, 31 October 1957, 782–785; Memo of Conversation Department of State, 4 October 1957, 747–748; Memo of Conversation, 13 November 1957, 793–794; see also, Memo of Conversation, 29 November 1957, 831–832, and Message from Dulles to Ben-Gurion, 12 November 1957, 792–793, FRUS 1955–1957 XVII. Memo William Rountree, NEA to the Secretary, 17 January 1959, file Israel, U.S.-Israel Relations 1959, RG 59, Lot file 61D124, Subject Files Relating to Israel and Lebanon 1954–1959, box 18, National Archives.

63. Memo Bergus to Dorman and Rockwell 30 September 1957, Department of State, RG 59, 250:49/18/7, Lot 59D582, box 5, National Archives; NSC 5801/1, 24 January 1958, file 1, NSC Policy Paper Subseries, White House Office for Special Assistant for National Security Affairs, box 23, Eisenhower Library; Deborah Dash Moore, "Bonding Images: Miami Jews and the Campaign for Israel Bonds," in *Envisioning Israel*, ed. Allon Gal, 263.

64. For example, Memo of Conversation, 30 June 1958, RG 59, 611.84a/6–3058, COO48, National Archives; Schoenbaum, *United States and State of Israel*, 129–132; Hahn, *Caught in the Middle East*, 230, 234; "Nasser's Next Move—Closing the Ring Around Israel?" *U.S. News and World Report*, November 7, 1958, 67.

65. Memo Rountree to Dillion, 20 June 1957, 652–653; Memo of Conversation, 24 June 1957, 654–656; see also, Memo of Conversation, 20 June 1957, 649–651, FRUS 1955–1957 XVII.

66. See Memo from Rountree to Dulles, 6 December 1957, 845–846, and Memo from Bell to Rountree, 11 December 1957, 851–852. See also Memo from Rountree to Acting Secretary, 13 March 1957, 412–413, FRUS 1955–1957 XVII.

67. Memo from Wilcox to Herter, 10 May 1957, 610–611; Memo from Wilcox to Herter, 2 July 1957, 661–677; and Memo from Villard to Herter, 6 August

1957, 699, 698–701; see also, Memo from Villard to Dulles 21 November 1957, 807–816, FRUS 1955–1957 XVII.

68. Abraham Ben–Zvi, *Decade of Transition* (New York, 1998), 78–80.

69. Telegram Eisenhower to Ben-Gurion, 25 July 1958, file Israel (2), and Ben-Gurion to Eisenhower, 24 July 1958, file Israel (1), International Series, Whitman File, box 32, Eisenhower Library.

70. NSC 5801/1, 24 January 1958, file 1, and NSC 5820/1, 4 November 1958, file 2, box 26, NSC Policy Paper Subseries, White House Office of Special Assistant for National Security Affairs, box 23, Eisenhower Library.

71. Memo Dulles to Eisenhower, 5 March 1958, file March 1958 (2), Dulles-Herter Series, Whitman File, box 10, Eisenhower Library.

72. Herzog OH, 9–10, Mudd Library.

73. Ibid., 8–9; Eban OH, 46, Mudd Library; Eban, *Abba Eban*, 263.

74. See "Can Israel Live?" *Newsweek*, April 21, 1958, 54–56+; "Recasting the Crucible," *Time*, April 21, 1958, 24; "Nine and Still Growing," *Time*, May 13, 1957, 32–33; "Exultant Birthday for Israel," *Life*, May 5, 1958, 32–34; William Attwood, "Ben-Gurion Talks," *Look*, April 15, 1958, 92+.

75. Gertrude Samuels, "New Roots, Old Land," *NYTBR*, April 27, 1958; Dana Adams Schmidt, "Forging a Nation," *NYTBR*, April 27, 1958, 3, 32; Walter Eytan, *The First Ten Years* (New York, 1958).

76. James Morris, "Four Clues," 98; Memo by the Secretary of State for the Assistant Secretary of State for Near Eastern, South Asian, and African Affairs Byroade, 10 April 1954, FRUS 1952–1954 IX: 1509.

77. The arms disagreement and solution was referred to in many places, for example, Israel, Background and Policy, 1959, and Memo from Parker Hart, NEA to the Secretary, 19 November 1959, file, U.S.-Israel Relations 1959, RG 59, Lot File 61D124, Subject Files Relating to Israel and Lebanon 1954–1959, box 18, National Archives.

78. Telegram from delegation at the Foreign Ministers meeting to the Department of State, 26 October 1955, FRUS 1955–1957 XIV: 659.

CONCLUSION

1. Leon Uris, "Exodus Revisited," *Look*, November 24, 1959, 98–104, 106.

2. Uris, *Exodus*, and *Exodus* (UA/Carlyle/Alpha, 1960).

3. Uris, *Exodus*, 10, 17, 367, 51.

4. *Solomon and Sheba* (UA/Edward Small, 1959).

5. Uris, *Exodus*, 572.

6. Ibid., 239, 455.

7. Ibid., 194, 219–220.

8. Ibid., 187, 357, 589.

9. *Ben-Hur* (MGM/Sam Zimbalist, 1959) and *Solomon and Sheba*, 1959.

10. Maxwell Geismar, "Epic of Israel," *Saturday Review of Literature*, September 27, 1958, 22–23.

11. Hertzberg, *The Jews in America*, 319.

12. Sidney Hyman, "Heroic Israel Today: The Legend and the Facts." *Harper's*, September 1960, 29–36, quotes from 31, 32.

13. Albert Maisel, "The Jews Among Us," *Reader's Digest*, April 1955, 26–31.

14. See for example, William Attwood, "The Position of the Jews in America Today," *Look*, November 29, 1955, 27–35; "Theological Coexistence," *Time*, September 28, 1959, 42+; "Threat of Assimilation," *America*, December 3, 1960, 334.

15. "Israel and the American Jew," *Look*, October 11, 1960, 42.

16. Ibid.

17. Nathan Perlmutter, "Bombing in Miami: Anti-Semitism and the Segregationists," *Commentary*, June 1958, 498–503; "Christians Condemn Bombings in South," *Christian Century*, April 2, 1958, 397–398; "Violent Act of Anti-Semitism in the South," *Life*, October 27, 1958, 43-44.

18. "Israel and Anti-Semitism," *Commonweal*, April 20, 1956, 63-64.

19. Truman address to sixtieth annual convention Zionist Organization of America, September 14, 1957, file 1957 September 14, Lloyd Papers, box 59, Truman Library.

Bibliography

NOVELS AND STORIES

Asch, Sholem. *Mary*. New York: G. P. Putnam's Sons, 1949.

———. *Moses*. New York: G. P. Putnam's Sons, 1951.

———. *A Passage in the Night*. New York: G. P. Putnam's Sons, 1953.

———. *The Prophet*. New York: G. P. Putnam's Sons, 1955.

———. *Tales of My People*. New York: G. P. Putnam's Sons, 1948.

Bellow, Saul. *The Adventures of Augie March*. New York: The Viking Press, 1949, 1952.

Fast, Howard. *My Glorious Brothers*. Boston: Little, Brown, & Company, 1948.

Green, Gerald. *The Last Angry Man*. New York: Charles Scribner's Sons, 1956.

Hersey, John. *The Wall*. New York: Alfred A. Knopf, 1950.

Hobson, Laura Z. *Gentleman's Agreement*. New York: Simon and Schuster, 1947.

Kaufmann, Myron S. *Remember Me to God*. Philadelphia: J. B. Lippincott Company, 1957.

Mailer, Norman. *The Naked and the Dead*. New York: Holt, Rinehart & Winston, 1948.

Roth, Philip. *Goodbye, Columbus and Five Short Stories*. New York: Houghton Mifflin Company, 1959.

Shaw, Irwin. *The Young Lions*. New York: Random House, 1948.

Slaughter, Frank G. *The Song of Ruth: A Love Story From the Old Testament*. Garden City, NY: Doubleday & Co., 1954.

Uris, Leon. *Exodus*. New York: Doubleday & Co., 1958.

Viertel, Joseph. *The Last Temptation*. New York: Simon and Schuster, 1955.

Weidman, Jerome. *The Enemy Camp*. New York: Random House, 1958.

Wouk, Herman. *Marjorie Morningstar*. New York: Doubleday & Co., 1955.

FILMS AND VIDEO

All—except as noted—from the Motion Picture Collection (abbreviated in notes as MPC), the Library of Congress, Washington DC; selected films also viewed on video and television.

Ben-Hur. 1959. MGM. Sam Zimbalist, producer; William Wyler, director; Karl Tunberg, writer. Based on the novel *Ben-Hur* by General Lew Wallace.

Crossfire. 1947. RKO. Adrian Scott, producer; Edward Dmytryk, director; John Paxton, writer. Based on the novel *The Brick Foxhole* by Richard Brooks.

David and Bathsheba. 1952. Twentieth Century Fox. Darryl F. Zanuck, producer; Henry King, director; Philip Dunne, writer.

The Desert Song. 1943. Warner Brothers. Robert Florey, producer and director; Robert Buckner, writer, adapted from 1929 version.

The Diary of Anne Frank. 1959. Twentieth Century Fox. George Stevens, producer and director; Frances Goodrich and Albert Hackett, writers. Based on the play by Goodrich and Hackett which was based on the diary.

The Eddie Cantor Story. 1953. Warner Brothers. Sidney Skolsky, producer; Alfred E. Green, director; Jerome Weidman, Ted Sherdeman, and Sidney Skolsky, writers.

Exodus. 1960. United Artists/Carlyle/Alpha. Otto Preminger, producer and director; Dalton Trumbo, writer. Based on the novel by Leon Uris.

Gentleman's Agreement. 1947. Twentieth Century Fox. Darryl F. Zanuck, producer; Elia Kazan, director; Moss Hart, writer. Based on the novel by Laura Z. Hobson.

Good Morning. Miss Dove. 1955. Twentieth Century Fox. Samuel G. Engel, producer; Henry Koster, director; Eleanore Griffin, writer. Based on the novel by Frances Gray Patton.

The Great Dictator. 1940. Charles Chaplin. Charles Chaplin, producer, director, and writer.

Home Before Dark. 1958. Warner Brothers. Mervyn Le Roy, producer and director; Eileen and Robert Bassing, writers.

I Accuse! 1958. MGM. Sam Zimbalist, producer; Jose Ferrer, director; Gore Vidal, writer.

The Juggler. 1953. Columbia Pictures. Stanley Kramer, producer; Edward Dmytryk, director; Michael Blankfort, writer. Based on the novel by Michael Blankfort.

Marjorie Morningstar. 1958. Warner Brothers/United States Pictures. Milton Sperling, producer; Irving Rapper, director; Everett Freeman, writer. Based on the novel by Herman Wouk.

Me and the Colonel. 1958. Columbia Pictures. William Goetz, producer; Peter Glenville, director; S.N. Behrman and George Froeschel, writers. Based on the play by Franz Werfel.

The Naked and the Dead. 1958. RKO Teleradio/Gregjac. Paul Gregory, producer; Raoul Walsh, director; Denis and Terry Sanders, writers. Based on the novel by Norman Mailer.

The Prodigal. 1955. MGM. Charles Schnee, producer; Richard Thorpe, director; Maurice Zimm, writer.

The Robe. 1953. Twentieth Century Fox. Frank Ross, producer; Henry Koster, director; Philip Dunne, writer. Based on the novel by Lloyd C. Douglas.

Samson and Delilah. 1949. Paramount Pictures. Cecil B. de Mille, producer and director; Jesse L. Lasky Jr. and Frederic M. Frank, writers.

Sands of Iwo Jima. 1949. Republic Pictures. Edmund Grainger, producer; Allan Dwan, director; Harry Brown and James Edward Grant, writers. (Home video copy.)

The Search. 1948. MGM/Praesens Film. Lazar Wechsler, producer; Fred Zinneman, director; Richard Schweizer, David Wechshler, and Paul Jarrico, writers.

Solomon and Sheba. 1959. UA/Edward Small. Ted Richmond, producer; King Vidor, director; Anthony Veiller, Paul Dudley, and George Bruce, writers.

The Sword in the Desert. 1949. Universal Pictures. Robert Buckner, producer and writer; George Sherman, director.

Take Me Out to the Ballgame. 1949. MGM. Arthur Freed, producer; Gene Kelly and Stanley Donen, directors; Harry Tugend and George Wells, writers. (Home video copy.)

The Ten Commandments. 1956. Paramount/Cecil B. de Mille. Henry Wilcoxon, producer; Cecil B. de Mille, director; Aeneas Mackenzie, Jesse L. Lasky Jr., Jack Gariss, and Frederic M. Frank, writers.

Three Brave Men. 1956. Twentieth Century Fox. Herbert B. Swope Jr., producer; Philip Dunne, director and writer. Based on the articles by Anthony Lewis.

The Young Lions. 1958. Twentieth Century Fox. Al Lichtman, producer; Edward Dmytryk, director; Edward Anhalt, writer. Based on the novel by Irwin Shaw.

TELEVISION

All from the Museum of Television and Radio, New York, NY; numbers refer to the cataloguing system at the museum.

CBS News: Israel/The Reality. T78:0330 004270.

Crossroads: CBS Reports. The Legacy of Harry S. Truman. 1984. T:04190 020216.

Directions '64: The Living Past. 1964. T81:0188 013925.

Meet the Press. February 24, 1957, and March 3, 1957.

President Eisenhower: Address on Eastern Eastern Europe and the Middle East. 1956. T13575 019874.

President Eisenhower: Address to the UN General Assembly. 1958. T81:0624 002553.

See It Now: Murrow at Wake Island. 1953. T82:0220 001920.

Toast of the Town: The Israel Anniversary Show with Ed Sullivan." 1951. T77:0074 005689.

ARCHIVE COLLECTIONS

David Ben-Gurion Archives, S'de Boker, Israel. Collections consulted: Subject File; Correspondence File.

Dwight D. Eisenhower Library, Abilene KS. Collections consulted: Dwight David Eisenhower Papers as President (Ann Whitman File); Papers of John Foster Dulles; Papers of James Hagerty; Papers of Christian Herter; Papers of

C.D. Jackson; Papers of Carl McCardle; White House Central Files; White House Office of the Special Assistant for National Security Affairs.

Oral histories: Elie Abel (1970), Joseph Alsop (1972), Andrew Berding (1967), Robert Clark (1978), Robert Donovan (1968), James Hagerty (1967–1968), Raymond Hare (1972), Loy Henderson (1970), Eric Hodgins (1968–1969), Jacob Javits (1968), Carl McCardle (1967), Max Rabb (1970, 1975), Ogden Reid (1967).

Library of Congress, Washington DC. Collections consulted: Manuscript Division, Papers of Joseph and Stewart Alsop; Motion Picture and Television Division.

Seeley G. Mudd Library, Princeton NJ. Collections consulted: Papers of John Foster Dulles; Papers of Adlai E. Stevenson.

Oral histories: Allen Dulles (1965); Abba Eban (1964); Dwight Eisenhower (1964); Yaacov Herzog (1964).

National Archives, College Park MD. Collection Consulted: General Records of the Department of State.

Harry S. Truman Library, Independence, MO. Collections consulted: Papers of Dean Acheson; Papers of Eben Ayers; Papers of Gordon R. Clapp; Papers of Clark Clifford; Papers of George M. Elsey; Papers of David Lloyd; Papers of Edwin A. Locke Jr.; Papers of Howard McGrath; Papers of Harry S. Truman; Papers in Weizmann Archives, Rehovoth, Israel (copies); Papers of Joel Wolfsohn.

Oral histories: Clark Clifford (1971, 1972, 1973), Matthew Connelly (1967–1968), George M. Elsey (1964, 1965, 1969, 1970), Mark Ethridge (1974), Oscar Ewing (1969), Abraham Feinberg (1973), A.J. Granoff (1969), Loy Henderson (1973), Edwin A. Locke Jr. (1967), James I. Loeb (1970), Max Lowenthal (1967), Joseph C. Satterwaite (1972), Walter Trohan (1970), Fraser Wilkins (1975), Edwin Wright (1974), Dr. Arthur Young (1974).

PERIODICALS AND NEWSPAPERS CONSULTED

Citations for individual articles are found in end notes.

American Home
Atlantic
Business Week
Christian Century
Christianity and Crisis
Cleveland Ohio Plain Dealer
Commentary
Fame
Harper's
Life
Look
Nation
New Republic
New York Herald Tribune
New York Herald Tribune Book Review (NYHTBR)

New York Post
New Yorker
New York Times (NYT)
New York Times Book Review (NYTBR)
New York Times Magazine (NYTM)
New York World Telegram
Newsweek
Reader's Digest
Saturday Evening Post
Saturday Review of Literature
Time
U.S. News and World Report
Variety
Wall Street Journal
Washington Post
Washington Star

BOOKS

Aburish, Said. *Children of Bethany: The Story of a Palestinian Family*. Bloomington, IN: Indiana University Press, 1988.

Acheson, Dean. *Present at the Creation: My Years in the State Department*. New York: W. W. Norton and Company, 1969.

Adler, Frank J. *Roots Moving in a Stream: The Centennial History of Congregation B'Nai Jehudah of Kansas City, 1870–1970*. Kansas City, MO: The Temple Congregation, 1972.

Adorno, T. W. et. al. *The Authoritarian Personality*. New York: W. W. Norton and Company, 1950.

Alteras, Isaac. *Eisenhower and Israel: U.S.-Israeli Relations, 1953–1960*. Gainesville, FL: University Press of Florida, 1993.

Ambrose, Stephen E. *Eisenhower, Vol. II: The President*. New York: Simon and Schuster, 1990.

Anderson, Benedict. *Imagined Communities: Reflections on the Origins and Spread of Nationalism*. London: Verso, 1991.

Andrew, Geoff. *The Film Handbook*. Harlow, Essex: Longman Group, 1989.

Bain, Kenneth Ray. *The March to Zion: United States Policy and the Founding of Israel*. College Station, TX: Texas A & M University Press, 1979.

Ball, George. *The Passionate Attachment: America's Involvement with Israel, 1947 to the Present*. New York: W. W. Norton and Company, 1992.

Bederman, Gail. *Manliness and Civilization: A Cultural History of Gender and Race in the United States, 1880–1917*. Chicago: University of Chicago Press, 1995.

Beilin, Yossi. *Israel: A Concise Political History*. New York: St. Martin's Press, 1992.

Benson, Michael T. *Harry S. Truman and the Founding of Israel*. Westport, CT: Praeger, 1997.

Ben-Zvi, Abraham. *Decade of Transition: Eisenhower, Kennedy, and the Origins of the American-Israeli Alliance.* New York: Columbia University Press, 1998.

———. *The United States and Israel: The Limits of the Special Relationship.* New York: Columbia University Press, 1993.

Bilik, Dorothy Seidman. *Immigrant-Survivors: Post-Holocaust Consciousness in Recent Jewish American Fiction.* Middletown, CT: Wesleyan University Press, 1981.

Blum, John Morton, ed. and intro. *The Price of Vision: The Diary of Henry A. Wallace, 1942–1946.* Boston: Houghton Mifflin, 1985.

Bodnar, John. *The Transplanted: A History of Immigrants in Urban America.* Bloomington, IN: Indiana University Press, 1985.

Boorstin, Daniel J. *The Image: A Guide to Pseudo-Events in America.* New York: Atheneum, 1961, 1987.

Breines, Paul. *Tough Jews: Political Fantasies and the Moral Dilemma of America.* New York: Basic Books, Inc., 1990.

Breitman, Richard and Alan Kraut. *American Refugee Policy and European Jewry, 1933–1945.* Bloomington, IN: Indiana University Press, 1987.

Brinkley, Alan. *Voices of Protest: Huey Long, Father Coughlin, and The Great Depression.* New York: Vintage Books, 1982.

Brodkin, Karen. *How Jews Became White Folks and What That Says About Race in America.* New Brunswick, NJ: Rutgers University Press, 1998.

Brown, Francis J., and Joseph S. Roucek. *One America: The History, Contributions, and Present Problems of Our Racial and National Minorities.* New York: Prentice-Hall Inc., 1952.

Bryson, Thomas A. *American Diplomatic Relations With the Middle East, 1784–1975: A Survey.* Metuchen, NJ: The Scarecrow Press, Inc., 1977.

Campbell, Richard H., and Michael R. Pitts. *The Bible on Film: A Checklist, 1897–1980.* Metuchen, NJ: The Scarecrow Press, Inc., 1981.

Carter, Paul A. *Another Part of the Fifties.* New York: Columbia University Press, 1983.

Ceplair, Larry and Steven Englund. *The Inquisition in Hollywood: Politics in the Film Community, 1930–1960.* Berkeley, CA: University of California Press, 1970, 1983.

Clifford, Clark with Richard Holbrooke. *Counsel to the President: A Memoir.* New York: Random House, 1991.

Cohen, Michael J. *Truman and Israel.* Berkeley, CA: University of California Press, 1990.

———. *The Origins and Evolution of the Arab-Zionist Conflict.* Berkeley, CA: University of California Press, 1987.

Cohen, Naomi W. *Jews in Christian America: The Pursuit of Religious Equality.* New York: Oxford University Press, 1992.

Combs, James. *Polpop: Politics and Popular Culture in America.* Bowling Green, OH: Bowling Green University Popular Press, 1984.

Cook, Blanche Weisen. *The Declassified Eisenhower: A Divided Legacy.* Garden City, NY: Doubleday & Co., Inc., 1981.

Curtiss, Richard H. *A Changing Image: American Perceptions of the Arab-Israeli Dispute.* Washington, DC: American Educational Trust, 1982, 1986.

Dean, Robert. *Imperial Brotherhood: Gender and the Making of Cold War Foreign Policy.* Amherst, MA: University of Massachusetts Press, 2001.

D'Emilio, John. *Sexual Politics, Sexual Communities: The Making of a Homosexual Minority in the United States, 1940–1970.* Chicago: University of Chicago Press, 1983.

Diner, Hasia. *Lower East Side Memories: A Jewish Place in America.* Princeton, NJ: Princeton University Press, 2000.

———. *A Time for Gathering: The Second Migration, 1820–1880.* Baltimore, MD: The Johns Hopkins University Press, 1992.

Dinnerstein, Leonard. *Antisemitism in America.* New York: Oxford University Press, 1994.

———. *Uneasy at Home: Antisemitism and the American Jewish Experience.* New York: Columbia University Press, 1987.

Divine, Robert A. *Eisenhower and the Cold War.* New York: Oxford University Press, 1981.

Dollinger, Marc. *Quest for Inclusion: Jews and Liberalism in Modern America.* Princeton and Oxford: Princeton University Press, 2000.

Doneson, Judith E. *The Holocaust in American Film.* Philadelphia: The Jewish Publication Society, 1987.

Dosh. *To Israel, With Love.* New York: Thomas Yoseloff, 1960.

Dower, John. *War Without Mercy: Race and Power in the Pacific War.* New York: Pantheon Books, 1986.

Drinnon, Richard. *Facing West: The Metaphysics of Indian-Hating and Empire Building.* New York: New American Library, 1980.

Druks, Herbert. *The Uncertain Friendship: The U.S. and Israel From Roosevelt to Kennedy.* Westport, CT: Greenwood Press, 2001.

Eagleton, Terry. *Literary Theory: An Introduction.* Minneapolis, MN: University of Minnesota Press, 1983.

Eban, Abba. *Abba Eban: An Autobiography.* New York: Random House, 1977.

Ehrenreich, Barbara. *The Hearts of Men: American Dreams and the Flight From Commitment.* New York: Anchor Books, 1983.

Ellwood, Robert S. *1950: Crossroads of American Religious Life.* Louisville, KY: Westminster John Knox Press, 2000.

Engler, Robert. *The Politics of Oil: A Study of Private Power and Democratic Directions.* New York: The Macmillan Company, 1961.

Erens, Patricia. *The Jew in American Cinema.* Bloomington, IN: Indiana University Press, 1984.

Evenson, Bruce J. *Truman, Palestine, and the Presidency: Shaping Conventional Wisdom at the Beginning of the Cold War.* New York: Greenwood Press, 1992.

Eytan, Walter. *The First Ten Years: A Diplomatic History of Israel.* New York: Simon and Schuster, 1958.

Faber, Eli. *A Time for Planting: The First Migration, 1654–1820.* Baltimore, MD: The Johns Hopkins University Press, 1992.

Feingold, Henry L. *Bearing Witness: How America and Its Jews Responded to the Holocaust.* Syracuse: Syracuse University Press, 1995.

———. *A Time for Searching: Entering the Maintream, 1920–1945.* Baltimore, MD: The Johns Hopkins University Press, 1992.

Feldblum, Esther Yolles. *The American Catholic Press and the Jewish State, 1917–1959*. New York: KTAV Publishing House, Inc., 1977.

Feldman, Egal. *Dual Destinies: The Jewish Encounter With Protestant America*. Urbana, IL: University of Illinois Press, 1990.

Ferrell, Robert H., ed. *The Eisenhower Diaries*. New York: W. W. Norton and Co., 1981.

———. *Truman in the White House: The Diary of Eben A. Ayers*. Columbia, MO: University of Missouri, 1991.

———. *Off the Record: The Private Papers of Harry S. Truman*. New York: Harper & Row Publishers, 1980.

———. *The Diary of James C. Hagerty: Eisenhower in Mid-Course, 1954–1955*. Bloomington, IN: Indiana University Press, 1983.

Fishman, Hertzel. *American Protestantism and a Jewish State*. Detroit, MI: Wayne State University Press, 1973.

Flanzbaum, Hilene, ed. *The Americanization of the Holocaust*. Baltimore, MD: The Johns Hopkins University Press, 1999.

Flapan, Simha. *The Birth of Israel: Myths and Realities*. New York: Pantheon Books, 1987.

Foucault, Michel. *The Archaeology of Knowledge*. Translated by Sheridan Smith. New York: Pantheon Books, 1972.

Frank, Anne. *Anne Frank: The Diary of a Young Girl*. Introduction by Eleanor Roosevelt. New York: Doubleday & Co., Inc., 1952.

Fraser, T. G. *The USA and the Middle East Since World War 2*. New York: St. Martin's Press, 1989.

Friedman, Lester D. *Hollywood's Image of the Jew*. New York: Frederick Ungar Publishing Co., 1982.

———, ed. *Unspeakable Images: Ethnicity and the American Cinema*. Urbana and Chicago, IL: University of Illinois Press, 1991.

Friedman, Thomas. *From Beirut to Jerusalem*. New York: Doubleday & Co., Inc., 1989, 1990.

Gabler, Neal. *An Empire of Their Own: How the Jews Invented Hollywood*. New York: Crown Publishers, Inc., 1988.

Gal, Allon, ed. *Envisioning Israel: The Changing Ideals and Images of North American Jews*. Jerusalem and Detroit: The Magnes Press, The Hebrew University, and Wayne State University Press, 1996.

Gallup, George. *The Gallup Poll, Public Opinion 1935–1971, Vol 1 1935–1948, Vol II 1949–1958*. New York: Random House, 1972.

Ganin, Zvi. *Truman, American Jewry and Israel, 1945–1948*. New York: Holmes & Meier Publishers, Inc., 1979.

Geertz, Clifford. *The Interpretation of Cultures: Selected Essays*. New York: Basic Books, Inc., 1973.

Gerges, Fawaz A. *The Superpowers and the Middle East: Regional and International Politics, 1955–1967*. Boulder, CO: Westview Press, 1994.

Gilboa, Eytan. *American Public Opinion Toward Israel and the Arab-Israeli Conflict*. Lexington, MA: D.C. Heath & Company, 1987.

Glazer, Nathan. *American Judaism*. Chicago: University of Chicago Press, 1957.

Gilman, Sander. *Jewish Self-Hatred: Anti-Semitism and the Hidden Language of the Jews*. Baltimore, MD: The Johns Hopkins University Press, 1986.

Goldberg, J. J. *Jewish Power: Inside the American Jewish Establishment*. Reading, MA: Addison-Wesley, 1996.

Goodwin, Doris Kearns. *No Ordinary Time: Franklin and Eleanor Roosevelt: The Homefront in World War II*. New York: Simon and Schuster, 1994.

Gordon, Albert I. *Jews in Suburbia*. Boston, MA: Beacon Press, 1959.

Graver, Lawrence. *An Obsession with Anne Frank: Meyer Levin and the Diary*. Berkeley, CA: University of California Press, 1995.

Green, Stephen. *Taking Sides: America's Secret Relations With a Militant Israel*. New York: William Morrow & Company, Inc., 1984.

Greenstein, Fred. *The Hidden Hand Presidency: Eisenhower as Leader*. New York: Basic Books, Inc., 1982.

Grose, Peter. *Israel in the Mind of America: The Untold Story of America's 150–Year Fascination With the Idea of a Jewish State, and the Complex Role Played by this Country and Its Leaders in the Creation of Modern Israel*. New York: Alfred A. Knopf, 1983.

Guttmann, Allen. *The Jewish Writer in America: Assimilation and the Crisis of Identity*. New York: Oxford University Press, 1971.

Hahn, Peter L. *Caught in the Middle East: U.S. Policy Toward the Arab-Israeli Conflict, 1945–1961*. Chapel Hill, NC: The University of North Carolina Press, 2004.

———. *The United States, Great Britain, and Egypt, 1945–1956: Strategy and Diplomacy in the Early Cold War*. Chapel Hill, NC: The University of North Carolina Press, 1991.

Halpern, Ben. *The Idea of the Jewish State*. Cambridge, MA: Harvard University Press, 1969.

Haskell, Molly. *From Reverence to Rape: The Treatment of Women in Movies*. New York: Holt, Rinehart & Winston, 1973, 1974.

Heald, Morrell and Lawrence S. Kaplan. *Culture and Diplomacy: The American Experience*. Westport, CT: Greenwood Press, 1977.

Hecht, Ben. *A Child of the Century*. New York: Signet Books, 1954.

Heller, Joseph. *The Birth of Israel, 1945–1949: Ben-Gurion and His Critics*. Gainesville, FL: University Press of Florida, 2000.

Herberg, Will. *Protestant-Catholic-Jew: An Essay in American Religious Sociology*. Garden City, NY: Doubleday & Co., Inc., 1955, 1960.

Hertzberg, Arthur. *The Jews in America: Four Centuries of an Uneasy Encounter*. New York: Simon and Schuster, 1989.

Higham, John. *Send These to Me: Jews and Other Immigrants in Urban America*. New York: Atheneum, 1975.

———. *Strangers in the Land: Patterns of American Nativism, 1860–1925*. New Brunswick, NJ: Rutgers University Press, 1955.

Hollinger, David A. *Science, Jews, and Secular Culture: Studies in Mid-Twentieth Century American Intellectual History*. Princeton, NJ: Princeton University Press, 1996.

Hoopes, Townsend. *The Devil and John Foster Dulles.* Boston, MA: Little, Brown and Company, 1973.

Hunt, Michael. *Ideology and U.S. Foreign Policy.* New Haven, CT: Yale University Press, 1987.

Immerman, Richard H. *John Foster Dulles: Piety, Pragmatism, and Power in U.S. Foreign Policy.* Wilmington, DE: Scholarly Resources, 1999.

Inge, M. Thomas, ed. *Handbook of American Popular Culture, Vol. 3.* Westport, CT: Greenwood Press, 1981.

Insdorf, Annette. *Indelible Shadows: Film and the Holocaust.* Cambridge: Cambridge University Press, 1983, 1989.

International Motion Picture Almanac. New York: Quigley Publishing; editions used: 1948–1960. Editors: 1948–1951, Terry Ramsaye; 1951–1952, Red Kann; 1952–1960, Charles Aaronson.

Jaher, Frederic Cople. *A Scapegoat in the New Wilderness: The Origins and Rise of Anti-Semitism in America.* Cambridge, MA: Harvard University Press, 1994.

Jarvie, I. C. *Movies and Society.* New York: Basic Books, Inc., 1970.

Kammen, Michael. *Mystic Chords of Memory: The Transformation of Tradition in American Culture.* New York: Alfred A. Knopf, 1991.

Kaplan, Amy and Donald Pease, eds. *Cultures of United States Imperialism.* Durham NC: Duke University Press, 1993.

Kaufman, Burton I. *The Arab Middle East and the United States: Inter-Arab Rivalry and Superpower Diplomacy.* New York: Twayne Publishers, 1996.

Kaufman, I. *American Jews in WWII.* New York: The Dial Press, 1947.

Kennan, George. *American Diplomacy, 1900–1950.* Chicago: The University of Chicago Press, 1951.

———. *Memoirs 1925–1950.* New York: Pantheon Books, 1967.

Kisohn, Ephraim and Dosh (Kariel Gardosh). *So Sorry We Won.* Tel Aviv: Ma'ariv Library, 1967.

Klein, Marcus. *After Alienation: American Novels at Mid-Century.* Cleveland, OH: The World Publishing Company, 1962.

Klingenstein, Susanne. *Jews in the American Academy 1900–1940: The Dynamics of Intellectual Assimilation.* New Haven, CT: Yale University Press, 1991.

Kollek, Teddy with Amos Kollek. *For Jerusalem: A Life.* New York: Random House, 1978.

Kolsky, Thomas A. *Jews Against Zionism: The American Council for Judaism, 1942–1948.* Philadelphia: Temple University Press, 1990.

Kreitzer, Larry. *The New Testament in Fiction and Film: On Reversing the Hermeneutical Flow.* Sheffield, England: JSOT Press, 1993.

———. *The Old Testament in Fiction and Film: On Reversing the Hermeneutical Flow.* Sheffield, England: Sheffield Academic Press, 1994.

Kunz, Diane B. *The Economic Diplomacy of the Suez Crisis.* Chapel Hill, NC: The University of North Carolina Press, 1991.

Kushner, Tony. *The Holocaust and the Liberal Imagination: A Social and Cultural History.* Oxford: Blackwell, 1994.

Kyle, Keith. *Suez.* New York: St. Martin's Press, 1991.

LaFeber, Walter. *America, Russia, and the Cold War, 1945–1984*. New York: Alfred A. Knopf, 1985.

———. *The American Age: United States Foreign Policy at Home and Abroad Since 1750*. New York: W. W. Norton and Company, 1989.

Laqueur, Walter. *A History of Zionism*. New York: Holt, Rinehart & Winston, 1972.

Lash, Joseph. *Eleanor: The Years Alone*. New York: W. W. Norton and Company, 1972.

Levine, Lawrence W. *The Opening of the American Mind: Canons, Culture, and History*. Boston: Beacon Press, 1996.

Levy, Zach. *Israel and the Western Powers, 1952–1960*. Chapel Hill, NC: The University of North Carolina Press, 1997.

Lewis, Bernard. *The Arabs in History*. New York: Harper Torchbooks, 1960.

———. *Semites and Anti-Semites: An Inquiry into Conflict and Prejudice*. New York: W. W. Norton and Company, 1986.

Liebman, Charles. *The Ambivalent American Jew: Politics, Religion and Family in American Jewish Life*. Philadelphia: Jewish Publication Society of America, 1973.

Lilienthal, Alfred. *What Price Israel*. Chicago: Henry Regnery Company, 1953.

Lipstadt, Deborah E. *Beyond Belief: The American Press and the Coming of the Holocaust, 1933–1945*. New York: The Free Press, 1986.

Liptzin, Sol. *The Jew in American Literature*. New York: Bloch Publishing Company, 1966.

Lutz, Catherine A., and Jane L. Collins. *Reading the National Geographic*. Chicago: The University of Chicago Press, 1993.

Marcus, Jacob Rader. *United States Jewry 1776–1985, Vol. IV*. Detroit, MI: Wayne State University Press, 1993.

Marty, Martin E. *Modern American Religion, Volume 3: Under God, Indivisible, 1941–1960*. Chicago: University of Chicago Press, 1996.

May, Elaine Tyler. *Homeward Bound: American Families in the Cold War Era*. New York: Basic Books, Inc., 1988.

McConnell, Frank. *Storytelling and Mythmaking: Images From Film and Literature*. New York: Oxford University Press, 1979.

McCormick, Thomas J. *America's Half-Century: United States Foreign Policy in the Cold War*. Baltimore, MD: The Johns Hopkins University Press, 1989.

McCullough, David. *Truman*. New York: Simon and Schuster, 1992.

McWilliams, Carey. *A Mask for Privilege: Anti-Semitism in America*. Westport, CT: Greenwood Press, 1947.

Medding, Peter Y. *The Founding of Israeli Democracy, 1948–1967*. New York: Oxford University Press, 1990.

Melman, Yossi and Dan Raviv. *Friends in Deed: Inside the U.S.-Israel Alliance*. New York: Hyperion, 1994.

Melnick, Ralph. *The Stolen Legacy of Anne Frank: Meyer Levin, Lillian Hellman, and the Staging of the Diary*. New Haven, CT: Yale University Press, 1997.

Miller, Merle. *Plain Speaking: An Oral Biography of Harry S. Truman*. New York: G. P. Putnam's Sons, 1973, 1974.

Miller, Perry. *Errand Into the Wilderness*. Cambridge, MA: Belknap Press of Harvard University Press, 1956.

Miller, Randall M. *The Kaleidoscope Lens: How Hollywood Views Ethnic Groups*. New York: Jerome S. Ozer, 1980.

Millis, Walter, ed. *The Forrestal Diaries*. New York: The Viking Press, 1951.

Moore, R. Laurence. *Religious Outsiders and the Making of Americans*. New York: Oxford University Press, 1986.

Morris, Benny. *Israel's Border Wars, 1949–1956*. New York: Oxford University Press, 1993.

Morse, Arthur D. *While Six Million Died: A Chronicle of American Apathy*. New York: Hart Pub. Co., 1967.

Mousa, Issam Suleiman. *The Arab Image in the U.S. Press*. New York: Peter Lang, 1984.

Myrdal, Gunnar. *An American Dilemma: The Negro Problem and Modern Democracy*. New York: Harper & Brothers, 1944.

Nadich, Judah. *Eisenhower and the Jews*. New York: Twayne Publishers, 1953.

Novick, Peter. *The Holocaust in American Life*. Boston: Houghton Mifflin Company, 1999.

Pinsker, Sanford. *The Schlemiel as Metaphor: Studies in the Yiddish and American Jewish Novel*. Carbondale, IL: Southern Illinois University Press, 1971.

Pogrebin, Letty Cottin. *Deborah, Golda, and Me: Being Female and Jewish in America*. New York: Crown Publishers, Inc., 1991.

Reich, Bernard. *Quest for Peace: United States-Israel Relations and the Arab-Israeli Conflict*. New Brunswick, NJ: Transaction Books, 1977.

———. *The United States and Israel: Influence in the Special Relationship*. New York: Praeger, 1984.

Ribalow, Harold U., ed. *Mid-Century: An Anthology of Jewish Life and Culture in Our Times*. New York: Beechhurst Press, 1955.

Riesman, David. *The Lonely Crowd*. New Haven, CT: Yale University Press, 1950.

Roosevelt, Eleanor. *The Autobiography of Eleanor Roosevelt*. New York: Harper & Brothers, 1958.

Root, Robert L. Jr. *The Rhetorics of Popular Culture: Advertising, Advocacy, and Entertainment*. New York: Greenwood Press, 1987.

Rosenberg, Emily. *Spreading the American Dream: American Economic and Cultural Expansion, 1890–1945*. New York: Farrar, Straus, Giroux and Hill and Wang, 1982.

Rubenberg, Cheryl A. *Israel and the American National Interest: A Critical Examination*. Urbana, IL: University of Illinois Press, 1986.

Sachar, Howard Morley. *The Course of Modern Jewish History*. New York: Harry N. Abrams, 1958, 1977.

———. *A History of Israel: From the Rise of Zionism to Our Time*. New York: Alfred A. Knopf, 1996.

Safran, Nadav. *The United States and Israel*. Cambridge, MA: Harvard University Press, 1963. Also, expanded reissue, *Embattled Ally*. Cambridge, MA: Harvard University Press, 1978.

Said, Edward. *Covering Islam: How the Media and Experts Determine How We See the Rest of the World*. New York: Pantheon Books, 1981.

———. *Culture and Imperialism*. New York: Vintage Books, 1993.

———. *Orientalism*. New York: Vintage Books, 1978, 1979.

———. *The Question of Palestine*. New York: Times Books, 1979.

Sampson, Anthony. *The Seven Sisters: The Great Oil Companies and the World They Shaped*. New York: Bantam Books, 1975.

Sartre, Jean-Paul. *Anti-Semite and Jew*. Translated by George Becker. New York: Schocken Books, 1948.

Scharf, Lois. *Eleanor Roosevelt: The First Lady of Liberalism*. Boston, MA: Twayne Publishers, 1987.

Schatz, Thomas. *The Genius of the System: Hollywood Filmmaking in the Studio Era*. New York: Pantheon Books, 1988.

———. *Hollywood Genres: Formulas, Filmmaking, and the Studio System*. Philadelphia: Temple University Press, 1981.

Schoenbaum, David. *The United States and the State of Israel*. New York: Oxford University Press, 1993.

Segev, Tom. *1949: The First Israelis*. New York: The Free Press, 1986.

Sha'ban, Fuad. *Islam and Arabs in Early American Thought: The Roots of Orientalism in America*. Durham, NC: The Acorn Press, 1991.

Shapiro, Edward. *A Time for Healing: American Jewry Since World War II*. Baltimore, MD: The Johns Hopkins University Press, 1992.

Shaw, Irwin and Robert Capa. *Report on Israel*. New York: Simon and Schuster, 1949, 1950.

Sheffer, Gabriel, ed. *U.S.-Israeli Relations at the Crossroads*. London and Portland, OR: Frank Cass, 1997.

Short, K. R. M., ed. *Film and Radio Propaganda in World War II*. Knoxville, TN: The University of Tennessee Press, 1983.

Sklar, Robert. *Movie-Made America: A Cultural History of American Movies*. New York: Random House, 1975.

Sklare, Marshall. *America's Jews*. New York: Random House, 1971.

———. *The Jews: Social Patterns of an American Group*. Glencoe, IL: The Free Press, 1958.

Slotkin, Richard. *Gunfighter Nation: The Myth of the Frontier in Twentieth Century America*. New York: Harper Perennial, 1992.

Smith, Huston. *The Religions of Man*. New York: Harper & Row Publishers, 1958.

Sorin, Gerald. *A Time for Building: The Third Migration, 1880–1920*. Baltimore, MD: The Johns Hopkins University Press, 1992.

Spiegel, Steven L. *The Other Arab-Israeli Conflict: Making America's Middle East Policy, From Truman to Reagan*. Chicago: The University of Chicago Press, 1985.

Stember, Charles Herbert et al. *Jews in the Mind of America*. New York: Basic Books, Inc., 1966.

Stivers, William. *America's Confrontation With Revolutionary Change in the Middle East, 1948–1983*. New York: St. Martin's Press, 1986.

Stookey, Robert W. *America and the Arab States: An Uneasy Encounter*. New York: John Wiley & Sons, Inc., 1975.

Suleiman, Michael W. *The Arabs in the Mind Of America*. Brattleboro, VT: Amana Books, 1988.

Svonkin, Stuart. *Jews Against Prejudice: American Jews and the Fight for Civil Liberties*. New York: Columbia University Press, 1997.

Terkel, Studs. *"The Good War": An Oral History of World War Two*. New York: Ballantine Books, 1984.

Thomas, Hugh. *Suez*. New York: Harper & Row Publishers, 1966.

Tillman, Seth. *The United States in the Middle East: Interests and Obstacles*. Bloomington, IN: Indiana University Press, 1982.

Tivnan, Edward. *The Lobby: Jewish Political Power and American Foreign Policy*. New York: Simon and Schuster, Inc., 1987, 1988.

Truman, Harry S. *Memoirs by Harry S. Truman, Vol. II: Years of Trial and Hope, 1946–1952*. New York: Doubleday & Company, Inc., 1956.

Tuveson, Ernest Lee. *Redeemer Nation: The Idea of America's Millennial Role*. Chicago: The University of Chicago Press, 1968.

Urofsky, Melvin. *We Are One! American Jewry and Israel*. Garden City, NY: Anchor Press/Doubleday & Co., Inc., 1978.

U.S. Department of State. *Foreign Relations of the United States, 1948–1960*. Washington, DC: U.S. Government Printing Office. (Applicable volumes cited in individual chapters.)

Weinstein, Allen and Moshe Ma'oz. *Truman and the American Commitment to Israel: A 30th Anniversary Conference*. Jerusalem: The Magnes Press, 1981.

Whitfield, Stephen J. *American Space, Jewish Time*. Hamden, CT: Archon Books, 1988.

———. *The Culture of the Cold War*. Baltimore, MD: The Johns Hopkins University Press, 1991.

———. *Voices of Jacob, Hands of Esau: Jews in American Life and Thought*. Hamden, CT: Archon Books, 1984.

———. *In Search of American Jewish Culture*. Hanover: Brandeis University Press/University Press of New England, 1999.

Whyte, William H. *The Organization Man*. New York: Simon and Schuster, 1956.

Wilkinson, Rupert. *American Tough: The Tough Guy Tradition and American Character*. New York: Harper & Row Publishers, 1986.

Wills, Gary. *Under God: Religion and American Politics*. New York: Simon and Schuster, 1990.

Wilson, Edmund. *Red, Black, Blond and Olive*. New York: Oxford University Press, 1956.

Wilson, Evan M. *Decision on Palestine: How the United States Came to Recognize Israel*. Stanford, CA: The Hoover Institute Press, 1979.

Wistrich, Robert S. *Antisemitism: The Longest Hatred*. New York: Pantheon Books, 1991.

Woll, Allen L., and Randall M. Miller. *Ethnic and Racial Images in American Film and Television: Historical Essays and Bibliography*. New York: Garland Publishing Inc., 1987.

Wyman, David S. *The Abandonment of the Jews: America and the Holocaust, 1941–1945.* New York: Pantheon Books, 1984.

Yergin, Daniel. *The Prize: The Epic Quest for Oil, Money and Power.* New York: Simon and Schuster, 1991.

Zucker, Bat-Ami. *U.S. Aid to Israel and Its Reflection in the New York Times and the Washington Post: the Pen, the Sword, and the Middle East.* Lewiston, NY: The Edwin Mellen Press, 1991.

ARTICLES AND ESSAYS

Adler, Frank J. "From Dream to Reality: Truman, Jacobson, and Israel." In *Roots Moving in a Stream: The Centennial History of Congregation B'Nai Jehudah of Kansas City, 1870–1970.* By Frank J. Adler. Kansas City, MO: The Temple Congregation, 1972.

Ahlstrom, Sidney E. "The Religious Dimensions of American Aspirations." In *An Almost Chosen People: The Moral Aspirations of Americans.* Edited by Walter Nicgorski and Ronald Weber. Notre Dame: The University of Notre Dame Press, 1976.

Bar-Siman-Tov, Yaacov. "The United States and Israel Since 1948: 'A Special Relationship'?" *Diplomatic History* 22, No. 2 (Spring 1998): 231–262.

Bataille, Gretchen and Charles L. P. Silet. "The Entertaining Anachronism: Indians in American Film." In *The Kaleidoscope Lens: How Hollywood Views Ethnic Groups.* Edited by Randall Miller. New York: Jerome S. Ozer, 1980.

Bender, Thomas. "Wholes and Parts: The Need for Synthesis in American History." *Journal of American History* 73, No. 1 (June 1986): 120–136.

Bercovitch, Sacvan. "The Rites of Assent: Rhetoric, Ritual, and the Ideology of American Consensus." In *The American Self, Myth, Ideology, and Popular Culture.* Edited by Sam B. Girgus. Albuquerque, NM: University of New Mexico Press, 1981.

Berelson, Bernard. "Who Reads What Books and Why?" In *Mass Culture: The Popular Arts in America.* Edited by Bernard Rosenberg and David Manning White. Glencoe, IL: The Free Press of Macmillan Publishing Co., Inc., 1957.

Bergoffen, Debra. "The Apocalyptic Meaning of History." In *The Apocalyptic Vision in America: Interdisciplinary Essays on Myth and Culture.* Edited and introduction by Lois Parkinson Zamora. Bowling Green, OH: Bowling Green University Popular Press, 1982.

Bové, Paul A. "Discourse." In *Critical Terms for Literary Study.* Edited by Frank Lentricchia and Thomas McLaughlin. Chicago: The University of Chicago Press, 1990.

Brunt, Rosalind. "Engaging With the Popular: Audiences for Mass Culture and What to Say About Them." In *Cultural Studies.* Edited by Lawrence Grossberg, Cary Nelson, and Paula Treichler. New York: Routledge and Kegan Paul, 1992.

Bryant, D. Darrol. "Cinema, Religion and Popular Culture." In *Religion in Film.* Edited by John R. May and Michael Bird. Knoxville, TN: The University of Tennessee Press, 1982.

Cassara, Ernest. "The Development of America's Sense of Mission." In *The Apocalyptic Vision in America: Interdisciplinary Essays on Myth and Culture.* Edited by Lois Parkinson Zamora. Bowling Green, OH: Bowling Green University Popular Press, 1982.

Combs, James. "The Western Myth and American Politics." In *Polpop: Politics and Popular Culture in America.* By James Combs. Bowling Green, OH: Bowling Green University Popular Press, 1984.

Costigliola, Frank. "The Nuclear Family: Tropes of Gender and Pathology in the Western Alliance." *Diplomatic History* 21, No. 2 (Spring 1997): 163–183.

Dinnerstein, Leonard. "Antisemitism in Times of Crisis in the United States: The 1920s and 1930s." In *Antisemitism in Times of Crisis.* Edited by Sander L. Gilman and Steven Katz. New York: New York University Press, 1991.

Divine, Robert A. "John Foster Dulles: What You See is What You Get," *Diplomatic History* 15, No. 2 (Spring 1991): 277–285.

Doneson, Judith. "The American History of Anne Frank's Diary." *Holocaust and Genocide Studies* 2, No. 1 (1987): 149–60.

Douglas, Susan J. "Notes Toward a History of Media Audiences." *Radical History Review* 54 (Fall 1992): 127–138.

Elkin, Frederick. "God, Radio, and the Movies." In *Mass Culture: The Popular Arts in America.* Edited by Bernard Rosenberg and David Manning White. Glencoe, IL: The Free Press of Macmillan Publishing Co., Inc., 1957.

Erens, Patricia. "Between Two Worlds: Jewish Images in American Films." In *The Kaleidoscope Lens.* Edited by Randall Miller. New York: Jerome S. Ozer, 1980.

Evenson, Bruce J. "A Story of 'Ineptness': The Truman Administration's Struggle to Shape Conventional Wisdom on Palestine at the Beginning of the Cold War." *Diplomatic History* 15, No. 3 (Summer 1991): 339–359.

Feldman, Egal. "American Protestant Theologians on the Frontiers of Jewish Christian Relations 1992–82." In *Anti-Semitism in American History.* Edited by David A. Gerber. Urbana, IL: University of Illinois Press, 1986.

Gans, Herbert J. "The Creator-Audience Relationship in the Mass Media: An Analysis of Movie Making," In *Mass Culture: The Popular Arts in America.* Edited by Bernard Rosenberg and David Manning White. Glencoe, IL: The Free Press of Macmillan Publishing Co., Inc., 1957.

Gerber, David A. "Anti-Semitism and Jewish-Gentile Relations in American Historiography and the American Past." In *Anti-Semitism in American History.* Edited by David A. Gerber. Urbana, IL: University of Illinois Press, 1986.

Gilman, Sander L., and Steven M. Katz. "Introduction." In *Antisemitism in Times of Crisis.* Edited by Sander L. Gilman and Steven Katz. New York: New York University Press, 1991.

Girgus, Sam B., "The New Covenant: The Jews and the Myth of America." In *The American Self, Myth, Ideology, and Popular Culture.* Edited by Sam B. Girgus. Albuquerque, NM: University of New Mexico Press, 1981.

Glanz, Dawn, "The American West as Millennial Kingdom." In *The Apocalyptic Vision in America: Interdisciplinary Essays on Myth and Culture.* Edited by Lois Parkinson Zamora. Bowling Green, OH: Bowling Green University Popular Press, 1982.

Glazer, Nathan. "The American Jew and the Attainment of Middle-Class Rank: Some Trends and Explanations." In *The Jews: Social Patterns of an American Group*. Ed. Marshall Sklare. Glencoe, IL: The Free Press, 1958.

Gleason, Philip. "Americans All: World War II and the Shaping of American Identity." *Review of Politics* 43, (1981): 483–518.

Hahn, Peter L. "Commentary: Special Relationships," *Diplomatic History* 22, No. 2 (Spring 1998): 263–272.

———. "The View From Jerusalem: Revelations About U.S. Diplomacy From the Archives of Israel." *Diplomatic History* 22, No. 4 (Fall 1998): 509–532.

Halpern, Ben. "Anti-Semitism in the Perspective of Jewish History." In *Jews in the Mind of America*. Edited by Charles Heibert Stember et al. New York: Basic Books, Inc., 1966.

Heinze, Andrew R. "*Peace of Mind* (1946): Judaism and the Therapeutic Polemics of Postwar America." *Religion and American Culture: A Journal of Interpretation* 12, No. 1 (Winter 2002): 31–58.

Henry, Patrick. "'And I Don't Care What It Is': The Tradition-History of a Civil Religion Proof-Text," *Journal of the American Academy of Religion* 49, No. 1 (1981): 35–47.

Herman, Felicia. "Hollywood, Nazism, and the Jews, 1933–1941." *American Jewish History* 89 (March 2001): 61–89.

Higham, John. "American Anti-Semitism Historically Reconsidered." In *Jews in the Mind of America*. Edited by Charles Herbert Stember et al. New York: Basic Books Inc., 1966.

Horowitz, Sara R. "The Cinematic Triangulation of Jewish American Identity: Israel, America, and the Holocaust." In *The Americanization of the Holocaust*. Edited by Hilene Flanzbaum. Baltimore: The Johns Hopkins University Press, 1999.

Jeffords, Susan. "Culture and National Identity in U.S. Foreign Policy." *Diplomatic History* 18, No. 1 (Winter 1994): 91–96.

Johnson, Willard. "Religon and Minority Peoples." In *One America: The History, Contributions, and Present Problems of Our Racial and National Minorities*. Edited by Francis J. Brown and Joseph S. Roucek. New York: Prentice-Hall Inc., 1952.

Kaplan, Amy. "Domesticating Foreign Policy," *Diplomatic History* 18 (Winter 1994): 97–106.

Kazal, Russell A. "Revisiting Assimilation: The Rise, Fall, and Reappraisal of a concept in American Ethnic History." *American Historical Review* 100, No. 2 (April 1995): 437–471.

Keller, Morton. "Jews and the Character of American Life Since 1930." In *Jews in the Mind of America*. Edited by Charles Herbert Stember et al. New York: Basic Books, 1966.

Kelley, Robin D. G. "Notes on Deconstructing 'The Folk'." *American Historical Review* 97, No. 5 (December 1992): 1400–1408.

Kracauer, Siegfried. "National Types as Hollywood Presents Them." *Public Opinion Quarterly* 13, No. 1 (Spring 1949): 53–72.

Levine, Lawrence W. "The Folklore of Industrial Society: Popular Culture and Its Audiences." *American Historical Review* 97, No. 5 (December 1992): 1369–1399.

Lewis, Bernard. "The Arab World Discovers Anti-Semitism." In *Antisemitism in Times of Crisis*. Edited by Sander L. Gilman and Steven Katz. New York: New York University Press, 1991.

Lippy, Charles H. "Waiting for the End: The Social Context of American Apocalyptic Religion." In *The Apocalyptic Vision in America: Interdisciplinary Essays on Myth and Culture*. Edited by Lois Parkinson Zamora. Bowling Green, OH: Bowling Green University Popular Press, 1982.

Louis, Wm. Roger. "Dulles, Suez, and the British," In *John Foster Dulles and the Diplomacy of the Cold War*. Edited by Richard H. Immerman. Princeton, NJ: Princeton University Press, 1990.

Mart, Michelle. "Tough Guys and American Cold War Policy: Images of Israel, 1948–1960." *Diplomatic History* 20, No. 3 (Summer 1996): 357–380.

May, Elaine Tyler. "Ideology and Foreign Policy: Culture and Gender in Diplomatic History." *Diplomatic History* 18, No. 1 (Winter 1994): 71–78.

McEnaney, Laura. "He-Men and Christian Mothers: The America First Movement and the Gendered Meanings of Patriotism and Isolationism." *Diplomatic History* 18, No. 1 (Winter 1994): 47–58.

Miller, Randall M. "Introduction." In *The Kaleidoscope Lens: How Hollywood Views Ethnic Groups*. Edited by Randall M. Miller. New York: Jerome S. Ozer, 1980.

Moore, Deborah Dash. "Bonding Images: Miami Jews and the Campaign for Israel Bonds." In *Envisioning Israel: The Changing Ideals and Images of North American Jews*. Ed. Allon Gal. Jerusalem and Detroit: The Magnes Press, Hebrew University, and Wayne State University Press, 1996.

———. "Jewish GIs and the Creation of the Judeo-Christian Tradition." *Religion and American Culture* 8, No. 1 (1998): 31–53.

Murolo, Priscilla. "History in the Fast Lane: Howard Fast and the Historical Novel." In *Presenting the Past: Essays on History and the Public*. Edited by Susan Porter Benson, Stephen Brier, and Roy Rosenzweig. Philadelphia: Temple University Press, 1986.

Nelson, John Wiley. "The Apocalyptic Vision in American Popular Culture." In *The Apocalyptic Vision in America: Interdisciplinary Essays on Myth and Culture*. Edited by Lois Parkinson Zamora. Bowling Green, OH: Bowling Green University Popular Press, 1982.

Oxtoby, Willard G. "Western Perceptions of Islam and the Arabs." In *The American Media and the Arabs*. Edited by Michael C. Hudson and Ronald G. Wolfe. Washington, DC: Georgetown University Press, 1980.

Pascoe, Peggy. "Miscegenation Law, Court Cases, and Ideologies of 'Race' in Twentieth Century America." *Journal of American History* 83, No. 1 (June 1996): 44–69.

Penslar, Derek. "Narratives of Nation Building: Major Themes in Zionist Historiography." In *The Jewish Past Revisited: Reflections on Modern Jewish Historians*. Edited by David V. Myers and David B. Ruderman. New Haven, CT and London: Yale University Press, 1998.

Radway, Janice. "Mail-Order Culture and Its Critics: The Book-of-The-Month Club, Commodification and Consumption, and the Problem of Cultural Authority." In *Cultural Studies*. Edited by Lawrence Grossberg, Cary Nelson, and Paula Treichler. New York: Routledge, 1992.

Reich, Bernard. "Themes in the History of the State of Israel." *American Historical Review*, 96, No. 5 (December 1991): 1466–1478.

Rosenberg, Bernard. "Mass Culture in America." In *Mass Culture: The Popular Arts in America*. Edited by Bernard Rosenberg and David Manning White. Glencoe, IL: The Free Press of Macmillan Publishing Co., Inc., 1957.

Rosenberg, Emily. "'Foreign Affairs' After World War II: Connecting Sexual and International Politics." *Diplomatic History* 18, No 1 (Winter 1994): 59–70.

———. "Revisiting Dollar Diplomacy: Narratives of Money and Manliness," *Diplomatic History* 22, No. 2 (Spring 1998): 155–176.

Rosenfeld, Alvin H. "Popularization and Memory: The Case of Anne Frank." In *Lessons and Legacies: The Meaning of the Holocaust in a Changing World*. Edited by Peter Hayes. Evanston: Northwestern Univesity Press, 1991.

Rosenzweig, Roy. "Marketing the Past: *American Heritage* and Popular History in the United States." In *Presenting the Past: Essays on History and the Public*. Edited by Susan Porter Benson, Stephen Brier, and Roy Rosenzweig. Philadelphia: Temple University Press, 1986.

Sarna, Jonathan. "A Projection of America as it Ought to Be: Zion in the Mind's Eye of American Jews." In *Envisioning Israel: The Changing Ideals and Images of North American Jews*. Edited by Allon Gal. Jerusalem and Detroit: The Magnes Press, Hebrew University, and Wayne State University Press, 1996.

Schiff, Ellen. "Shylock's Mishpoceh: Anti-Semitism on the American Stage." In *Anti-Semitism in American History*. Edited by David A. Gerber. Urbana, IL: University of Illinois, Press, 1986.

Schoenbaum, David. "Commentary: More Special Than Others." *Diplomatic History*, 22, No. 2 (Spring 1998): 273–283.

Short, K. R. M. "Hollywood Fights Anti-Semitism, 1945–1947." In *Feature Films As History*. Edited by K. R. M. Short. Knoxville, TN: University of Tennessee Press, 1981.

Silk, Mark. "Notes on the Judeo-Christian Tradition in America," *American Quarterly* 36 (Spring 1984): 65–85.

Singer, David G. "From St. Paul's Abrogation of the Old Covenant to Hitler's War Against the Jews: The Responses of American Catholic Thinkers to the Holocaust 1945–76." In *Anti-Semitism in American History*. Edited by David A. Gerber, Urbana, IL: University of Illinois Press, 1986.

Singerman, Robert. "The Jew as Racial Alien: The Genetic Component of American Anti-Semitism." In *Anti-Semitism in American History*. Edited by David A. Gerber, Urbana, IL: University of Illinois Press, 1986.

Smith, Geoffrey S. "National Security and Personal Isolation: Sex, Gender, and Disease in the Cold War United States." *International History Review* 14, No. 2 (May 1992): 307–337.

———. "Security, Gender, and the Historical Process." *Diplomatic History* 18, No. 1 (Winter 1994): 79–90.

Smith, Judith. "Celebrating Immigration History at Ellis Island." *Atlantic Quarterly* 44, No. 1 (March 1992): 82–100.

Snetsinger, John. "Truman and Israel: The Politics of Mythology." *Diplomatic History* 16, No. 3 (Summer 1992): 463–467.

Steedman, Carolyn. "Culture, Cultural Studies, and the Historians." In *Cultural Studies*. Edited by Lawrence Grossberg, Cary Nelson, and Paula Treichler. New York: Routledge, 1992.

Stein, Kenneth. "A Historiographic Review of Literature on the Origins of the Arab-Israeli Conflict," *American Historical Review* 96, No. 5 (December 1991): 1450–1465.

Stern, Guy. "The Rhetoric of Anti-Semitism in Postwar American Literature." In *Antisemitism in Times of Crisis*. Edited by Sander L. Gilman and Steven Katz. New York: New York University Press, 1991.

Suleiman, Michael W. "American Public Support of Middle Eastern Countries: 1939–1979." In *The American Media and the Arabs*. Edited by Michael C. Hudson and Ronald G. Wolfe. Washington, DC: Center for Contemporary Arab Studies, Georgetown University, 1980.

Weingertner, James J. "Trophies of War: U.S. Troops and the Mutilation of Japanese War Dead, 1941–1945." *Pacific Historical Review* 61, No. 1 (February 1992): 53–68.

White, David Manning. "Mass Culture in America: Another Point of View." In *Mass Culture: The Popular Arts in America*. Edited by Bernard Rosenberg and David Manning White. Glencoe, IL: The Free Press of Macmillan Publishing Co., Inc., 1957.

Wolfenstein, Martha and Nathan Leites. "The Good-Bad Girl." In *Mass Culture: The Popular Arts in America*. Edited by Bernard Rosenberg and David Manning White. Glencoe, IL: The Free Press of Macmillan Publishing Co., Inc., 1957.

Zamora, Lois Parkinson. "Introduction," and "The Myth of the Apocalypse and the American Literary Imagination." In *The Apocalyptic Vision in America: Interdisciplinary Essays on Myth and Culture*. Edited by Lois Parkinson Zamora. Bowling Green, OH: Bowling Green University Popular Press, 1982.

UNPUBLISHED MATERIALS

Balboni, Alan Richard. "A Study of the Efforts of the American Zionists to Influence the Formulation and Conduct of United States Foreign Policy During the Roosevelt, Truman, and Eisenhower Administrations." PhD diss., Brown University, 1973.

Bick, Etta Zablocki. "Ethnic Linkage and Foreign Policy: A Study of the Linkage Role of American Jews in Relations Between the United States and Israel, 1956–1968." PhD diss., City University of New York, 1983.

Dean, Robert. "'Firmness' and Foreign Policy: John F. Kennedy and the Cult of Masculinity." Paper presented at the Dusquesne University History Forum, Pittsburgh, PA, 1992.

Dohse, Michael Arthur. "American Periodicals and the Palestine Triangle, April 1936 to February 1947." PhD diss., Mississippi State University, 1966.

Fishman, Hertzel. "American Protestantism and the State of Israel: 1937–1967." PhD diss., New York University, 1971.

Goldstein, Eric. "Race and the Construction of Jewish Identity in America, 1875–1945." PhD diss., University of Michigan, 2000.

Huff, Earl Dean. "Zionist Influences Upon U.S. Foreign Policy: A Study of American Foreign Policy Towards the Middle East From the Time of the Struggle for Israel to the Sinai Conflict." PhD diss., University of Idaho, 1971.

Klingenstein, Suzanne. "Sweet Natalie: What Happens to Femininity in Holocaust Fiction." Paper presented at "Developing Images: Representations of Jewish Women in American Culture." Brandeis University, Waltham, MA, March 1993.

Nasir, Sari Jamil. "The Image of the Arab in American Popular Culture." PhD diss., The University of Illinois, 1962.

Rosenthal, Alan. "Selling Zion." Article in the author's possession, 1992.

Index